LIFE IN A TIN

STORIES FROM A FLYING LIFE

By Mark Blois-Brooke

with Dick Gilbert

First Published January 2022

Second Edition January 2023

Skyline Aviation Books

"There is no such thing as a natural-born pilot. Whatever my aptitudes or talents, becoming a proficient pilot was hard work, really a lifetime's learning experience. For the best pilots, flying is an obsession, the one thing in life they must do continually."

Chuck Yeager

"Anyone can do the job when things are going right. In this business, we play for keeps."

Ernest K. Gann - 'Fate Is The Hunter'

CONTENTS

Introduction	i-ii
Prologue	iii
White Waltham	Page 1
Chess Wing	Page 18
Skyguard	Page 27
South East Air	Page 37
Interflight	Page 40
Air Contractors	Page 150
BP	Page 179
TAG Aviation	Page 183
Tiger Moth	Page 203
Glossary and Slang	Page 230
Appendix 1 Companies in Date Order	Page 232
Appendix 2 Aircraft Types Flown	Page 233
Appendix 3 Foreign Countries and Airfields Visited	Page 234
Index	Page 243

INTRODUCTION

This is not by any means meant to be an autobiography since leaving home, for two reasons; there is no mention of the seven years I spent working in the oil industry in the North Sea, which would fill another book and I would have to have led a much more interesting life to warrant an autobiography. This is just a series of anecdotes from the 15,000 hours flown, the 110 countries and the 500 or so airports I have visited over the years. A lot of them are from an era where health and safety and work practices were a world apart from those of today. They are in no particular order other than whom I was flying for at the time. Some names have been changed but this has no impact on the stories.

I'm no storyteller but I hope they give an insight into flying in the world of not only airline but instruction, charter, air taxi and business aviation, a pathway that has been closed off to pilots now entering the world of aviation who expect to go directly onto jet aircraft with major airlines. I feel sorry for them, I think a world of solid experience where survival skills are learned the hard way has been shut off, to their detriment. This is also in a small way a tribute to the guys I have flown with over the years, trained and been trained by, all of whom in varying degrees (with one notable exception as you will discover) have been a pleasure to fly with and some of them, in my opinion, giants in the industry. I count myself very lucky in this regard. I maintain that for the most part, aviators are the best people around.

I have tried to keep the arcane technical details of aviation to a minimum so the stories can be understood and hopefully enjoyed by non-fliers. I have added a short Glossary of terms and aviation slang which may help a little with some of the abbreviations. To any pilot into whose hands this may fall, my apologies for the occasionally simplistic nature of some of the stories; they are written for those unfortunate people who are forever confined to the surface of the Earth.

Also, if the language gets strong at times, no apologies; this is the world of aviation where there are shovels not spades and black humour is the norm.

This is dedicated to my beautiful wife Amanda and my amazing children Henry and Eleanor who mean all the world to me. They have benefited from some of my flights but have also had to put up with my absences from important events from time to time – such is aviation.

M.H.B-B, January 2022

PROLOGUE

I am aware that something is wrong, but I can't put my finger on it. For the last hour, something unknown has been troubling me. I repeatedly scan the engine instruments and they tell me nothing, everything is as it should be and yet I have this hunch that something is not right. Looking into the purple of the darkening horizon, where the sky merges into the grey, flecked sea, I focus on the rain on the windscreen, listening intently to the engine sound. Nothing. Then I'm sure I hear it again, a slight roughness, a missing beat to the symphony of the engines.

Am I imagining it? No, after hundreds of hours sitting between these engines, I am certain something's not right. I look at the cherry-red exhaust stack of the left-hand engine for reassurance and again fine-tune the engine controls. There it is again, a definite change in tone and I fix my gaze on the engine instruments noticing that the power on the left engine has dropped slightly and the cylinder head temperature seems to have crept up a little. I experience a churn in my stomach. In my head, I think the problem through and start to make contingencies. Should I inform ATC of my problem? No, there is no emergency yet. Should I wake the passengers or let them sleep? I glance behind me and in the dim light, I can see they are dozing, oblivious to my dilemma and shifting uncomfortably in the cramped seats. Fifty miles to a landing at Aberdeen. I can just make out lights in the distance through the blur of the wet windscreen and I will them to get closer; small hamlets and the headlights of traffic throwing beams onto the coast road and, beyond, the yellow sodium lights of the airport.

I decide not to wake the passengers unless things get worse - time enough when it happens to let them know we have had an engine failure over an unforgiving North Sea.

WHITE WALTHAM

Let's start at White Waltham airfield.

I was introduced to the West London Aero Club (WLAC) by my brother-in-law Nigel in late 1978 after I returned from America where I had enjoyed a wonderful eighteen months flying in Vermont. His cousin Rob from South Africa had been there during the 1970s working in the engineering hangar. Rob lived in a mildewed old caravan that was for years parked next to the flight office. It was owned by Phyllis who ran the bar and restaurant, such as it was in those days. Anyway, Phyllis was frequently entertained in its musty interior and rumour had it that Rob enjoyed free rent.

I arranged for an interview with the owner of the flying club Maurice Looker. Looker was an old school flying instructor, known to the instructors as 'Mog' as he was deemed a 'Miserable Old Git'. Grumpy he might have been but he was an interesting character. He must have once been a heavy smoker as his large handlebar moustache was stained with nicotine and he wheezed heavily. His long-suffering and bird-like wife Olive ran the accounts from the office next to the Operations room. On the day of my interview, he summoned me into his office and fixed me with a wary eye for a few seconds from behind his desk. To my surprise, his first question was,

"Have you ever crashed an aeroplane?" When I said no, I never had, he responded, "Well, I suppose you can start next month then." He turned to shuffle some papers so I guessed that was it, the interview must be over.

Looker, although a cantankerous character, was a renowned aviator and an experienced instructor although long retired by the time I joined the Club. When Mog was the Chief Flying Instructor, he used to wake up the ATC cadets, who lived in the prefab bedrooms at the rear of the bar known as 'the eggboxes', by running the wheels of his Auster along the corrugated tin roof over their heads first thing in the morning. That had the cadets spilling out of their beds as if by magic. To those that had never experienced it before, it must have sounded like the end of the world. In his younger days, legend has it that Mog flew his little Auster from North Denes airfield near Great Yarmouth to Scroby Sands, a sandbank five miles offshore to cull seal pups. He would land at low tide, cull as many pups as the Auster could lift from wet sand and fly back to North Denes.

It takes a tremendous leap of faith to do this at all on an incoming tide. Anyway, my demanding interview over, I started as an Instructor at WLAC on the 1st of February 1979. I was considered a bit of a novelty as I already had a Commercial Pilot's Licence and Instrument Rating at this point, albeit an American one, as well as both FAA and my recently acquired CAA instructor ratings. White Waltham was very much a sleepy backwater in 1979 with only a handful of aircraft parked outside on the grass as most aircraft, apart from the flying club aircraft, were hangared. Douglas Bader, the famous fighter ace of the Battle of Britain, kept his pale blue 1959 Beechcraft 'Travelair', registered G-APUB, in the hangar. This was a parting gift to him from Shell when he retired from their Aviation Department.

Bader was a famous character, usually turning up unannounced in his beautiful drophead Alvis with his glamorous wife Joan in the passenger seat. He would stomp into the flight office on his prosthetic legs, filling the doorway with his stocky frame and demand his aircraft pulled out of the hangar and refuelled. As he flew infrequently, his aircraft was usually at the back of the hangar so the poor 'hangar rats' had to disgorge maybe twenty aircraft from the hangar to reach Bader's before dragging it outside. Bader would then stride stiff-legged to his aircraft, clamber in with surprising agility, start up and set off with minimal fuss. I once plucked up the courage to ask him where he was going and he replied simply, "Newcastle, old boy."

He was a known menace to ATC as he never went anywhere other than in a straight line and didn't bother with anything as boring as a Notam. This meant he flew straight across busy airfields, RAF bases, military ranges etc. with various ATC units frantically trying to clear him a path. When challenged once he allegedly replied, "They are not going to ground me, old boy," which was probably true; it was hard to imagine a newspaper headline declaring 'BADER GROUNDED – LICENCE WITHDRAWN'. Although headstrong and blunt and a known difficult character, you had to admire his achievements during the war and afterwards, especially the work he did with the disabled. He was certainly a force of nature and, interestingly, a personal friend of the Luftwaffe ace Adolf Galland. He last flew his Travelair in June of 1979 and died of a heart attack in 1982 at the relatively young age of seventy-two.

I was lucky and caught the end of a golden period at White Waltham. The Club was full of large characters and the bar was always open so the nine months I was instructing there, living in one of the 'eggboxes' and surviving on beer and pizza, was no hardship. At last, I was flying and being paid for it although the rates were close to slave labour even then; Mog paid a very small salary topped up according to the number of instructional hours flown each month. The hourly rates were £2 for the first twenty hours, £3 for the next twenty hours, £4 for the next twenty and so on. If you flew non-stop you could make £250 a month all of which was spent in the club bar or other local pubs. We usually ended at 'The Star' in Waltham St. Lawrence which was one of the few local pubs that put up with our boorish behaviour probably as the landlord was an ex-flight engineer and was undoubtedly aware of the arrested development inherent in most pilots.

Once Mog had left for the day, normally around 4 pm, we would each grab a club aircraft and practice our 'Bob Hoovers'. This involved marking a spot halfway down the longest runway, taking off from that point, climbing overhead the airfield and shutting down the engine, reducing speed to stop the prop completely and then gliding down to a landing. The game was to land and roll out to stop exactly where you took off from without touching the brakes as the supremely talented Bob Hoover used to do, among other things, in his famous displays with his Shrike Commander.

Another favourite pastime was to beat up the clubhouse. The trick was to come in low and fast over the airfield and leave the pull-up until you could see your landing light reflected from the mirror over the bar. That meant being very low and very close to the clubhouse, missing the two chimney stacks by only a few feet as you roared overhead. Understandably, this used to terrify Phyllis and she would storm, apoplectic, into the flight office demanding to know who was responsible. Phyllis in a rage was a fearsome sight. There would be no beer or pizza for the offender that night.

My first student at the Club was Liz Inwood. Liz was a talented artist and seemed to live on a slightly different planet than anyone else. She had an ethereal connection with aircraft, to her they were all beautiful in their own way. But nothing compared to the Spitfire in her eyes. She was totally in love with them and used to drive up the road to Wycombe Air Park just to gaze at the one

West London Aero Club, clubhouse

that was resident there and then reproduce it on canvas. She smoked like a chimney which turned out to be the end of her years later. Since I was the 'new boy' instructor, Liz was offloaded to me as she was, in the nicest possible way, a demanding student. She took a bit of time to prepare for her first solo but eventually, the day came and after a few circuits practising engine failures after takeoff, I announced to her that today was the day. Her look was the usual one of all first solo pilots - one of shock and excitement rolled into one.

"Off you go," I said as I climbed out of the cockpit, "Do one circuit and come back in. If you are not happy with your approach, go around and have another go. There's no shame in that. Good luck!" I jumped off the wing and began walking back to the flight office. So started a worrying twenty minutes.

As I returned to the flight office I glance back and saw Liz just getting airborne in the Piper Cherokee. So far so good, I thought, in five minutes she'll be back on the ground and the first major milestone for any pilot, the first solo, will be completed. She will buy me beer in the bar that evening, as is traditional, so it's happy days. I wandered into the flight office where there was an air of excitement. Paul Stanton, the office chief and resident Total Aviation Person was talking excitedly on the radio. Two Spitfires were joining the circuit to land for the following day's celebrations for surviving members of the wartime Air Transport Auxiliary (ATA). White Waltham was a big ATA airfield during the war and every year they had a reunion with Spitfires attending.

"Tell them there's a first solo in the circuit and to hold off for a while!" I said urgently to Paul as I looked out of the flight office window.

I could see Liz now on the crosswind leg of the circuit and about to turn downwind. To my alarm, I could also see two dots that were the Spitfires moving quickly across the sky to join directly on downwind. Christ, I thought as my blood ran cold, I can see this going horribly wrong.

"Paul, for God's sake tell them again there is a first solo in the circuit, just turned downwind! Tell them to go wide and slow down!"

"I have," he replied, "but only Number Two has a radio and he is following Number One!"

I watched with my heart in my mouth as the three dots in the sky rapidly merged into one. I closed my eyes for a few seconds and when I opened them again I could see, thank God, that three dots had reappeared downwind, rapidly separating as the Spitfires left Liz behind. My worry now was what would the effect be on Liz. She would surely have seen and heard the two Spitfires howling past her and, knowing her, would probably freak out with excitement and lose all her concentration. I kept my gaze on Liz. Come on…. time to turn base leg now…. what are you doing? I watched horrified as she kept flying downwind with no sign of her turning towards the airfield. Then the flight office phone rang and I knew instinctively who it was.

"Hello, West London Aero Club," I said trying to sound calmer than I felt. The voice was brisk and direct.

"Heathrow Director here. One of your aircraft is outside your ATZ. Are you aware of this?"

"Yes", I replied lamely, "it's a first solo. I'm sorry if it's causing any problems." The reply was curt.

"If it doesn't turn in the next mile, we will have to stop all departures from 28R." Christ, that was serious.

"OK I'll contact the pilot, thank you." I slammed the receiver back and grabbed the radio mic to call Liz. As I did so, I could see her finally turning towards base leg.

While all the other instructors were intent on watching the Spitfires that were now taxiing in, I watched Liz as she flew down finals and made a safe, if bumpy, landing. She came to a stop on the runway, engine running, not making any attempt to taxi back to the flight line. I jumped into the fire truck and raced over to her, pulling up alongside her and jumped out. Liz was staring straight ahead in a daze. I wiggled the right aileron to let her know I was there before jumping up onto the wing and opening the door.

"Liz, are you OK? What happened?" She was staring straight ahead, as if in a trance.

"Thank you so much! Spitfires on my first solo!" she whispered hoarsely, "I couldn't have wished for anything more." Well, who was I to disappoint a lady?

* * * *

Flying students come in all varieties as anyone who has instructed can attest to. There is a broad spectrum of motivations amongst their ranks. There are the young lads, sometimes RAF cadets, who live and breathe aviation and want one thing only and that is to fly and have a career in aviation. Next are the boasters who want to fly for the sole purpose of joining in with the bar talk. They are generally lazy and just want the licence as quickly as possible. Next, come the middle-aged plodders who try hard and progress slowly but are well-intentioned; they secretly never want to fly on their own without an instructor next to them. And then there are characters like Peter Scammell. Peter was an estate agent who went on to have a successful string of agencies in and around Berkshire. As far as I could make out, he had only one real agenda and that was to look at properties from the air. We would be happily flying along with me droning on about some finer points of aviation when he would suddenly grab my arm.

"Hang on, can we have a look at this place for a minute?" and he would put the Cherokee into a 45° steep turn with one hand while furiously scribbling in a notebook with the other.

A Spitfire at the annual ATA reunion

history but then nothing that I ever flew was any newer and most were a lot older, so I wasn't unduly worried. Dick Gliddon, the Chief Engineer at the Club, told me it was full of sand as it had allegedly spent time in the Sinai desert before being imported from Israel. Anyway, I took it for a quick flight and liked it; powerful and reasonably quick with around a 140 kts cruise speed.

The day arrived for the first flight to Dublin. I had flown the aircraft to Oxford Airport earlier in the day and arranged to meet Mr Myers in the cafe at 1100. Off we went, wearing our life jackets with a VFR flight plan filed for the international flight. The flight was uneventful. We negotiated the Irish Sea with fingers crossed, cleared Customs in Dublin, picked up some fuel and then departed for a little farm strip in Co. Wicklow just south of Dublin. This took some finding in the days before GPS. It was a remote farmhouse with several fields all of which looked like they might be suitable but nothing stood out as the designated landing field.

Mr Myers shouted in my ear that they had all been walked over and were suitable for landing although the thought crossed my mind as I circled above – when and by whom? None of the fields looked that great. Anyway, it was his aircraft. I selected what looked like the best field and set up the approach across its diagonal and roughly into wind touching down and rolling out with no problems, the undercarriage oleos thumping on the rough ground. I taxied to the corner of the field which was shielded by a small copse and shut down.

As I secured the aircraft, a Land Rover bounced over the field towards us. We piled in and the driver told drove us to the client's farmhouse to clean up and have dinner ahead of Mr Myers's meeting the next day. Mr Myers then took me aside and mentioned something that focused my mind considerably.

"The people here are lovely but just be careful and be aware. People talk a lot in Ireland."

This made me think – here we were during the worst times of the Troubles, flying a UK-registered aircraft to remote country airstrips in rural Ireland. Hmm, I should be careful. And the next stop was to the west of Ireland, to Adare Manor the home of the Earl of Dunraven. Hang on, could this get worse? We were to visit a member of the British aristocracy only a few miles from Limerick, the most republican town in southern Ireland. I began to take this trip a bit more seriously.

In the morning, we flew from Wicklow to Adare Manor. Having been given a reality check, I approached the aircraft carefully. What if it had been tampered with? Suppose there was a trip wire attached to a few pounds of C4 or Semtex? What if someone had contaminated the fuel? Anyone could easily remove the fuel caps, they weren't lockable. Or the control cables tampered with? I walked around the aircraft a few times looking intently for any signs of interference before deciding to approach it. I have to say this was one of the most thorough pre-flights I have ever done. I found nothing wrong with the aircraft and later that day we departed for Adare Manor. The takeoff was brisk but bumpy on the rough grass field, the undercarriage oleos thumping and banging in complaint, but we got airborne in no time thanks to the 300 horses under the cowling and set heading to Adare.

Adare Manor is a beautiful 19th-century manor house on the banks of the River Maigue in Co. Limerick. In 1984, a few years after our visit, the last Earl sold it off and it was converted into one of the top hotels in Ireland with a championship golf course but at the time it was still the Earl's private residence. Anyway, forty-five minutes after leaving the farm in Wicklow we arrived overhead and I circled the Manor a few times before locating the prepared landing strip that I had been promised had been cut next to the long driveway. The strip was easy to spot and I landed on the smooth grass. Perfect. I spent three days there at the Dunraven Arms Hotel in Adare while Mr Myers had his meetings with the Earl. With instructions from the Manor for everything to be paid for, I had an enjoyable time, walking, eating well and drinking a lot of Guinness.

However, when it came time for the flight home, via Shannon Airport to clear Customs, I was in for a bit of a shock. My concerns about terrorism were replaced by a more immediate problem. The beautifully cut grass strip that had I landed on had disappeared. The grass must have been six inches tall and was covering the wheel spats and almost touching the bottom blade of the propeller. I wasn't aware of how fast the grass can grow in Ireland after a week of warm, wet spring weather.

What to do? I decided to do a fast taxi and see how the aircraft accelerated and maybe, if that was OK, get airborne and do a quick circuit. If I wasn't happy

Adare Manor

with the acceleration, I would have to ask for the strip to be cut again, something I viewed as a last resort after all the Earl's hospitality. The big Lycoming engine started easily and settled into its lazy, deep rumble. I knew that I had enough fuel to get to Shannon but not much more, so the aircraft was very light. I completed the engine run-up carefully, set two stages of flap for takeoff and taxied to the very end of the now barely visible strip. I wanted as much takeoff distance as possible. With full power selected against the brakes, the aircraft began to skid forward on the wet grass. I was attempting what shouldn't really be done – a takeoff on very long, wet grass, the very worst combination for performance. However, when I released the brakes, the aircraft accelerated briskly and at 80 kts I lifted it off with no drama and turned left to complete a quick circuit to land back on the strip. With the problem of getting off the strip solved, my concerns returned to security issues and not making myself too visible locally for obvious reasons. However, without doubt, everyone in the local area knew by now two English chaps were staying in the area. After I landed, I walked around the aircraft for a careful post-flight inspection – the propeller, wheels and underside were all covered in a dark green slime from the grass.

Piper Cherokee Six, G-BAXJ

The flights back to White Waltham via Shannon and Shoreham were uneventful. Mr Myers seemed pleased with how it had all gone and as he left the airfield, he said that I could expect another trip back to Ireland in a couple of weeks if I was free. Yes, please! This never happened, however, as the day before I was due to fly him again, someone had thrown a brick through the aircraft's windscreen while it was parked at White Waltham overnight. Clearly, the amiable Mr Myers had enemies somewhere.

* * * *

A few weeks later I was asked to do another flight for some club members, this time a day trip to Leeds-Bradford Airport for a business meeting. All these flights were technically charter flights and even in those days when there was a fairly lax approach to legality, you had to be careful. To get around any accusation of operating illegal charters we referred to them as 'cost-sharing flights'. With hindsight, I doubt whether this would ever have stood up in court.

The day came and me and the two passengers boarded a Club Cherokee 180 and set off for Leeds. The weather was fine with a slight tailwind and although the forecast was for a warm front to come in from the west later in the day, I didn't pay much attention to it. After all, I had an Instrument Rating (even though it was an American one and so not technically legal in the UK). Nonetheless, it gave me the confidence that I could always land somewhere if the weather got bad.

The flight up to Leeds was fine and I enjoyed going somewhere for once rather than the endless local flying and circuits that instructing inevitably entails. The plan was for the passengers to spend a couple of hours in the city and then return to the airport for the return flight at around 5 pm. With sunset at 8 pm that gave us sufficient time to make the flight back to White Waltham in daylight. I thought about refuelling but decided against it. I calculated I had enough for the return flight and anyway fuel was expensive at Leeds Airport and I would have to pay for it myself and claim it back from the passengers later which I would rather avoid.

The passengers didn't arrive at 5 pm and all I could do was wait by the Information Desk, as we had agreed. In the days before mobile phones, I had no way of contacting them for an estimated arrival time. I was starting to get a little concerned about the delay when I saw them walking towards me at 5.15. As we passed through Security and out to the aircraft, I glanced to the west. The sky had a grey haze to it; the warm front was certainly in its way. I did a quick pre-flight and boarded the passengers, one in the back and the other in the front next to me. A quick call to the Tower and I had the airfield information and clearance to taxi to the active runway.

We got airborne at 5.40 and set heading to Gamston VOR, my first turning point. I glanced again to the west. The sun was just visible through the haze but I was alarmed to see some clouds lower than I would have liked. Never mind, we will still get back to White Waltham in a decent time. I glanced at the groundspeed readout from the DME. It was 15 kts slower than on the way north in the morning. The wind had definitely shifted and was now a pronounced headwind. I glanced at the fuel gauges and for the first time wished I had taken on some fuel at Leeds. We passed overhead Gamston and I turned right towards Daventry VOR.

This track would take me safely clear of East Midlands Airport. A slight left turn at Daventry would have me tracking towards the Stokenchurch mast and home. The two passengers were chatting and joking and enjoying the flight while I remained quiet. I was doing some quick calculations and was getting increasingly uncomfortable with the way things were going. The ground speed had dropped further and the air was becoming more unstable with a slight chop that increased my workload considerably. Worse, the cloud base was dropping and there were the first drops of rain appearing on the windscreen. The warm front was upon me.

It was also noticeably darker than half an hour earlier and I leant forward to switch on the navigation lights on the wings but left the instrument panel lights switched off to conserve my day vision for as long as possible. With Daventry VOR passed, I started the left turn towards the Stokenchurch mast. This mast is a useful landmark situated on the Chilterns. It rises to 1100ft above sea level. I was now in the cloud at 2500 ft so I dropped down to 2000 ft. I was aware that this was as low as I should be if flying visually but I was also aware that soon the cloud would force me to drop down lower. I tried to think. Should I climb and carry on IFR? That would involve ATC and a diversion to a big airport. If so, where? East Midlands and Birmingham airports were now behind me. Luton? Possibly. But if I could make Luton then surely I can make White Waltham? Also, what about the cost and inconvenience to my passengers? Luton is the last place they would want to end up. I decide to press on.

By now the rain was light but persistent. I tried to call RAF Benson for radar assistance but it was past 5 pm and they were closed. In a way, I was pleased as a call to them would achieve little but alert them to my plight. Also, what could they do to help? Another glance at the fuel gauges. They were both indicating just under a quarter full each but what did that really mean? Fuel gauges on light aircraft are notoriously inaccurate – as the saying goes the best fuel gauge is a full tank and a stopwatch. I tried to do some maths in my head. Let's see, I had set off with around 150 litres of fuel ….it took one hour and 45 minutes to Leeds at 32 litres/hour…… I had flown 55 minutes since departing Leeds….I estimated another hour to White Waltham……

I stopped, I was getting too tired to do the maths and needed to concentrate on my instrument flying. All I knew was that thanks to this headwind, I was burning much more fuel than I had anticipated. Approaching the Chiltern hills the cloud got a lot lower and I was forced to drop down to 1500ft then 1000ft. It was now too dark to see the instruments properly, so I was forced to switch on the instrument panel lights. Instantly day became night. It is very hard in a confined space to hide being anxious; I was getting worried and I was sure the passengers had noticed. I had stopped chatting and they too had stopped their banter and were now starting to ask some questions. Is this weather OK? Shouldn't we be there by now…. it didn't take this long on the way up….is everything OK? My answers were terse and I knew they sensed all was not well.

They fell silent as we flew on. I was low on fuel, in worsening weather and too low to be safe over the hills, the stuff of countless accident reports. And where the hell was the Stokenchurch mast? It should be here by now. I descended further to 800ft. Houses were visible but only as darker patches lit from inside with the warm glow of lights. What I would give to be down here rather than here. Then out of the murk, I saw Stokenchurch mast ahead and slightly to my right approaching fast. It's 330 feet tall and I was below its top and flying in and out of low stratus. It flashed past me and my heart was thumping, Christ, I could have hit it if I wasn't looking out! I wanted to land more than anything else in the world at that moment.

I called ahead on the radio to White Waltham praying that someone would still be there and that they weren't all in the bar or on their way home. No answer. I tried again, trying to keep the nervousness out of my voice. Please answer! On the third call, an answer from Paul Stanton. Thank God. Of course, if anyone would still be there it had to be Paul, the Club's 'Total Aviation Person'.

"G-SC, good evening! I was just about to pack up for the night. Go ahead," he responded in his usual jolly fashion. I passed my ETA and explained as discretely as I could my predicament. There was no point in broadcasting this to all and sundry.

"White Waltham, G-SC, estimating overhead the airfield at time 55. I will need some lights please if you could arrange it?"
There were no runway lights available at White Waltham at the time but I hope Paul understood what needed to be done.

As I arrived, at what I estimated was the overhead of the airfield, discernible only as a dark patch of ground, it was raining heavily and almost completely dark. There was no sign of any lights on the airfield. Come on, where are you? And then, all of a sudden, I saw the headlights of four cars pointing in two 'V's down what I assumed was a runway although it was too dark to see at this stage. Thank God. Paul must have pulled some guys out of the bars to drive their cars onto the airfield. I turned quickly so as not to lose sight of the lights, switched the landing light on and lined up to approach over the top of the cars. As it was dark, I flared too high and landed heavily with a thump but was too relieved to be on the ground to care much. For the first time, but by no means the last, I was so pleased to be on the ground.

* * * *

Saturday nights at the club were disco nights and this being the end of the carefree, pre-Aids 1970s, suburban morals were pretty loose; in fact, it seemed most people left them at the door of the Club on these occasions. As instructors, we staked our claim at the bar early in the evening to get some beers in and observe events. By 7 pm the first of the social members started to arrive, usually

Stokenchurch Mast

couples but a few single guys too, all wide lapels, garish shirts and big hair. Naturally, we totally ignored them. The big attraction at the Club was the 'one-armed bandit' slot machine at the end of the bar by the entrance to the dining room. This had a jackpot of £100, which was a lot of money in 1979. Some members would spend all night on the machine pressing money in and spinning the wheels hoping for the big payout. I only witnessed the jackpot a couple of times. It wasn't exactly Las Vegas but the sight and sound of £100 in metal vouchers cascading out of the machine and spilling onto the floor was impressive. By 9 pm the disco would be in full swing and the social members would be bumping and grinding on the gloomy dance floor lit only by the spinning glass disco ball. The bar would be thick with cigarette smoke mixed with the smell of aftershave and perfume. From our barstools, we would watch the entertainment degenerate and lay bets on how the evening would play out, who would melt into the shadows with who. It wasn't exactly 'car keys in a basket' but it wasn't far removed and there was a group of couples whom we knew as regular swingers and we watched them with particular interest.

CHESS WING

At the end of 1979, with my CAA Commercial Pilot Licence exams passed, I got my first break. After a year of instructing at White Waltham a chance encounter at the flying club in November with Geoff Wass, the Chief Pilot at Chess Wing landed me a job flying from Leavesden Aerodrome, near Watford. Leavesden is now the home of Warner Brothers and closed as an airfield in 1994 but at the time was a small airfield with a 950m runway and a Rolls Royce factory that manufactured small gas turbines for helicopters. Geoff offered me a job flying the two Beechcraft Barons the company operated with the promise to move on to the pressurised Cessna 421C 'Golden Eagle' as I gained more experience. I was pretty happy, to me this was a perfect break. As an authorised examiner, Geoff would complete the necessary training on the aircraft.

Chess Wing, named after the small River Chess that runs to the west of the airfield, was a family business run by Geoff and Diana Wass. Geoff was a clever chap; he had been a flight test engineer with Handley Page in his younger days and had the air of distraction and slight bemusement typical of a boffin. Diana was brisk and efficient and did the accounts and admin which was just as well – I think that if Geoff had been involved with the money side of things, the company would have lasted a month.

There were only three pilots at Chess Wing; me, Bill Driver and Barry Bristow. Geoff flew occasionally to fill in. All the aircraft belonged to a leisure company called ABI Caravans based in Beverley, Yorkshire and were used to take their salesmen around the UK and also, on a regular basis, to their factory in Rotterdam. The flying involved positioning empty from Leavesden to Brough Aerodrome on the north side of the river Humber early in the morning, picking up the passengers (normally just one or two) and completing the day's flying. It was interesting flying, almost always to airfields on the coast, where the caravan sites were mostly located. A lot of the aerodromes were disused and neglected and in poor repair, so some care was required.

Brough Aerodrome was owned by British Aerospace whose factory next to the airfield made wings for various military aircraft such as the Hawk trainer and was located just west of the Humber Bridge, which was under construction at the time. At night, the 1000m runway was lit by old-fashioned 'gooseneck' paraffin lanterns that needed setting out and lighting, so advance notice was always needed for arrivals after sunset. We pilots often stayed overnight at the Brough Flying Club, a 1930s art deco clubhouse where a room, a decent breakfast and a comfy lounge were available for very little.

The Baron is a great aircraft, good looking with a 190 kts cruise speed and I was really happy to have this as my aircraft in my first proper flying job. Chess Wing operated two variants, the Model 55 which was a four-seater and the Model 58 which was larger, with a club four cabin and six seats in total. Nice handling and well put together with either two 285hp or 300 hp Continental engines. Most of my friends were flying lesser aircraft, so I was a happy guy.

Leavesden was also the home of Eagle Aircraft Services which were a Beechcraft Service Centre. This was the remnants of British Eagle the airline owned by Harold Bamberg until it came to an end in 1968. Eagles looked after all the Chess Wing aircraft.

One day, I arrive as usual at the airfield at around 7.30 for the usual 8 am takeoff having driven up from my flat in South Kensington. I walk into the flight shed with my flight bag, collect the aircraft keys, chat briefly with the guys and walk over to the aircraft that's parked near the fuel pumps as usual. It has just come out of some maintenance with Eagles and is looking pristine in the early morning sunshine. While the refuelers are topping off the tanks, I complete the walk round. Battery on, a quick check of the lights and pitot heat, battery off, brakes set. I remove the control lock and start the walk-round ritual that's as old as flying itself. General condition, propeller condition, fluid levels, tyre pressures, control surfaces etc, etc. Aware that the aircraft has just come out of maintenance, I take special care in the inspection. Well, I think I did but I didn't. I miss one thing and it causes me my first proper scare in any aeroplane.

The external checks complete, I do a final check of the fuel caps, remove the chocks and settle myself in the cockpit. With the battery on, fuel on, cowl flaps open, fuel pumps and magnetos on, I start each engine in turn. They start instantly and settle quickly into a deep rumble. I switch the avionics master switch on and make a quick call to ATC with the usual morning pleasantries before taxiing the short distance to the threshold of Runway 06, checking as I go the fuel, controls, cowl flaps, trim settings, radios and engine instruments. ATC clears me to takeoff with a left turn towards Bovingdon VOR climbing to not above 2400ft to keep me below controlled airspace.

The weather is lovely, with no wind, a pale blue sky and cool so the acceleration is brisk. As the aircraft accelerates down the runway it dawns on me that something is not normal, the elevator feels heavier and heavier as the aircraft picks up speed. The 100 mph lift-off speed arrives quickly at which point I'm aware there is a big problem as the elevator is now very heavy. The runway is not overly long and stopping is not an option as I would probably overrun the runway. So, using all my strength, I pull the aircraft into the air. What's going on, is the trim out of position? No, a quick glance down confirms it's indicating in the takeoff position.

The Baron is powerful and accelerates quickly and when airborne the elevator control force is extreme and I have to think fast. I try to trim nose up but the nose down force only increases dramatically. I quickly reset the trim to where it was. What's going on? I reach for the throttles to try and reduce power but am unable to hold altitude when I do this; with only one arm to hold the control yoke, I am not strong enough to keep the nose up. I quickly snatch a handful of power off before placing both hands on the yoke again. The aircraft dives momentarily but the aircraft slows quickly and as it does so the control forces reduce but are still considerable. With my heart in my mouth, I make a quick call to ATC that I need an immediate return due to control problems which they acknowledge calmly in the usual laconic way of all ATC.

As I turn downwind at 120 kts the aircraft is more controllable although still trying to dive for the ground if I release backward pressure the least bit. My arms are shaking partly with the strain and partly with the adrenaline pumping through my body. I try and formulate a plan. Not knowing what the problem is, I decide to land flapless in case lowering the flap makes things worse. I turn base leg and final and settle at the 115 mph flapless approach speed. The gear is still down as I didn't even have the chance to raise this after takeoff. I'm aware that I will need to touch down right at the end of the runway with this approach speed on such a short runway. As I cross the runway threshold, I chop the power and the aircraft lands heavily with the nose gear thumping down as I release the back pressure. I am now concerned with stopping as the runway end is approaching fast so I brake hard and I can hear the tyres complaining as I do so.

With heavy braking and some swerving, I bring the aircraft to a stop in the last few yards of tarmac and vacate the runway. Parking in the spot I had left only ten minutes earlier, I switch the avionics master switch off, shut down both engines and switch the mags and battery switch off. I sit there shaking for probably five minutes, composing myself, before I consider getting out of the aircraft and I am still shaking as I see the Chief Engineer of Eagles walking towards me with a puzzled look on his face.

"Got a problem?" he asks.

"Yes, there is something seriously wrong with the aircraft and I bloody nearly crashed!" I splutter, or words to that effect probably not as polite.

I'm still full of adrenaline, still shaking. I explain the problem to him and we walk around the aircraft together. And then we spot it. The elevator trim tab had been reassembled upside down so that the tab was projecting upwards and not downwards as it would normally do. This explained it – as I accelerated this would cause an increasing nose-down force and trimming nose up, as it tried, would only increase the nose-down force as the tab was now operating in a reverse sense.

How had I missed this on my walk around despite my taking extra care, or so I thought? It was so obvious. And how on earth had a flight control maintenance task (a so-called 'critical task' in aviation maintenance-speak) that requires two independent engineer inspections been wrongly signed off? The Chief paled. He was shocked and was clearly very worried that I would file a MOR, the official channel for reporting serious issues, but to be honest, I was just too pleased to be in one piece on the ground to even consider this and I had other things to attend to like calling Geoff to explain that the passengers waiting for me at Brough would have to make other plans. I learned a valuable lesson though – always treble-check everything after maintenance! I mentally kicked myself for my carelessness in not being more observant. If I had taken off into a low cloud base or had an engine failure as well, this could have killed me.

* * * *

There are those pilots that have landed wheels up and those pilots that have yet to do so, so the old saying goes. Luckily, I never have but one experience made me realise how easily it could be done. On a routine flight back from Rotterdam in the Baron I was lined up on finals to Brough's Runway 30, a long way out with approach flap and the gear extended. However, the headwind was stronger that day than I expected and I realised that it was going to take a long time to get to short finals where I could lower the final stage of flap before landing. So, I raised the gear again to pick up some speed, reduce the noise and continued the approach.

In a small aircraft, even with a good headset, you can still just hear passengers talking and I had been aware all the flight that one of them was a know-it-all and was giving a running commentary on the progress of the flight. As we neared the runway, I heard him say,

"He will lower the undercarriage soon."

God! I had forgotten to lower the gear again having retracted it! My hand twitched instinctively towards the gear handle but stopped – I didn't want Know It All's conversation to be seen as a trigger for me to lower the gear. After a few seconds, I slowly reached for the gear handle and lowered the wheels. With an electrical whine and thump the wheels locked into place. The act of putting the gear down a few minutes earlier had ticked the box in my mind that the gear was down and raising it again hadn't reset the thought process. A classic 'gotcha' and another lesson learned.

* * * *

Flying out of Leavesden was great except for the long drive, often in rush hour traffic, from my flat in South Kensington. This could easily take an hour and a half on a bad day. To get to the airfield in time for an 8 am takeoff I had to leave the flat by 6 am at the latest to arrive at the airfield at 7.30, do the preflight and be ready in time. On one awful occasion, after a late night with friends the evening before, I overslept. When I say overslept, I mean, really overslept. For some reason, I slept right through the alarm and when I opened a bleary eye and looked at the clock it was 7.30. Christ, it can't be! I'm meant to be at Leavesden now and taking off in thirty minutes! We have all experienced that brief moment of disbelief when we oversleep. I'm dreaming! The clock must be wrong! It must have gained an hour in the night! I look at my watch

Beechcraft Baron 58 – stock photo

and yes, it really is 7.30. Fuck! Heart thumping, I jump out of bed and try and get dressed in a hurry, which always takes twice as long. I struggle to get my uniform trousers on while simultaneously buttoning my shirt and forcing my feet into my shoes, hopping around the room like a Dervish. In some semblance of 'dressed' I grab my flight bag and bolt through the front door and into my car, driving like a madman through the streets of Kensington and up Edgware Road. The rush hour traffic is building and progress is slow but by driving at breakneck speed and taking stupid risks I arrive at the airfield at just after nine o'clock. I throw the car into the car park, skidding to a halt in a cloud of dust and run to the flight shed in a sweat. The passenger is there glaring at me with a face like thunder, saying nothing which makes me feel even worse. I offer profuse apologies as we walk to the aircraft and I start my pre-flight. We are airborne at 9.30, one hour and a half hours late. Ouch. I'm wondering if this is my glorious career ended before it has even started but Geoff somehow manages to smooth things over with ABI Caravans.

* * * *

One of the contracts Geoff brought to Chess Wing was to supply a pilot each Saturday to fly for the high-street boutique chain 'Chelsea Girl'. The Lewis family, who owned the chain at the time, had a Cessna 421 similar to Chess Wing's, appropriately registered G-GIRL and known to ATC everywhere as 'Gee Girl' rather than the correct phonetic version. The Lewis family had an interesting approach to auditing their stores. Each Saturday they would descend, unannounced, to three shops around the UK, walk in and inspect the books. I imagine this approach kept the shop managers on their toes as the visits were never pre-warned and so the frequency of the visits was completely unpredictable. I often volunteered to do these flights as the passengers were fun to fly and it was a busy day, a typical day's flying one day taking in Newcastle, Glasgow and Bristol and another maybe Norwich, Leeds and Plymouth. We would land, the passengers would disembark, get into a taxi and return one to two hours later either full of smiles - or not, depending on what they found. The Lewis family, although courteous to me, were a ruthless north London business family with long experience in the 'rag trade' and I wouldn't have liked to be the manager on the receiving end of an inspection that went badly.

Eventually, I was made redundant from Chess Wing. Geoff approached me one evening and very apologetically told me that ABI Caravans had decided to sell two of their aircraft in the 1982 recession and therefore business wasn't what it was. Although we did some air taxi charter work, the ABI contract was the 'bread and butter' of the company so the loss of this contract was a big blow. As the last man in, I would have to be the first man out. I was disappointed but understood and for a year or so flew freelance, finding work where I could. I picked up work flying old Chieftains on night freight for a fly-by-night company called, appropriately, Nightflight based at Luton Airport. I was living in Battersea in South London at the time. I would drive to Luton, go flying, (typically to Brussels and back) and drive home again. All for £50 a night which, even then, was a pittance and barely covered my costs but it kept me flying and current. One night, I turned up at Luton airport as planned and got a lift out onto the ramp with the handling agent to find heavy chains locked around the undercarriage of the Chieftain and a lien stuck to the entry door. The company was bust - game over.

From time to time I flew for Air Foyle, which was also based at Luton, doing similar cargo and mail runs. Chris Foyle himself called me at 10 o'clock one night when they were desperately scratching around for a freelancer to operate the night's service to Brussels that normally departed at 1 am. I had just got in from the pub.

"Mark, it's Chris at Air Foyle. Could you help us out? We need a pilot tonight for the Brussels run, our regular guy has called in sick. Any chance you can help?" he wheedled.

Bloody cheek, I thought, obviously I'm not his first call. Never mind. I bit my tongue.

"Chris, I'd love to, but I've just come back from the pub." There was a long pause. "Well, how much did you have?"

* * * *

Apart from the less-than-glamorous work flying night mail, I also had some memorable trips over this freelancing period. I was asked by Peter Veasey of Heathrow Air Ambulance fame - known to one and all as 'Sleazy Veasey' due to his shambolic appearance - to fly him and six colleagues down to Cannes for the annual ABTA conference in May 1982. Peter had all the ambulance contracts at Heathrow and made a lot of money from this business. I first had to find a suitable aircraft and after hunting around a bit found a private Cessna 421 that I could dry lease cheaply at Staverton Airport. I drove down to Staverton, met the owner, wrote a large cheque for the anticipated flying hours plus a deposit and flew the aircraft to White Waltham. Life was simple then, no background checks, contracts etc. I just showed my licence, wrote a cheque and flew off.

The flight to Cannes the next day was uneventful, arriving on a warm, balmy evening. It was a wonderful week. The party, with me included, stayed at the five-star Majestic Hotel on the beach front and I had a fabulous suite on the top floor overlooking the blue sea, all expenses paid for by Peter. I had a great time, spending the week eating and drinking and watching the working girls steam the bar for custom. Come the day to leave, I decide that the luxurious fluffy towelling robe that was hanging in the room wardrobe was too good to pass up.

Cessna 421C, G-GIRL, parked at Leavesden

It had a gold 'M' embroidered on the front. Naughty, but how could I possibly resist a robe with my initial on? So, as I leave the room, literally as the last act, I pop the robe into my grip. The bill has already been settled by Peter, so I go downstairs, put the key on the front desk say my goodbyes and walk outside to get a cab to the airport. As I am loading the bag into the boot of one of the waiting taxis, the uniformed concierge comes down the front steps and walks slowly over to me. My heart sinks with a guilty feeling.

"Monsieur, I'm sure zere is a mistake but I have been asked by ze front desk if you have accidentally taken something from ze room," he says, smiling charmingly. I can't believe it - it can't be that more than five minutes have elapsed since I left my room. I can feel myself sweating.

"I don't think so," I say, trying to look puzzled "but, please, take a look."

I unzip my grip and there right on the top is the dazzling white robe. I have now gone bright red and don't know where to look. He looks up at me directly and smiles,

"I am so sorry. Monsieur. Obviously, a mistake was made. Please, have a safe journey." And he touches his cap and walks off, duty done and clearly not wanting an embarrassing scene on the front steps of the hotel. Beautifully managed. Heart pounding, I get into the cab. I have seldom been so embarrassed and vowed never to do that again.

SKYGUARD

After a while, I needed a steady income. Freelancing was too hit and miss and my occasional returns to my previous life, working as a hydrographic surveyor in the North Sea wasn't really working out. In theory, some North Sea work with its tax-free cash and some freelance flying seemed like a perfect mix, however in reality I found that I just got out of practice at both. I needed a permanent flying job. Enter Alan Joyce.

Alan owned a company called Skyguard and was a colourful character, to put it mildly. He was a wealthy scrap merchant from Pinner, north London, who had originally made his money by recycling the precious metals found on discarded printed circuit boards from large electronic companies such as Ferranti, English Electric and Plessey. However, stories circulated about consignments of gold being flown to and from Europe in his Beech Baron so I think there was more to his acquired wealth than circuit boards. In any event, Alan was always very keen to keep his nose clean with everything to do with the police. The Skyguard offices were over a baker's shop in Rickmansworth High Street which was about as anonymous as can be.

Alan was a classic self-made man, partial to Jaguars, golf, whisky and explosions of temper. Caught driving home in his Jaguar XJS one time after an extended 19th hole at the Pinner golf club he was stopped by the police on suspicion of drunk driving. To avoid the breathalyser, Alan stepped out of the car and theatrically clutched his chest, falling to the ground, feigning a heart attack. He was taken to the hospital but was still over the limit hours later and promptly charged.

The company had two aircraft when I joined, Alan's personal Baron 58, G-BEUL, and a Piper 'Chieftain', G-SAVE. I was employed as Chief Pilot working closely with the Operations Manager, John Morgan. John was a retired Gulf Air pilot who had been there at the beginning of the airline, flying the BAC1-11. He was a large man with bushy 'mutton chops' who was an encyclopaedia of knowledge with all things aviation, particularly the history of CAA rule-making. For every CAA regulation, John could cite, chapter and verse, the accident that led to the regulation - the so-called 'Tombstone Imperative'. He also edited the Operations Manual for the company. In it was included a hilarious section on the hazards of flying at altitude concerning bodily functions and gas production – a reference to the fact that people tend to break wind more at altitude than at sea level. It was the only reference I have ever seen to farting in any Operations Manual. John was old school and kept a bottle of Dewar's in his bottom desk drawer which he would enjoy in large measures with soda after lunch in the pub. Needless to say, his only really productive hours were in the morning. Around 4 pm, John would shuffle off with his parting phrase "Well, sufficient unto the day is the evil thereof" and somehow drive home. Drinking and driving were rife in those days. I really enjoyed his company, he had a wealth of knowledge and I learned a lot from him, not just about flying but his general philosophies on life. He loved to compare the stupidity of human behaviour with the regimentation and industry of insects.

The accountant at the company was an Indian fellow called Mr Soneji who worked under several aliases. Whether Alan knew this or not, he also ran his own businesses from Skyguard's office; corner shops, off licences, launderettes etc. When he answered the phone, he could switch seamlessly and in different dialects between Mr Patel, Mr Soneji and Mr Khan without batting an eyelid, depending on who the caller was. He wasn't a qualified accountant but he was as sharp as a tack and knew every trick in the book. Which was exactly what Alan wanted.

I was living in Southfields in south London at the time and Skyguard's aircraft were based at Leavesden and Birmingham airports, which wasn't convenient so I asked Alan if he could offer me one of the company cars as a runabout. The only car he had available was an old Lada estate, a truly awful Russian buzz box that set my teeth on edge and practically fell apart as I went along. Every time I drove it, something else would fail or fall off; the sun visors, then the window winder, followed by the rear-view mirror and the indicator stalk. However, a free car with petrol paid for is a free car after all so I was happy to take the inevitable ribbing from friends. I heard all the Lada jokes a thousand times. When I took the car for its MOT after the first year the mechanic gave me some sobering facts.

"This car has failed on fourteen major points," he told me, looking down at his clipboard. "Where have you been driving it?"

I didn't dare tell him the truth that for twelve months I'd mostly been hammering up and down motorways. I would leave Southfields early morning, drive through London, up the M1 and M6 to Birmingham do a day's flying and, as often as not, drive home again. Talk about young and keen.

* * * *

Alan was always up for a quick buck so when a call came in one wet Friday evening for a charter, I was dispatched to do it. The task was to collect one passenger from Southend Airport and fly him over to Amsterdam. Alan assured me he would pay for the flight in cash when I met him at Southend. I drove over to Leavesden to collect the aircraft and positioned it across to Southend. It was around 9 pm when I arrived at Southend and the airport was almost deserted. I met the passenger in the departure lounge and accepted the cash payment for the flight in a large envelope. He was mid-30s, well dressed but I thought it was strange that he had nothing with him apart from a briefcase and a teddy bear.

"It's for my daughter," he explained, straight-faced, when he saw me glancing at it. I smiled and mentally shrugged; this was none of my business and I escorted him through Customs and Immigration to the aircraft parked outside. The officers paid no particular interest to him, a cursory glance at his passport and a couple of questions and we were through.

Airborne and halfway over the North Sea, I glanced back to check he was OK. He was sitting in one of the forward-facing club seats with the briefcase open and his hands busy inside. The bear sat on the seat next to him, looking blankly at me with its button eyes. He glanced up, nodded a smile and went back to his briefcase. We landed at Amsterdam and parked on a central stand, unusually, but I was pleased as this meant we would clear Customs and Immigration quickly. Again, no official paid him any notice, even though he had nothing with him but the briefcase and the bear. How suspicious does that look? I was amazed he didn't attract more attention but it was now around midnight and things were quiet even in Amsterdam. We said our goodbyes, shook hands and he disappeared into the concourse. When I got back to Southend, I had to stay the night as Leavesden was now closed. I called Alan as was customary just to let him know how the trip went.

"Did he pay you in cash?" he demanded, interrupting me mid-sentence.

I could sense something was not right. I assured him that he had - and the full amount.

"Well get it into the bloody bank first thing in the morning, we need to lose it fast. The bastard has just done a building society in Hastings for twenty grand!"

That explained it; he had been busy counting the money when I looked around during the flight.

The next morning, I was waiting outside Barclays Bank in Southend on the stroke of opening time at 9.30 and paid the stolen cash into the Skyguard account. In those days, banks didn't question the deposit of large amounts of cash. When I returned to the office in Rickmansworth the next day, after positioning back to Leavesden, Alan was looking nervous.

"The Old Bill has been in touch. You need to go to Vine Street police station as soon as you can, CID wants a statement from you."

A little anxious, I caught the train into London and made my way to the police station. On the way into town, I mentally ran through my actions the day before. I couldn't see that I had done anything wrong; I had filed a flight plan, cleared Customs and Immigration at Southend and escorted the passenger through the Immigration channels in Amsterdam. Everything was above board; surely, I couldn't be held responsible for assisting an armed robber to leave the country? Fortunately, the police saw it that way too.

"Thanks for your cooperation, sir. We have Interpol looking for him," the detective told me after I had given him my account. "We will pick him up eventually, we always do," he added wearily, putting away his notepad. And, sure enough, they did, three days later in a hotel near Liege.

I did another dodgy charter a few months later in Skyguard's Chieftain G-SAVE this time from Exeter Airport down to Madrid. Again, it was late on a wet Friday night. This was the modus operandi in those days if you wanted to escape – choose a sleepy airport late at night and no one will look too closely. The four male passengers wanted out of the country in a hurry. They were tense and certainly in a rush to get going and were visibly relieved once the wheels were tucked away and we were on our way south. It turned out they were one step ahead of the police who wanted them to 'help with enquiries' regarding a

£20m financial fraud in Edinburgh; it was all over the news the next day. Their relief when we touched down in Madrid, four and a quarter hours later, was palpable; suddenly they were all laughs and jokes. In those days there was no formal extradition from Spain which was why it was full of robbers and other undesirables enjoying life in the sun on the 'Costa del Crime' rather than the inside of Parkhurst prison.

* * * *

"We've got a charter on Saturday from Denham down to Exeter with two guys. Can you do it?" asked Trish, the Skyguard secretary, over the phone. Exeter again.

"Sure, no problem. What are the details?"

It turned out it was to take two young guys, George Michael and Andrew Ridgeley to the city for the day. They were well-known celebrities apparently and I had vaguely heard of them but no more than that. Departure was planned for 9 am from Leavesden and the planned return at 4 pm. This was going to involve a long day sitting around the sleepy airport but that was usual in air taxi work, you get used to it. Read the paper, drink too much coffee, go for a walk, drink more coffee and then do an extended pre-flight, maybe even revise the flight manual; anything to pass the time.

The guys show up and we walk over to the Baron. They are all loose jackets and big hair as was 'a la mode' in the early 1980s, friendly and kidding around. Off we go and forty-five minutes later we land at Exeter and I escort them into the Terminal building. Their limo pick-up is late, so we sit at the café and have a coffee together. They get some car magazines out and start looking at the cars they are going to buy when they have passed their driving tests. I realise then that these guys are even younger than I thought but are obviously planning on getting rich – they are looking at Aston Martins, Ferraris, and Lamborghinis. I'm aware of a couple of the girls serving in the café nudging each other, whispering, giggling and pointing at us. Eventually, the limo arrives and off they both go with a wave.

"What's funny, why are you laughing?" I ask one of the girls. "Was that really 'Wham!'?" she asks "I can't believe it, so amazing! Can I ask for an autograph when they come back?"

* * * *

Skyguard was heavily involved with Securicor at Birmingham and because of their security interests, they got involved with 'Cash in Transit' flights. These CIT flights, as they were known, involved returning Irish Punt banknotes to Dublin on behalf of the Allied Irish Bank - and it involved a lot of money. I heard anecdotally that it was often in the region of £500,000 in cash, a great deal of money in the early 1980s and as a result, all the pilots had to be security-vetted by Securicor. Once I was settled in the pilot's seat, sacks and sacks of notes would be loaded behind me in the empty cabin, the seats since removed.

As access to the only door on the aircraft – at the rear of the aircraft - was blocked by the piles of sacks, there was no proper escape path in the event of an accident, so Alan thoughtfully offered me one of his scrap-merchant axes so I could bash my way through the windows if need be. Once fully loaded, a portly, middle-aged security guard clambered in and the door was closed behind him. He lay among the sacks making himself as comfortable as possible for the flight. No seat belt or anything. (I would love to run this arrangement past a modern-day risk assessment.) The guard mostly fell asleep during the flights and I did idly daydream sometimes about how easy it would be to take some extra fuel and alter course while the guard was asleep and head off to pre-extradition Spain with the money. Having paid off the guard, I would be a rich man….

For reasons that I never understood, some clever fellow in Securicor decided that the flight should leave Birmingham at exactly 11 am every Tuesday, week after week. Bearing in mind the security risk these flights posed and that the IRA was very active at the time and would surely have loved some ready cash, this struck me as a curious decision. With the Chieftain emblazoned with Securicor colours and loaded with bank notes, I would then fly to Belfast, where the army would provide security with soldiers and armoured vehicles, collect more banknotes and after an hour on the ground, continue to Dublin. Here, security was even tighter – both the Irish army and the Garda surrounded the aircraft as the Punt notes were unloaded. I then loaded up with UK pound notes and made the return flight via Belfast back to Birmingham.

Skyguard's Baron 58 G-BEUL

Piper PA31 Chieftain, G-SAVE, in Securicor colours

* * * *

6th June 1984 and I am flying a group to Caen in Normandy in the Skyguard Baron as part of the 40th D-Day commemorations. On board are Selina Scott and Frank Bough, well-known TV presenters and the actor Richard Todd. On the same day forty years earlier, he was part of the 6th Airborne Division that was parachuted into Normandy near Pegasus Bridge. Along with a few other aircraft in the area also heading to Caen, I am listening in on the Paris Information frequency as a US Marine Corps helicopter, carrying President Reagan, crosses the Channel and heads to the Pointe du Hoc where he will deliver his famous speech at the US Ranger memorial. I can see the Sikorsky in the distance, a tiny spot against the sea. Paris Information are notorious for not replying, so we are all listening with amused interest as the Marine pilot tries to make contact.

"Paris Information, this is Marine One," he calls with a voice full of authority. Silence. "Paris Information, this is Marine One," he calls again. Again, silence. Several times the pilot calls with the same result; Paris Information, true to form, is ignoring everyone. The pilot is becoming more and more irritated. After all, he is carrying the leader of the free world in the back and justifiably expects some acknowledgement. Eventually, someone butts in.

"Marine One, I wouldn't bother mate, they never reply to anyone."

"Yeah", comes the reply, "I kinda figure that."

* * * *

One of the more challenging series of flights I did with Skyguard was flying low-grade medical isotopes for the Wellcome Trust, the health research charity based in London. Flying radioactive substances is not permitted by international law unless the carrier has a Dangerous Goods (DG) certificate, but I don't think Alan Joyce worried about that too much. I was sent off on a two-day DG course at Heathrow to learn about the management of Class 7 DGs (radioactive substances) but that's probably as far as our compliance with the regulations went. These isotopes were very temperature sensitive and if they got too cold were rendered useless, so I did a series of flights with a max/min thermometer in the nacelle baggage bays behind the engine which I reckoned would be the warmest place in flight. Sure enough, the temperature in the nacelles never got below freezing even at 10,000ft so that's where the packages went. However, occasionally I was asked to carry an isotope that was referred to as a 'generator'. I have no idea what a 'generator' is, but I do know that it is pretty 'hot' radioactively speaking. It was placed in the middle of a barrel the size of a small beer keg and weighed probably 25 kgs due to the amount of lead that surrounded the isotope which I was told was only the size of a large peanut. The Geiger counter still went haywire when placed anywhere near the barrel. Due to its level of radiation, according to the regulations it had to be a certain distance from a living person, the so-called Transport Index. This distance was just achievable in the Chieftain with it sitting on the very rear position in the cabin, safely lashed down with ties. I wore a dosimeter clipped to my shirt which would turn black if I received too high a dose of radiation. I never did but it was never explained to me what would happen in that event anyway.

* * * *

Alan Joyce decided, with a little helpful prompting from John Morgan, that as Chief Pilot I should become an IRE/TRE - the coveted Instrument Rating and Type Rating Examiner qualification. The company was growing and operating a Handley Page 'Herald' on a Securicor contract in addition to the company's three Chieftain and one Baron aircraft. For me, with barely 2000 hours of flying experience, this was a great opportunity. The course was prestigious and generally offered to senior airline captains not someone with my limited and chequered background and no time on jet aircraft, so I counted myself very fortunate.

In March 1985 I went up to Stansted to enrol in the course run by CAAFU, the CAA Flying Unit that was disbanded in 1996. The course was demanding and designed to test you. The first week involved ensuring you had a very thorough knowledge of the regulations and understood the responsibility of signing someone's licence to allow them to continue flying using their Instrument Rating. The second week was to hone your briefing and debriefing skills. The CAA trainers were skilled at this and played the difficult, stroppy candidate who would argue with you, the 'examiner', whenever possible. They were also very good at demonstrating flying just on the limit of a pass or fail, even after a pint or two at lunch in The Dog and Duck where - unbelievably - we went for lunch each day. Which was it, a pass? Or a fail? This is what you had to decide and be prepared to justify with the argumentative candidate in the debrief, all the while being filmed so you could cringe on replay. I was taught to forget the small misdemeanours and concentrate on the big gotchas that the 'candidate' couldn't argue with, for example, an incorrect altimeter setting or flying below minima. You had to avoid being drawn into arguments at all costs. It was undoubtedly hard work and I spent every evening practising my briefs.

I was paired in the simulator (an ancient Series 1 Hawker) with an old hand from BWIA, British West Indies Airlines. He was a captain on their Lockheed L1011 'TriStars'. We flew left seat, and right seat alternately. This guy was British but had lived in Trinidad long enough to have the slooow island mentality. You simply couldn't rush him. While I was desperate to impress the examiners with my speed and efficiency, born of single pilot flying, he would deliberately take his time. An engine fire? He would acknowledge my call of the fire, ask me to cancel the fire warning bell, give me control of the aircraft and slowly reach for his half-moon glasses. Then he would pick up the checklist, read the index, confirm with me the correct section before handing it back to me, take back the controls and ask me to read the agreed checklist. This probably took thirty seconds but seemed a lifetime with the light of a big fire warning light staring me in the face. He taught me a valuable lesson and one that I hadn't learned previously. All my experience to date had been flying solo in piston aircraft in which, if you didn't act quickly following an engine failure, you would not survive. It's a lesson everyone should have engrained when transitioning to jet aircraft: don't rush, sit on your hands before doing anything.

The simulator sessions were run by the legendary Tony Angel. He was reputed to be the world's most experienced simulator instructor when he finally retired with tens of thousands of hours in simulators. Tony was excellent at playing ATC in the sim and mimicking beautifully other airlines in their native accents, Russians, Africans, Egyptians you name it. He was hilarious and this helped provide light relief when things started to get stressful in the 'box'.

SOUTH EAST AIR

After a while, it was time to move on from Skyguard and for a short time I flew for South East Air (SEA), based at Biggin Hill. This was started up by Don Daines, an ebullient character typical of the sort of enthusiastic amateur that was found at Biggin in those days. In fairness, however, Don at least had a solid track record, having started up Euroair and running that company successfully for a few years.

Don explained to me at the interview, held over lunch at his favourite curry restaurant in Biggin Hill, that he was starting up SEA with a brand-new Britten-Norman 'Islander' and he wanted me to join as Chief Pilot. He had two contracts secured. One was for Evergreen Cargo carrying packages on a nightly service between Gatwick and Maastricht and the other was with Jersey European Airways on a passenger run between Shoreham Airport and Jersey. As I enjoyed my curry, I could see that this would make it a very busy aircraft. The plan was for the nightly run to start at Gatwick with the seats removed by the resident gopher. After loading the freight, the aircraft would fly to Maastricht, the freight would come off and the return load brought back to Gatwick. There, after unloading, the seats would be re-installed and in the early morning, another pilot would fly empty to Shoreham on the south coast. There it would do the run to Jersey with passengers, spend the day there and return to Shoreham in the evening. The same pilot would fly back to Gatwick empty after disembarking the passengers, the gopher would remove the seats and the cycle would start again. He had plans to add a much larger ATR42 to the fleet which is why I was interested in the position.

To anyone that doesn't know the 'Islander' let me describe it briefly. It was designed in the 1960s and is a good aircraft for what it is best at doing which is to fly between rough and very short airstrips. It is basic, tough and has great short-field performance. At this it excels; for anything else it's dreadful. It's slow and noisy and the undercarriage is not retractable, so it picks up ice at the drop of a hat. Additionally, it has a petrol-fuelled Janitrol heater in the rear of the aircraft that never provides any heat in the cockpit and is almost guaranteed to fail immediately after takeoff, so the flights at night and in winter could be grim.

The moment ice was picked up on the airframe, (guaranteed in cloud at 8,000ft unless it's the height of summer) the airspeed washed off by 20 kts. You didn't have much speed to start with so if heading into a strong westerly wind on the way back from Maastricht, you sat there slowly freezing to death watching the trucks travelling at almost the same speed as you on the Belgian motorways - quite a dispiriting experience. In icing conditions, your speed over the ground could be as little as 80 kts. I once got close to diverting into Southend Airport for fuel because the flight took so long – and this was just from Maastricht, a flight of only 195 nm. Madness.

I used to listen to the BBC World Service on the ADF to pass the time on these flights and this was where I first heard of the explosion at Chernobyl in April 1986. I didn't pay too much attention to this at the time but later understood that by the time the western news agencies heard of the explosion it was already hours after the event. And the drift of the radioactive cloud was westerly and had reached across Germany and the Netherlands and into the UK. Had I been sitting in the fallout on my way to Maastricht that night? Who knows.

The passenger flying was different, however. Flights on the Shoreham-Jersey-Shoreham route were enjoyable, especially in summer – a day in Jersey was no hardship after all. Jersey European Airways was testing the water on this route using the little 'Islander'; if the route proved popular then they would put a bigger aircraft on the route, hopefully the ATR42 Don had plans for. We could carry up to nine passengers in the Islander, day trippers with hand luggage only, with one of them often sitting up the front next to the pilot. The passengers approached the aircraft with the usual apprehension of seeing a 'dinky toy' machine with 'those propeller things' but for the most part, they were happy enough unless it got bumpy in which case the chatter went quiet and they quickly started searching the seat backs for the sick bags.

South East Air's Britten-Norman Islander G-OSEA

Don had great plans to expand into airline flying with an Airbus 320 aircraft; in those days, airlines were starting up all the time and usually disappearing just as quickly. He had the airline name sorted out – he wanted to use 'Imperial Airways' although I'm not sure British Airways, who have historical rights to this name, were aware of this. He had already designed the crew uniforms. All he hadn't thought about was the tedious things such as sourcing and financing the aircraft, obtaining route licences, recruitment and crew training. Don was a lovely guy but a classic cart-before-the-horse dreamer.

INTERFLIGHT AIR CHARTER

In May 1986 I joined Interflight at Gatwick as Chief Pilot. Interflight was owned by Simon Masey and Terry Rawlings, two British Airways pilots who had been to BOAC's Hamble College of Air Training as cadet pilots in the late 1960s. Masey, (as he was known to us), left BA in 1982 during one of the company's furlough schemes while Terry stayed on retiring at 55, as was then the norm, as a senior 747 captain. Masey was a very good pilot, one of the best handling pilots I have flown with. His energy management of the aircraft from the top of descent to landing was a pleasure to behold. He taught me a lot and his technical skills and knowledge of the industry were second to none. Terry was the other director but, being busy at BA, didn't fly the Interflight aircraft very often, although he was rated on some of the aircraft.

To Masey there was no special kudos in owning a certain type of aircraft – if it was the right aircraft for the current market conditions he would operate it, if not he wouldn't. He would probably have bought a Wright Flyer if he thought it could make money. In the late 1980s, when cash was everywhere as a result of London's 'Big Bang', he took a huge gamble. Seeing an opportunity to make money from all the liquidity in the economy, he took a leap into the executive jet market and bought a Learjet 35. As always, his instincts were spot on. This aircraft was exactly right for the market at the time and was incredibly busy in its first two or three years when we would often 'back-to-back' trips and always at top dollar. VIP, medical evacuation, AOG spares for airlines, news crews – Masey would accept anything as long as the price was right. If not, we wouldn't fly. To him, there was no point in flying just to keep the cash flow moving, unlike other companies. The company needed to make money to succeed - and it did.

In the early days at Gatwick, Interflight was based in 'The Beehive' building on the south side of Gatwick. The Beehive is the original circular 1936 airport terminal which had the control tower protruding up in the centre. Still visible are the rail tracks that originally had covered walkways that led passengers to their waiting aircraft. The building is full of original Art Deco features and it is easy to imagine the check-in desks and cafes full of chatting passengers back in the day preparing to board their 'Heracles' airliners to Paris or further afield. It is frequently used for film sets, which really brings it alive and is reputed to be haunted although I never encountered anything paranormal even though I used to come and go at all times of day and night.

To watch Masey quote for a charter was to watch a master at work. He would sit at his desk with a cigarette in his hand cradling the telephone while he scrawled some figures on the packet of his Benson & Hedges with a biro, squinting through the curling smoke. In his head, he instinctively knew which other companies were likely to have competing aircraft available on the day of the charter and could price accordingly. For example, our big rival in the Learjet market was Northern Executive at Manchester who operated a couple of similar model Lears. Within thirty seconds he would give a price to the charter broker, literally off the back of a fag packet. Quoting for trips is a black art and Masey was the master.

It's all too easy to get charter quotes wrong though. Pat Morgan, (also known as Jabbit as her only French extended to "J'habite…") was a Yorkshire girl who did the accounts and occasional charter quotes but got it beautifully wrong on one occasion. When asked to quote for a trip while Masey was away, she thought she heard the American client on the end of the phone say,

"Please can you quote me for an aircraft to Peterborough, near York? Five passengers."

Looking at a map she found Sibson airfield not far from Peterborough and seeing it was a short flight, offered a price on the piston-engined Piper Aztec.

"Are you sure?" enquired the client. "That seems a very reasonable price. I'll take it!"

What the client had actually said was, "Please can you quote me for an aircraft to Teterboro, New York?" expecting a price for the Learjet.

"Well 'eck, he was American," she explained. "I couldn't 'ear him properly."

To his credit, Masey worked very long hours, drove old wrecks for cars and ploughed everything back into the company. In 1991, when the country was in recession and pilots were being laid off everywhere, he kept us all in employment, not making anyone redundant. The recession was bad and the office phones almost stopped ringing overnight. Single, but with a big mortgage, I will always be grateful to him for keeping me in work.

When he started Interflight in the mid-1970s, (or Berrard Aviation as it was called then), doing pleasure flights in a Cessna 206 off the beach at Blackpool), Masey accepted any job if it paid well and contributed to the coffers. He had some great stories. In those days British Airways gave pilots a lot of time off and he used this to do work as a ferry pilot, delivering aircraft all over the world. Masey had a characteristic, slightly pigeon-toed gait which was the result of foot frostbite after the heater failed on an Atlantic ferry flight in a De Havilland 'Heron' in sub-zero conditions with six hours of the flight remaining. When he finally landed at Keflavik in Iceland, he had to be carried out of the aircraft unable to walk. Masey also ferried Britten-Norman 'Islanders' from the factory in Romania, where they were made under licence, to the Far East. On one of these long trips, he fell asleep over the Bay of Bengal and woke up suddenly, startled to see lights below him. Convincing himself that these were stars and that he must have rolled upside down while asleep he then rolled the aircraft - only to put himself inverted. What he has actually seen - when he was still the right way up - were the bright lights of a fishing fleet in the ocean. He once force-landed a DC3 in the Egyptian desert south of Cairo when both engines started to run roughly. After retrieving his bag and the all-important dollar float, he saw a young chap on a motorcycle travelling down a nearby road. Flagging him down to ask for assistance, he was astonished to be answered in impeccable English. He had stumbled across an Egyptian army officer who had been commissioned at Sandhurst. He also ferried a WW2 'Mosquito' and a Junkers 52 from Spain to the UK for Doug Arnold's aircraft collection.

The Junkers 52 flight was an interesting one. Filling to full tanks in Spain for the flight, which should have been plenty of fuel, Masey set off feeding the engine from the left wing tank. Mid-France, the engine unexpectedly surged and then spluttered to a halt. Without wasting time trying to find out why Masey pulled the big metal fuel selector lever to the other tank and looked at his watch. The left-wing tank had lasted one hour so presumably, the tank in the right wing will last the same amount of time. The engine running sweetly again, Masey tried to work out how he had run out of fuel so quickly but couldn't come up with an answer. After all, he had set off with full tanks that should have given hours of endurance. He decided to make a precautionary landing at Nantes. As he taxied in the right engine stopped, luckily at the very moment that he pulled up to the fuel pumps so no one was any the wiser and no local gendarme was asking awkward questions as happens in France after any incident. As Masey filled the tanks, he got his answer as to why he had run out of fuel; filling the tanks from empty to full the uplift was only half what it should have been. It later transpired that the Spanish Air Force had wire-locked half of each fuel tank without telling anyone – he had set off with only half the fuel he thought he had.

The Beehive' at Gatwick Airport, showing the original control tower

On another occasion, ferrying a Piper Pawnee from Goose Bay in Canada to the UK, seriously overweight with fuel for the fifteen-hour flight as is permitted on ferry flights, Masey got airborne only to discover that he had left his cigarette lighter behind. He always did his best thinking whilst drawing on a ciggy and so the prospect of that long flight without one proved too much for him. He returned to Goose, landing so, so gently and hugely overweight to retrieve his lighter.

The big break financially for Masey, however, involved a trip into the desert south of Tripoli to collect some Dutch oil workers who were being held illegally by Gaddafi's regime. Masey got this job through his friend Dick at Rijnmond Air Service in Rotterdam. The Dutch government wanted the guys

Two of Interflight's Piper Chieftain and C404 Titan aircraft, G-IFTA and G-IFTD, with Gatwick's North Terminal under construction in the background

out of Libya but couldn't be seen to be involved. The task involved flying low-level, below radar, into the desert to a remote airstrip where the 'oilies' would be waiting. His brief was to fly them to Marseilles. Masey duly arrived at the airstrip, landed and waited in the blistering heat. And waited. For hours no one showed up. Just as he was considering getting out of there before he was detected, from nowhere a pickup truck burst through the wire perimeter fence, pursued in the distance by two other vehicles. The pickup skidded to a halt and six guys ran over and piled into the Chieftain. Masey started up and took off, flying fast and low over the desert and then over the sea to Marseilles. He landed three hours later where the authorities were waiting to fast-track the oil workers through Immigration. This had all been sanctioned at a high level by the Dutch and French governments. Masey was never shy about telling a story but he never revealed how much he got paid for this trip. I have no doubt it was enough to set him up in business.

At Interflight we operated a mixture of aircraft; the Cessna 404 'Titan', Piper Navajo 'Chieftain', Piper Aztec, Beechcraft King Air, Learjet 35a and various Hawker 125s. All good aircraft for their particular markets. Masey's policy was for everyone to fly all the aircraft if possible with the proviso that new pilots started on a jet rather than a piston aircraft which made sense; handling a complex turbocharged piston engine takes a lot more savvy than a jet engine. Jet engines either work or don't - and mostly do faultlessly for thousands of hours - whereas piston engines talk to you and need careful managing. Young, inexperienced pilots who joined the company couldn't believe their luck. They started on a jet and later 'graduated' to the piston fleet.

The Cessna 404 'Titan' was similar to the Cessna 421 'Golden Eagle' I flew at Chess Wing but unpressurised, much more utilitarian and in my view a good aircraft although they had a bad reputation for engine failures. This was mostly due to poor handling techniques – the engines certainly needed looking after. It had the same 375 hp geared and turbocharged Continental engines as the 421 but weighed nearly 1000lbs more at maximum takeoff weight – the clever engineers at Cessna somehow got this to work although the climb out on one engine was very marginal when heavy. We always treated the 'Titan' as a single-engine machine until safely through 1000ft – any problems before that we would land straight ahead and not attempt a climb out. As the old saying goes, if you're not careful an engine failure on a twin-engine aircraft will result in the remaining engine merely taking you to the scene of the crash. Above 1000ft you maybe had some options, depending on circumstances - if you flew accurately.

We used the aircraft for passenger charter when you could take up to 10-12 passengers and also cargo; stripped of seats it would carry around 950 kgs of cargo making it a very useful aircraft. The staple work was flying the post on contract for Royal Mail from East Midlands Airport to Aberdeen, Glasgow, Liverpool, Dublin and Belfast among other airports. We picked up a lot of unusual flights in the Titan; one day 'just in time' items for Ford down to their factory in Valencia, Spain, with 800 kgs of wing mirrors or wiring looms, the next day 500 kgs of Mars bar wrappers for Mars UK.

The Valencia trips meant flying over the Pyrenees wearing an oxygen mask and being very mindful of the possibility of an engine failure over the 11,000ft mountains. Checking into the hotel in the early mornings after such a flight, the receptionist would step back in alarm despite my cheery "Buenos dias!" My face would be scarred with the marks from the tight-fitting oxygen mask. Ferrying day-old chicks was another occasional challenge. Not a few – 5000 of the little yellow fluffballs. One or two are cute but 5000 make a hell of a racket and absolutely stink to high heaven, a smell that might get you a place at the bar in the evening but was ruinous for your love life.

The Beaujolais Nouveau run was an annual event. Every year on the third Thursday prescribed in November one wine importer or another would charter the Titan or the Chieftain to go to France and take part in the race to bring the first bottles back to the UK. Naturally, the importer would invite a few guests to go along for the ride. We would land, they would disappear for a couple of hours and then return with the crates of the wine, all jollied-up having been guests of the vineyard in the meanwhile. The flight back to Gatwick would be a party atmosphere all the way. One year, I am landing at Gatwick when one of the more lubricated passengers thinks the runway approach lights just before landing would make a great photo and leans forward to take a picture. POP! The flash goes off and, in an instant, all my night vision has completely disappeared and all I can see are pulsating orbs of white on my retina. I am literally blinded. I can't see to land and I can't see to go around and have another go, so my only option is to close the throttles, close my blinded eyes and grit my teeth. Hoping for a good outcome, the aircraft touches down softly (God bless Cessna for the forgiving undercarriage) and we roll out down the runway. Turning off the runway, I swung around.

"Who the hell thought that would be a good idea?" I snarl down the cabin my sense of humour somewhat diminished after a long day. There are mumbled apologies and the party atmosphere becomes more subdued.

This was single-pilot flying although occasionally we took a 'pilot assistant'. At Interflight this was a character called Ian McEwan. Ian was the company gopher who organised the refuelling of all the company aircraft and reconfigured them from passenger fit to cargo fit and vice versa as necessary. He had a moniker of BC2 This was no fault of his own, it came from his predecessor who was known by Masey as 'bollock chops' as he was lazy and a bit dense. It was inevitable that Ian, as his successor, would be known forever as Bollock Chops 2 – BC2. Ian was a Walter Mitty character who we all felt would have preferred to have made a living on the flight deck of a US aircraft carrier launching fighters; he certainly dressed accordingly on the ramp complete with helmet, ear defenders and Ray-Bans. Instead, he had to make do with dispatching our aircraft from Gatwick although he was prone to making the same elaborate arm gestures. However, he was very resourceful and could get, borrow or otherwise acquire virtually anything and at short notice. His thick Filofax, bound with heavy elastic bands, was crammed with useful contacts; there was no one useful he didn't know at or around Gatwick.

One of the Titans had a cassette player fitted and the custom amongst the pilots on cargo flights or when flying empty was 'gear up, tunes on'. The only tape we had in the aircraft was an old cassette of Meat Loaf's 'Bat Out of Hell' which was just fine with us. You had to remember to turn the volume down before speaking to ATC or they would invariably ask if there was a party going on but at 3 am on the night mail runs ATC was very quiet. I can remember one early morning in summer flying back to Gatwick from Dublin skimming the tops of the cloud as the eastern horizon turned lemon-red with the sunrise, the engines thrumming in perfect harmony and Meat Loaf belting out 'Bat out of Hell' in the cabin behind me – truly magical.

Once, I experienced the worst turbulence I have ever experienced including, later in my career, thunderstorms in the Far East and Africa. The route from East Midlands to Dublin took me down an airway that paralleled the north Wales coastline. I was in one of Interflight's Chieftains flying at FL80 when, completely unexpectedly, I hit violent turbulence. There are officially four levels of turbulence; light, moderate, severe and extreme and I was, for the only time in my life, in extreme turbulence. This is defined as the aircraft being violently tossed about, practically impossible to control and possibly suffering structural damage. On this occasion, the turbulence was so bad that I struggled to read the instruments or even make a call to ATC to explain why my altitude readout would appear erratic on their radar screens.

My headset flew off my head and even with the seat harness pulled as tightly as possible I felt in danger of being injured. The aircraft reached extreme bank angles and my altitude varied by plus/minus 500ft. I was concerned about the aircraft holding together, it was that bad. It lasted about five minutes and then abated as quickly as it started. The wind was southerly and in hindsight, I realised that this turbulence was curl-over from the mountains in Snowdonia. I had been caught in turbulent rotors coming off the high ground which would have been identifiable in daylight as lenticular clouds, the type, along with cumulonimbus, that all aviators give a very wide berth to. Of course, being night-time, I flew straight into it. Nasty. I arranged for a thorough post-flight engineering inspection in Dublin and the aircraft was given a clean bill of health, not even a single distorted panel. Thank you for your build quality, Mr Piper.

* * * *

Interflight operated several Hawkers on charter and Medevac flights over the years, including a Hawker-600 aircraft. Many of these flights were into Africa but this was always an adventure as this variant of the Hawker was definitely not the ideal aircraft for Africa due to its limited range. Some pilots claimed you were fuel critical the moment you started engines. That's a little hysterical, however you had to watch the fuel consumption very carefully. Although it was a tough aircraft, like all Hawkers, the reason for its thirst was that it was powered by the Rolls-Royce 'Viper' turbojet engine. The Viper was developed in the early 1950s by Armstrong Siddeley as a powerplant for the 'Jindivik' target drone used by the military. Because these drones were routinely shot down, niceties such as engine design life and fuel economy were unimportant - the original Viper engines boasted a life of around 10-20 hours. For unfathomable reasons, someone at Hawker Siddley Aviation decided it would be a good idea to mate this crude engine to an airframe and so was born the first HS-125 'Hawker' aircraft. The -600 was the last variant with this engine.

The Viper was a very early-generation jet engine. It had a 'total loss' oil system because, as explained, engine longevity wasn't remotely a concern for its original purpose. The rear turbine bearing was designed to burn oil constantly (hence the 'total loss') at the rate of just over a pint an hour.

This was normal - if it didn't burn oil you could expect the high-pressure turbine to seize with catastrophic consequences as did happen once at Interflight, fortunately not when I was flying. A pint an hour in jet terms is a huge amount of oil to burn, as modern jet engines will consume this maybe every fifty hours, but this was the total loss oil system at work. This consumption meant that for long trips you carried tins and tins of spare oil to top up the oil reservoirs. Unlike later fan jets, the Viper had no bypass ducts at all to reduce noise and improve fuel efficiency; it was a true turbojet. It was incredibly noisy outside with a high-pitched shriek although, from the inside of the aircraft, all you heard was a faint and distant whine. It had a thirst like a drunken sailor - at low level, you could literally see the fuel gauges dropping. I did a flight once from Tenerife South to Paris Le Bourget, around 3hrs 50 minutes which was at the limit of its endurance and got badly caught out when Paris ATC descended me early, as they often do. This hugely increased the fuel flow and my eyes became glued to the fuel gauges. The fuel consumption low down was frightening. I don't know what I landed with on that occasion, but I knew I never wanted to experience that again. I doubt there was enough fuel in the tanks for a go-around if that had been necessary, put it that way.

On another occasion, I was groping around low level in the haze that surrounds Port Harcourt in Nigeria desperately trying to find the airport visually as none of the radio beacons were working, as usual, and watching the gauges drop lower and lower with no backup plan. Not a good feeling.

For a while, our Viper-powered Hawker had the reputation of being the noisiest aircraft at Gatwick, quite an achievement in the days of BAC 1-11s and DC-9s. Masey, in his usual style, devised a homemade noise abatement procedure to try and keep us out of trouble with the airport authorities. This meant departing flapless, raising the gear and immediately reducing thrust to the minimum we could climb away with. It was not very scientific and completely ignored the regulatory second segment climb-out for obstacle clearance, but it worked. Well, after a fashion; we still regularly bust the noise monitors.

However, for all its faults, this Hawker, like all variants of the type, was a forgiving aircraft. One day Roy 'The Boy' Cobb and I stopped in Tamanrasset for fuel while northbound from Nigeria. Usually, we used Ghardaia but this time it was Tamanrasset. We fuelled up to full tanks to make our next stop on the way north to the UK and then it occurred to me that at our maximum takeoff weight of 25,000 lbs, we may just be overweight for the current conditions.

This was something of an 'oops' moment. Tamanrasset is 4,500ft above sea level and the temperature then, even at night-time, was 28°C. I reached for the aircraft's Performance Tables and turned to the WAT tables. WAT stands for Weight, Altitude and Temperature, the starting point for all aircraft performance. From these tables, you can check if you have very basic performance in the given conditions (altitude and outside air temperature) for a safe takeoff at your weight. To my dismay the graph showed that we were outside the limit – we were simply too heavy for the conditions, even using the time-honoured 'thick pencil' on the graph. I kicked myself for being so sloppy but I was tired after some challenging days in Nigeria.

Roy and I chat it through. With no other real option, we decided to go anyway, reasoning that there is always some margin in the tables. Off we go. We taxi out, turn onto the runway, set full thrust and started rolling down the runway. The acceleration was terrible, the notional 3750lbs of thrust from each Viper severely degraded in the hot, thin air. 80 kts came slowly….90 kts…then 100 kts. We needed 110 kts to rotate at our maximum weight. The airspeed indicator reached 105 kts and simply stopped there. The aircraft just wouldn't accelerate anymore and it was clear that speed was all we were going to get. The long Tamanrasset runway was disappearing very quickly and the runway end lights were fast approaching. And an abort would mean very hot brakes, possibly blowing a tyre and staying overnight in Algeria, which has never been recommended if it can possibly be avoided.

I gently increased the back pressure on the yoke and the aircraft responded. The nose wheel lifted and a few seconds later I felt the main wheels also leave the runway. We were airborne and accelerating in the ground effect but painfully slowly. I watched the airspeed gradually build until we achieved V2, our takeoff safety speed. We climbed into the inky black desert night. An engine failure at this point would have been fatal without a doubt. Holding our breath, we slowly climbed away.

Lesson learned – don't try and beat the book.

Interflight's Viper-powered HS125-600, G-FFLT....

.....and the fan-engined HS125-700, G-IFTE

* * * *

One major design flaw with the Viper-powered Hawkers was the system used to clear fuel filter ice. The engines didn't have any oil/fuel heat exchanger system like most jets where the hot engine oil is routed around the fuel filter to keep it free of ice. Instead, it relied on methyl alcohol liquid being squirted from a small reservoir directly into the fuel filter to melt any ice that may have formed from the small amounts of water that always exist in fuel. Anytime a fuel filter bypass light illuminated (indicating that the filter was clogged due to ice and the fuel was bypassing the filter) all that was required was to squirt some methyl alcohol into the filter for three seconds and, bingo, the ice was cleared and the light extinguished. Fuel filter icing wasn't common but could happen from time to time and was no big deal.

The pump was operated by a spring-loaded rocker switch on the overhead panel. However, the reservoir was ridiculously small, one and a half gallons from memory, which lasted no time. The AFM clearly stated that if the fuel filter continued to bypass due to icing, the pilot should land as soon as possible as engine failure was very likely. There are two recommendations found in most aircraft AFMs: *'Land as soon as practicable'* means land when you reasonably can. *'Land as soon as possible'* is much more urgent; it means land without delay. With that background information in mind, dear reader, read on.

Masey and I are on our way back to Gatwick from Port Harcourt. We must have picked up some water contamination there, which wasn't unusual, because the whole flight we keep getting FUEL FLTR alerts and were having to clear the fault as described above. Just before the top of descent into Tamanrasset we get another CAS message: FUEL FLTR 1 on the left engine. I press the rocker switch. It doesn't feel right, there's no spring to it and it doesn't pop back to the centre position. I look closely at the rocker switch and can see that it has got stuck over-centre which means that since the last application, the pump has been running continuously and needlessly for several minutes.

The CAS message stays illuminated. Two minutes later we get the same CAS for the right engine. I press the other rocker switch - again nothing. We are completely out of methyl alcohol and the filters are iced up. I look at Masey and he stares back at me. He says nothing but reaches for a cigarette, a sure sign that he's thinking. We both know what this means - according to the AFM a blocked fuel filter can lead to engine failure; so now we could expect a double engine failure at any moment. At this stage, we are ninety miles from landing at Tamanrasset and those twenty-five minutes seem a lifetime. The terrain south of Tamanrasset is mountainous and barren and although it was a bright moonlit night, we both know that a successful forced landing among the sharp rocky peaks and ridges at night, if both engines quit, would be impossible.

We have a chat and decide to leave the thrust levers exactly in their current position knowing that that gives us the best protection; jet engines often defy the odds and remain working as long as the power remains the same. They have even been known to run on zero oil pressure as long as the thrust levers are left alone. I watch the engine gauges intently looking for even the tiniest fuel flow fluctuations that might signal imminent engine failure. Thank God, nothing. Eventually, I see the runway lights, a bright trapezoid seemingly dancing against the pitch-black desert surround. We make a fast approach and both breathe a huge sigh of relief as the wheels hit the runway - we don't care what happens now.

Once parked on the apron, Masey says, "Right, I'm going to drain some fuel off and check it for water."

He has the cowlings off in no time and the fuel lines to the FCU disconnected. He has the handling agent collect two huge plastic bins and asks me to run the fuel boost pumps while he aims the fuel line in the direction of the first bin. Starting with the left engine, fuel pours into the bin under pressure from the fuel pumps.

Sure enough, there is a lot of water mixed in with the fuel, evidenced by the glassy-looking globules. This would have frozen at altitude and caused the fuel filter to bypass. We run the right engine pump too with the same result. Having cleared as much as we can out of the system, we reconnect the fuel lines and button up the engine cowls. Of course, there is no methyl alcohol available at Tamanrasset at 2 am – or probably ever. We load some fresh (and warmer) fuel and file a flight plan for Seville, flying lower and faster than usual to keep the fuel temperatures warm. The flight is uneventful and, after a short tech stop there for more fuel, we continue to Gatwick, another African epic completed.

The desert terrain south of Tamanrasset

* * * *

One of the freelance pilots that Masey used from time to time, who shall remain nameless to save his blushes, was on a trip from Biggin Hill to Jersey. He was known to everyone as 'The Unmade Bed' as he was a scruffy individual who usually turned up to work looking as though he had slept in his shirt and just fallen out of bed. As this trip involved a night stop, The Bed decided to take his girlfriend along for the trip and leave his wife at home. While the two love birds were on the island, they hired a car for a bit of sightseeing around the coast taking in all the sights. Unfortunately, they took a wrong turn at speed on one of the coastal lanes and careered over a humpback, leaving the road and ending up on a sandy beach. The tide was coming in and despite their frantic efforts they were unable to move the car up the beach in time; it was sunk deep into the sand. The water rose and it ended up in three feet of water, wrecked beyond repair. The Bed and his girlfriend made their way back to the airport for the return flight home. On arrival back at Biggin Hill, no one said a word to them but when The Bed got to his car, an inflated yellow lifejacket was hanging on his car aerial, flying gently in the breeze. News travels fast in the aviation world.

* * * *

For a while, during 1988, Interflight had a contract with Nixdorf Computer. Nixdorf was a large privately-owned computer company based in Paderborn, Germany, and was the fourth largest in Europe at one time until bought out by Siemens in 1990. They contracted Interflight to carry executives and data packages between their UK and German offices. Only 25 nm south-west of Paderborn airfield is the Möhne dam, the most famous of the three dams that were attacked by the RAF during the famous 'Dambusters' raid. It is on a direct line from Gatwick to Paderborn and on the flight over it was easy to see the dam slightly to the right as you started the descent into Paderborn.

The Möhne Dam, looking to the east

Inevitably, during the several flights into Paderborn, my thoughts wandered to re-enacting the bombing run of May 16th 1943. Could I do it and get away with it? I decided to give it a go and take the risk of being reported; it was too tempting and you only live once. Also, it was the month of May and this seemed a fitting time if I ever was to do it. So, without telling anyone (I was flying VFR so was responsible for my routeing) I turned right during the descent to the airport and lined up with the huge east-west reservoir. I could see the dam with its distinctive two towers at the far western end of the reservoir as I dropped down to 200ft over the lake and ran in. I was flying at 190 kts and the surface of the water seemed very close, sparkling black in the summer sun. The enormous dam grew bigger and bigger as I approached and, before I knew it, I was there. I flashed over the top of the dam wall between the towers, pulled up and peeled away quickly, making sure that the underside of the wing, which showed the aircraft registration, wasn't visible to anyone on the dam. Looking back over my shoulder, I could just spot out of the corner of my eye startled tourists on the dam wall staring up at me. If there is one golden rule in low flying it is don't linger and don't repeat so, without delay, I set course again for Paderborn airport.

My heart rate was up as it was undoubtedly exhilarating but as I flew away I thought about how it must have been to do the same flight forty-five years earlier in a heavy and unresponsive Lancaster bomber only 60 ft above the water and flying 20 kts faster – at night, whilst under intense anti-aircraft fire and carrying four tons of high explosive. What can you say about that kind of courage?

* * * *

A few years after my scare with the Baron, I had another interesting moment with flight controls. I was flying the Learjet from Nice to Dublin on a medevac flight, me in the left seat with Martyn Bayley in the right. We were at FL430 and ready for the descent. Clearance received from ATC, I thumbed the conical 'coolie hat' autopilot trim button forward, as usual, to start down.
Seconds later the autopilot disconnected. I tried to reset the autopilot but it would reengage only to disconnect seconds later. Curious. This could only mean

that the horizontal stabiliser, which was driven by the A/P servos, was not trimming to the commanded elevator position; it was 'frozen' in its current position. Martyn and I had a discussion. The aircraft would fly quite happily and remain in trim as long as we didn't change the indicated airspeed – that is the nature of aeroplanes. Our indicated airspeed at FL430 was around 230 kts in the thin air even though our true airspeed was 420 kts. We could descend at 230 kts but obviously couldn't land at this speed so at some point we would have to slow up and configure the aircraft for landing by extending the gear and flaps. We had practised a jammed stabiliser in the simulator and knew it could take a lot of muscle depending on the speed at which the stab became jammed. 230 kts wasn't a good speed to start at because the arm strength required to hold the control column back for any length of time against the trim to reduce to a reasonable landing speed, say 140 kts, would be considerable.

Martyn and I briefed on how we were going to manage this. We decided we would do as we had practised in the sim; Martyn would clasp his hands behind the control column to take the strain as he kept the nose up and I would manage the roll and power using the yoke and thrust levers. On short finals, with the aircraft stabilised and on-speed, we would manage the pitch load together. We decide to alert Dublin ATC that we had a control problem and to ensure the emergency vehicles were on standby for our landing but we asked them to ensure they kept behind us during the landing to prevent the passengers from being unduly alarmed. As we didn't carry a flight attendant on the Lear as it was too small, we asked the lead paramedic to come forward and we briefed him regarding the situation and that he and the others may see fire engines as we landed. He was cool about it - not much fazed these guys - and went back to his patient and the other medic. Briefings complete, we started descent maintaining the same 230 kts. I kept trying the pitch trim more in hope than expectation when suddenly, at around FL100, the aircraft lurched. I tried the trim again to be sure and yes it was definitely free, working fine in both directions. Phew, that was a relief as neither of us needed the heroics of landing with a jammed stabiliser. It must have come free as we passed into warmer air. We kept our special status just in case but the subsequent landing was uneventful, the fire engines in attendance but off at a discrete distance. The next day we discussed the problem with Masey. It was decided that we would ferry the Lear across to Manchester for our maintenance facility, Northern Executive Aviation, to investigate. Martyn and I briefed that we would fly the short flight with the trim's circuit breakers pulled to prevent any possible further malfunction; we would get airborne and fly at 150 kts the whole way, this way we would barely need to trim at all. Inconceivable in these days of compliance and risk assessments but that's what we did and it was fine. The investigation at Northern Exec showed that the stab trim screwjack was badly corroded, probably from repeated applications of de-icing fluid during the preceding winter and most of the lubricating grease was missing. It was a mess and had to be replaced.

* * * *

Terry Ramsden was a colourful character from the 1980s. He was a multi-millionaire who made his money from racehorses and betting. By 1985, aged 33, he was worth around £100m. He loved his cars, horses and women in equal measure and was an ardent Chelsea football fan, at one time owning 35% of the Club. He was a regular passenger with us for a while when we used to fly him to Nice and was always a popular passenger because of his generous tips. Terry would arrive at the GAT with a different catwalk model on his arm every time and they would settle themselves in the plush leather seats of the Lear without fuss. He was lovely and never wanted anything apart from a glass of Perrier but could never be convinced to wear a seat belt. On arrival in Nice, he would drop us £50 each (a decent amount at the time) with the words:

"Here you are lads, thanks a lot. Have a cup of tea in the canteen. See ya later."

The idea of a 'canteen' anywhere on the Côte d'Azur was novel. After a while, he stopped coming and then in 1991 I saw footage of him on the news being arrested in Los Angeles and escorted in handcuffs to a police car. He was £100m in debt and being extradited for fraud. No more 'tea in the canteen' at Nice for us, then. He bounced back though - after a short jail term, he started a market trading company that was very successful. It goes to show, you can't keep a good man down.

John Elliott was another product of the booming global economy of the late 1980s. Described as having an 'eccentric, crass and often controversial style of business and politics he was a tough businessman from Australia who was the boss of the giant Elders corporation. Along with Robert Holmes à Court and Kerry Packer, he was one of three Australian movers and shakers of that decade. A heavy smoker, he looked like a bare-knuckle fighter with a tough round face and squashed nose whose favourite term of abuse about anyone and anything was 'pig's arse'. The broker told us that for catering he only wanted two things for the flight: meat pies and Australian Graves Hermitage vintage red. An interesting mix! The meat pies were easy, the vintage red a bit harder.

Masey went off to find this rare wine at short notice, as he fancied himself something of a wine connoisseur. To his credit, he finally tracked down two bottles of exactly the correct wine which he handed over the BC2 to safekeeping. Big mistake. When I got to the aircraft on the day of the flight there was one of the bottles - sitting comfortably in the ice tray of the aircraft. BC2 for reasons known only to himself had decided that this beautiful red should be served cold from a bed of ice. That move truly was a pig's arse. Elliott munched through his pies on the flight. He never said a word about the ruined wine but on the next flight asked for some tins of his own Foster's lager instead.

* * * *

"Turn that bloody dirge off!" Dave Newcomb, the Operations Manager at Interflight, shouted as he walked into the GAT. 'In the Air Tonight' was playing on the radio and Dave was grumpy and in no mood for music. Someone coughed from behind the counter and discreetly pointed to the passenger area on the other side of the counter. Dave turned around to meet, face to face, Phil Collins himself waiting for his flight. Phil stared at him, smiled thinly and turned away; he didn't take any offence. He sold millions of records every year, so I don't suppose he cared too much if he wasn't one person's favourite. But we enjoyed Dave's acute embarrassment as he turned red and for once was lost for words.

Phil was a regular passenger for a while and during his well-publicised affair with Orianne Cevey– subsequently his third wife - we took a lot of trouble to help him avoid the paparazzi who dogged his life for months and were at every airport he was flying into or out of. The lengths these weevils went to get 'the picture' of Phil and Orianne were unbelievable and we did what we could to throw them off the scent. We would leak that we were flying Phil to Northolt, then go to Luton, or Frankfurt-Main and go to Frankfurt-Hahn. He was very appreciative and it added a bit of a challenge to the flights.

We flew Phil mostly on the Hawker 600 that had the Viper engines, mentioned previously. He loved the aircraft until he witnessed an engine start at night in Dusseldorf as he approached the aircraft after which, quite understandably, he flatly refused to get on board. The Viper was truly spectacular during a night start-up. Although it was perfectly normal, the engine shot a jet of blue flame out of the jet pipe as it lit up, something you never see on modern jet engines. This was a pure turbojet after all, with no pussy bypass features.

"There's no way I'm getting on that thing again," he said as he witnessed the howl and flame of the trusty Viper. "Get me something else."

* * * *

It's 7 am on a beautiful summer's Saturday morning and I am just airborne in the Titan from Runway 26L at Gatwick. My destination is Cardiff where I will collect an Air Europe crew and take them to Manchester, standard weekend work. Like a lot of charter airlines, Air Europe often had crews end up at the wrong airport for the next day's schedule and so these crew positioning flights were commonplace and good business for companies like Interflight. It's been an early start but I'm wide awake with a flask of coffee next to me in the empty co-pilot's seat. Just the way I like it. The air is still, smooth like silk and without a ripple, the sun not up long enough yet to heat the land and produce turbulence. The sky is the palest blue and gently merges into the low-lying early morning mist.

As I pass abeam Bath at 2000ft, the mist turns into a soft cotton wool stratus and I am just skimming along the top, the engines running in their familiar deep rumble. The propellers are set at 1750 rpm, the fuel flows are leaned to exactly 240 lbs/hour and the prop synchro-phase is on. All's well with the world. With the sun behind me, the 'pilot's angel' – the shadow of the aeroplane - is dancing on the clouds beside me sometimes close, sometimes distant as the occasional cloud tops come and go. It's a morning to relish and I am loving being aloft on my own and am looking forward to meeting and joking with the cabin crew who fill the aircraft for a short time with laughter, drinks and perfume. And then, as if by magic, I am woken out of my thoughts by a truly surreal sight. Rising slowly through the mist and maybe three miles ahead of me appears a giant castle. As I stare, transfixed, at this apparition the top of a Fyffes banana appears. And then Mickey Mouse pops up followed by a Duracell battery, a pint of foaming beer, an ice cream and a huge owl. The apparitions hang there, motionless, facing the sun. I turn thirty degrees to the right to keep clear still looking at this amazing sight and then remember, as I see the occasional pinprick of flame at the base of these ghosts, that today is the annual Bristol hot air Balloon Fiesta, the largest balloon event in Europe.

* * * *

GPS was something of a novelty in the early 1990s and to us who were used to only basic radio aids backed up by the unreliable Omega VLF, it was greeted with what's known in the aviation world as PFM – Pure Fucking Magic. Although these GPS receivers were not fitted equipment at the time and were placed in the aircraft as carry-on items, they made life so much easier for us, allowing for precise navigation at last. Had we had GPS fitted that time over Bulgaria, we wouldn't have had the excitement of being shot at for one thing (see later). However, we soon learned first-hand one of the limitations of the equipment; that the US Department of Defense (DOD), who provides this wonderful and accurate navigation for free, can also take it away at will.

During the ugly Balkan Wars of 1992-1995, we frequently carried Foreign Office personnel to and from Split. Baroness Lynda Chalker was a regular passenger, a lovely person to have on board, humorous and very down to earth. The airport at Split was under UN control at the time but there was evidence of recent heavy fighting in the form of a huge and jagged piece of shrapnel, maybe two feet across, embedded in the wall of the control tower. Our route into Split took us southbound through Slovenia and into Croatia which the DOD deemed to be unfriendly territory because of the brutal civil war. This is when we discovered that the DOD can very accurately disable GPS in certain geographical regions. Almost within a mile as we passed the FIR separating the

Bristol Balloon Fiesta

Interflight's Cessna 404 'Titan' G-IFTD

two countries, the GPS would stop working; the receiver still showed satisfactory satellite reception, but the internal computations stopped and so there was no navigational output. And as we flew northbound on the same route on the return journey, bingo, the GPS navigation came alive again. This wasn't signal jamming - as happens often these days in regions close to conflict - but geographical targeting.

Around the same time, I had a trip to Tirana the capital of Albania. Albania was then a strange and secretive country and although emerging from President Hoxha's communist rule when it endured decades of isolation from the international community, it was still a largely unknown country. A kind of European Burma. Hoxha was paranoid about the possibility of invasion although why any power would bother to invade this small, backward country with its peasant economy is a long-standing mystery. However, as a result of this paranoia, he must have deliberately falsified the declared positions of the main civil airport, Rinas International. This came to light after we landed when we found that the correct position of the airport as shown on the GPS was 1-2 miles from the position declared to ICAO and thus indicated on the charts. There's no hiding from technology.

* * * *

One of the routes we operated for Royal Mail in the Titan had us finishing in Belfast in the early hours. We had accommodation arranged in a nearby farmhouse where the couple who lived there ran a B&B. This was a lovely place set in the rural countryside not far from Aldergrove airport. When I first arrived, in the company runabout (a clapped-out Datsun Cherry that was so rusty you could see the road going past under your feet) no one was around. It was probably around 6 am. The heavy front door was unlocked so I walked in, calling out softly in case someone was up but, apart from an old terrier in a basket by the Aga who gave me a weary and uninterested look before going back to sleep, no one was around. Still, knowing I was expected, I decided to go upstairs and just find a bedroom. Leaving a note on the kitchen table, I climbed the stairs and found a bedroom that looked unused and clean enough and crashed out. I woke up at around 1100, washed and wandered downstairs to introduce myself. The lady of the house was there in a dressing gown and drinking what I naively assumed to be weak black tea from a china cup until I saw the neck of a bottle of Jameson poking up from behind the cornflakes. She started frying the eggs and bacon and was very chatty. I soon realised she was completely pissed. Soon her husband joined us.

"When you have finished your breakfast, I'll take you down to the office for a couple of hours," he said, winking. Why not, I thought. I've nothing to do all day before tonight's flight.

I finished off the breakfast and climbed into his old Land Rover and we set off into the local village, pulling up outside a bar. "Welcome to the office!" he grinned as we walked inside and he headed straight for the bar. Three hours later, after he had completed his 'paperwork' we stumbled into the Land Rover for the short drive back to the farmhouse. He headed for the sitting room and slumped in front of the TV to watch the racing while I rested in readiness for the night's work.

The gopher we employed in Belfast was Freddie Dayne. His job, like BC2's at Gatwick, was to reconfigure the aircraft as necessary, refuel them and generally rob, borrow or otherwise procure anything we needed to keep the operation running. He was also a staunch Protestant and rumoured to be a member of the hard-line UDA although, naturally, that was a subject you would never raise; you pick your conversations very carefully in Northern Ireland. Freddie and I used to knock around together some evenings when I wasn't flying. On one occasion we were in the Datsun Cherry between pubs when it spluttered to a halt. You never knew how much petrol was in the tank as the old Cherry's petrol gauge had long since stopped working. We were out of petrol. This was sobering as we were in the middle of nowhere, down a country lane at the height of the Troubles. All of a sudden, I felt distinctly uncomfortable. I felt that the hedgerows suddenly had eyes and we were being watched. Here we were, me a Brit and Freddie a died-in-the-wool 'Prod', out of petrol and smack in the middle of bandit country. We started to sober up fast.

"Freddie, we have got to get out of here," I said to him, stating the bloody obvious. "Oi know that," he replied looking around nervously. "Have you got anything to get this heap started again, anything at all?" I asked more in hope than expectation and tried to keep the nervousness out of my voice.

"Hang on, oi moight have," he said and wrenched open the squeaky boot, lugging out a container of de-icing fluid we used to clear the aircraft wings of ice on frosty nights. "Let's troi this," and he poured a gallon or so into the tank. I jumped inside and turned the key. The engine burst into life – the de-icing fluid was pretty much pure ethanol.

"Let's get the fuck out of here," I suggested and Freddie agreed with a nod, piling in. We roared off. The old Cherry never went so well as with the ethanol. In fact, I don't think it ever ran again. We had probably burned all the valves out but it got us home and that's all I cared about at the time. One day Freddie didn't show up for work and we never saw him again.

* * * *

At Interflight, all the six-monthly proficiency checks (known then as Base Checks) were done on the aircraft rather than in a simulator. This was for two reasons. One reason was there are no simulators for light piston-engined aircraft (they don't exist) and the other was the only Learjet simulator at the time was in the US and there was no way Masey was going to spend money flying pilots out there for training any time other than for the initial rating. I'm not sure about Hawker sims, they probably didn't exist in Europe either at the time. Completing checks on the aircraft definitely has benefits as it takes place in a real machine rather than the synthetic world of simulation, although of course, you can't safely replicate malfunctions in an aircraft in the same way as in a simulator. However good a simulator is and they are very good indeed, nothing replicates the feel of the real thing. These days, as a result of a series of accidents, aviation authorities insist on simulator training on all aircraft unless there is no suitable sim available. Along with Masey, I was a CAA-authorised examiner on all the types that Interflight operated so I did a lot of the checking of the pilots.

For a while, Masey employed freelance pilots to help out from time to time. One of these was a captain from a major airline whose name I won't reveal to save his blushes. Let's call him Paul. He was a very competent pilot as you'd expect, who took flying these smaller aircraft as seriously as he took his 747 flying, always jotting down notes as aide memoires. Come the day, it was time for his Base Check on the Chieftain.

We meet up at the GAT and have the usual briefing to cover all aspects of the flight, as is normal and make our way out to the Chieftain, looking pretty on the apron in the spring sunshine. Start-up and taxi out are all normal and all of Paul's checks and airmanship are excellent. So far, so normal. I'm sure this will be a good check. Gatwick Tower clears us to line up on the runway, Paul smoothly advances the throttles and we accelerate down the runway. Up come the wheels and they tuck away with a clunk. As we are passing around 300ft and safely climbing away, I go to work. I hide the throttles from Paul's view and slowly bring the left engine to idle to simulate an engine failure after takeoff, all standard stuff and the normal way to start a Base Check. The pilot is expected to control the aircraft, keeping it straight with the rudder while climbing out at the correct single-engine speed. Once this is done, he talks through his subsequent actions simultaneously touching with a finger the appropriate controls, the so-called 'touch drills': full power on the good engine, failed engine throttle closed, propellor to feather etc. For good safety reasons, the failed engine isn't ever actually shut down while still close to the ground in case you need it. However, for other, unrelated, reasons Paul nearly kills us.

As I bring the left throttle to idle, I expect Paul to smoothly apply the right rudder to keep the wings level. But he doesn't; he applies the left rudder, absolutely the wrong action! Now the right engine and the rudder are working together to head us into the ground. The right wing rises sharply as the left wing drops and, suddenly, I'm looking at the grass of a field through the windscreen. My heart is in my mouth. "I have it!" I shout, grabbing the controls and simultaneously applying full right rudder and aileron. The aircraft slowly rights itself but the speed has bled off and we are below the safety speed. I very gently ease the nose down, acting more in instinct than with any thought, there simply isn't time. Gently adding power from the idling left engine, we slowly gain speed and climb away. Gatwick Tower makes no comment and hands us off to Gatwick Radar, although they must have seen what happened in the previous thirty seconds. I look at Paul. "What the hell were you doing?" He is white-faced and living that horrible moment that all pilots know so well when they mess up royally in front of their peers. I know what he's thinking and it's along these lines: "I'm a senior 747 captain with thirty years and tens of thousands of hours experience, a training captain to boot, making a pig's ear of flying a simple aeroplane". He is clearly shocked not so much for nearly killing us but for his inexplicable actions. "I'm so sorry, I don't know why I did that."

People are flawed and sometimes react strangely to events even when they know what they should do and are hugely experienced. When training in an aircraft, it pays, yet again, to expect the unexpected.

* * * *

One charter involved taking six roadies from Rotterdam to Marseilles for the rock band U2. I got the trip and positioned the Titan over to Rotterdam the day before as it was an early morning departure. I decided to take maximum fuel out of Rotterdam as it was cheap and would mean I wouldn't have to refuel in Marseilles. Good plan. I worked out I could take full fuel and the five guys and not be overweight, so on arrival at Rotterdam, I called Shell and they duly turned up and topped off the tanks. I left the aircraft with 2000 lbs of Avgas overnight, all ready for the departure the next morning.

After a decent sleep at the airport hotel, I turned up at the aircraft in good time and started my pre-flight inspection. As I had time, I decided to do the fuel drain check to test for water. This entailed pushing a plastic vial into the spring-loaded fuel drain under the wing and taking a sample of fuel. Holding the vial with its fuel against the sky you could see if there was any water or particles present; this could mean possible fuel contamination. I confess that, like most pilots, I didn't always do this check but I liked to when time permitted even though Masey was never that keen in case the drain valve stuck open, as they were occasionally prone to do. Anyway, I started with the drains under the left wing and they were all clear and then moved to those underneath the right wing. Crouching down, I pushed the fuel tester vial into the first spring-loaded drain near the wing root, removed it to look at the contents but saw that the valve hadn't shut off; in fact, it had remained fully open. Fuel, driven with 1000lbs of weight from that wing's fuel tank, was pouring onto the concrete. Quickly I pushed the vial back into the drain and wiggled it – often this was enough to jiggle the valve back into place and shut off the flow of fuel but on this occasion, it didn't work; fuel was cascading out of the tank and onto the concrete. I quickly pushed my thumb over the leak to stop the flow but the force of fuel pushing against my thumb was considerable. I frantically looked around for some assistance but being parked on a remote part of the airfield in the early morning there was no one to be seen anywhere. I knew I couldn't hold pressure on the valve for much longer as the pressure was too great and my wrist was starting to ache with the strain.

In the distance, maybe two hundred metres away, I could see a figure and I shouted as loudly as I could. Eventually, he heard me but just stood there looking at me. People shouting on airfield ramps are a rare sight and there must also have been something in my voice that made him realise that this was urgent and he walked over. Christ, hurry up I thought to myself. When he got closer, I shouted, "Get an engineer quickly, I have a serious fuel leak and I can't hold it back!" sounding a bit like the boy with his finger in the dyke. Well, at least in Holland this analogy should ring a bell, I thought. He nodded and jogged off. After what seemed like an age but probably not more than ten minutes and with my arm muscles aching under the strain, he came back with a KLM engineer on the morning shift at the airline. I explained the problem as quickly as I could and without fuss, he whipped out a screwdriver from his back pocket and pushed my arm away. With a deft movement and with fuel pouring down his arm he thrust the screwdriver into the drain socket and twisted it closed. The flow stopped and I breathed a huge sigh of relief. There was petrol all over the ramp but, not being jet fuel, I knew that it would evaporate quickly. Otherwise, we would have had to call the airport fire service who always take a dim view of fuel on their aprons.

Panic over and massaging an aching arm, I closed up the aircraft making a mental 'note to self' never again to test a fuel drain on anything bigger than a light aircraft and I never have. To me, this is an engineer's task pure and simple. An hour later the roadies appeared at the terminal and after the normal pleasantries, I escorted them through security and out to the aircraft. As we boarded the bus to the aircraft, I thought I could detect a whiff of something mixed with the alcohol - they had obviously had a good night in the best traditions of rock and roll. I got them settled onboard the aircraft, gave the usual safety brief and started the engines. On the taxi out I could hear them through my headphones laughing in the back and generally having a good time. And then I smelt the dope again, but stronger. I glanced back and they were lighting up large spliffs and the cabin was gradually filling with the purple haze. I stopped the aircraft, set the brakes and turned around, taking my headset off to talk to them. "Guys," I said, "I really don't give a stuff if you smoke but bear in mind that if you do, after a while I will be stoned too and maybe that's not a good idea?" I left the question hanging but could see the realisation slowly dawn on their faces that their lives were in my hands and that a stoned pilot living in a dream world could be a bad thing. Laughing and nodding in agreement, they stubbed out the spliffs and we were on our way.

* * * *

For a while, Interflight had a freight contract with FedEx between Birmingham and Glasgow. This was the very early days of FedEx in Europe and they were testing the water to see if there was a market that could be developed. It was a good contract as we got paid for the route even if there was no cargo to carry. However, sometimes the load was so small, perhaps 50 kg, it was difficult to even get the aircraft in balance. With this amount placed right at the rear of the aircraft, it was just possible to get the calculations to work. Each pilot did a week's stint on this route. I elected to stay at a farmhouse B&B in the Warwickshire countryside not far from Birmingham airport. It was a really nice rural lodging and at times it was hard to believe it was only fifteen minutes from a major airport. Each day I would drive to the airport, collecting some sandwiches from a petrol station on the way to sustain me during the day. Just under two hours flying up to Glasgow, wait a while for the return load and two hours back; that was the schedule each day. After a few days of this routine, subsisting largely on sandwiches, crisps and Coke, I found myself becoming somewhat of a stranger to the lavatory. As luck would have it one day's work required me to do two rotations, so before the first flight up to Glasgow, I decided to take matters into my hands and take a laxative. In Boots, there was a pleasing array of laxatives to choose from all promising 'gentle relief' so I bought the strongest version. Why not? My plan was that on arrival in Glasgow, I could nip into the airport Excelsior Hotel and let nature take its course.

The flight up to Glasgow was normal but when I got there – nothing. Disappointing but no problem, I was sure that there would be some result when I returned to Birmingham; clearly, things were just taking longer than I thought. However, when I got back to Birmingham two hours later, still nothing. So, I decided to take another laxative and set off again for Glasgow. On the way north for the second time, I became aware of movement in my stomach. Serious movement. It felt like a giant hand was slowly rearranging my insides.

By the time I was abeam Leeds, I realised that things were certainly on the move but there was still an hour to go before I landed in Glasgow. I began to get concerned. What should I do? Pretty soon I was going to have to go - but how? I was on my own in an aircraft with no autopilot. I glanced back in desperation, was there anything I could use in an emergency? I spotted a black gash bag a few feet back but how could I get this without leaving my seat and losing control of the aircraft? Thoughts of the future accident investigation ran through my head, 'the crash was due to loss of control in flight due to the pilot becoming incapacitated by bodily functions'. Normally, that would be funny but right now it definitely was NOT funny and I was sweating and losing the power to focus on the flight. All my thoughts were concentrating on relieving myself - or rather not doing so - and I was flying purely by memory with no spare capacity for anything else. I stared at the DME groundspeed readout willing it to increase. How much longer before I land? What if there are delays to the approach at Glasgow? Should I land somewhere before I get there, maybe declare an emergency? "What is the reason?" ATC would ask – what would I say to that? And what would my mates say when I told them the reason, I'd be a laughing stock! No, there was no choice, I had to carry on.

By now my stomach was in open revolt and gurgling like erupting lava. 45 minutes left, 40, 35……the time couldn't go quickly enough. It was like my world had come to a standstill as I concentrated desperately on keeping things together. At last Glasgow airport was in sight and I asked ATC for a straight-in approach. Luckily for me, it was mid-afternoon and things were quiet. I did a high-speed approach to Runway 23, landed in some fashion and taxied quickly to the freight sheds. With barely a thought of any unnecessary checks, I set the brakes, slammed the mixture levers to shut off, switched the magnetos and battery off and stumbled to the door at the rear of the aircraft, bolting past the astonished FedEx rep without a word. I sprinted cross-legged across the apron to the Port-a-Cabin where I knew there was a loo of sorts. God, what a sweet, sweet relief.

This was funny (well, in retrospect!), but being sick down route away from the comforts of home can be no fun. I have picked up amoebic dysentery from a beach restaurant in Turkey after eating a bad kebab which had me curled up with the most excruciating stomach cramps for days and feeling like I wanted to die. And have been as sick as a dog in a decrepit hotel in Baku, Azerbaijan, after swimming in the Caspian Sea which I subsequently found out is heavily polluted. Both seemed good ideas at the time but most definitely were not.

* * * *

At night the exhaust pipes of the Chieftain could be seen through the grilles in the cowlings glowing hot from the heat of the turbochargers. It was possible to lean the engines on colour alone without any reference to the exhaust gas temperature (EGT) gauge that was fitted for that purpose; too lean and the exhausts would be a bright orangey red, too rich and they would be a dull red. Just right and the colour would be cherry red and a glance at the EGT gauge would confirm an exhaust temperature of 1350°F, slightly on the rich side of lean; exactly right. We had two Chieftains at Gatwick which we flew from the General Aviation Terminal (now lost underneath the North Terminal) on any work that came our way.

Interflight did a lot of airline crew positioning, as mentioned earlier, which involved repositioning a crew to or from their base after a day's flying. Having the aircraft filled up with lovely cabin crew was not so bad and I always invited a cute one to sit next to me in the front seat. The positioning pilots, if they were decent guys and neither nervous nor interfering, generally left me alone and sat at the rear and got stuck into the well-stocked bar box. We also had two Chieftains based in Aberdeen leased to Air Ecosse. These were in support of the oil industry and flew men and urgent oil parts mostly to places in Norway such as Tromso, Bergen, Andoya, Bodo and Stavanger.

For a while, we had a contract with these Aberdeen-based Chieftains with Wimpey Offshore, an oil support company that employed contract workers and ran some supply ships in the North Sea. The contract was to fly their guys back and forth between Aberdeen and Stavanger. These guys were typical 'oilies' - hard, rough-edged characters who liked a drink once they 'hit the beach'. On one such trip, the passengers were no exception; they had clearly been on the lash in Stavanger the night before I picked them up, probably the infamous Dickens Bar near the harbour, the pub favoured by offshore workers. Having worked in the oil industry in the North Sea in a previous life, I recognised the signs well enough; bleary, unshaven and grumpy from lack of sleep.

We were mid-North Sea between Stavanger and Aberdeen when a fight broke out in the cabin between two of the guys. I turned around to see the cabin in uproar with the fight happening near the main exit door. The aircraft was rocking slightly in sympathy with the shifting bodies. The Chieftain is an unpressurised aircraft so the door could easily open if forced, certainly the weight of two big guys crashing onto it might do the trick. I was mid-way through the flight with 140 nm to go to the safety of Aberdeen so this was the last thing I needed; if the door opened the aircraft could become uncontrollable. Sitting 8,000ft above the North Sea with a fight in the cabin is certainly a lonely place to be but eventually they stopped fighting as the others intervened to separate them and an uneasy truce was apparent. Being miles from anywhere I felt exposed in case the fight should restart. I had few options apart from the one trick that all pilots that have time in twin-propeller aircraft know. I was aware that the guys would probably fall asleep after the night before, given half a chance, so I climbed slowly to 10,000ft which put me nicely above the overcast and into the bright, warm sunshine. Carefully adjusting the propellors to put them 50 rpm different to each other, the rhythmical 'thrum' of out-of-synch propellors started. Wha-um…wha-um… wha-um. Glancing back quickly ten minutes later I could see they had all dozed off. Warm sunshine and the thrum of the props had done the trick. However, I wasn't prepared to let them get away with this behaviour. I don't like being scared by over-refreshed passengers and as soon as I was within radio range of Aberdeen, I called ahead and asked for the police to meet me on landing. I taxied on to stand and a reception of burly policemen and as the passengers disembarked, the officers herded them all into the waiting vans. To give Wimpey their due they sacked the lot, no questions asked and shortly afterwards the contract ended anyway.

* * * *

"Hi, can you take a drill bit to Kristiansund for Schlumberger ASAP? BC2 is at the aircraft with the loaders, and they're ready to load it. Call when airborne."

No preamble as usual and no further details - Masey always just left you to get on with it. I'm in jeans and a sweater and, as luck would have it, close to Gatwick Airport, supposedly on a day off. Masey has caught me on my mobile phone. Somehow, I knew phones would be a bad idea when they were introduced. I always have my licence, ID and passport with me so I'm OK to go and Masey didn't care about such trivia as uniform if it meant getting a job done.

The drill bit is duly loaded on spreader boards and tied down securely with straps. It's a heavy piece, maybe 300 kg but it's loaded centrally so there are no centre of gravity problems. I get airborne from Gatwick in good time and set heading. As I coast out over Norfolk, I am about to file an airborne flight plan with Eastern Radar when an interesting thought occurs to me: did Masey say Kristiansund or did he say Kristiansand? I can't file the flight plan if I don't know what my destination is. The problem is, as hard as I rack my brains I can't remember which airport Masey had said during our brief conversation. These are two towns that sound the same but are actually miles apart, Kristiansand in the south of Norway and Kristiansund on the west coast, 300 nm further north. Luckily, I have just enough fuel for both. By now I am out of radio range to call back on the company frequency to check and I have no other way of contacting Interflight so I mentally toss a coin and guess, from my days in the oil industry in the North Sea, that Kristiansund would be more likely and luckily I am right.

Flying to and around Norway was always an adventure. At Stavanger airport, for example, the refueller was an unusually grumpy character who refused to come out on his bicycle to dispense Avgas unless you had a bottle of Scotch to offer him, spirits being so expensive in Norway. So, when going to Stavanger a last-minute visit to the duty-free before leaving the UK was essential (this being in the days of duty-free in Europe).

One year, I did a flight on the Titan up to Bodø in northern Norway, again with oil parts, in early June. Bodø is just above the Arctic Circle so in midsummer the sun never sets.

The midnight sun, Norway

I arrived at midnight but it was still broad daylight. As I flew northwards, I watched the sun dip to the horizon and then slowly rise back up again; beautiful and disorientating at the same time. I suppose, driven from deep within our lizard brains, we expect the sun to rise, peak and set, and not bounce along the horizon. It is curiously disconcerting. The next day, with the tanks filled to the brim, I flew back the 1,000 nm to Norwich just off the coastline of Norway, at a thousand feet just cruising along, the engines rumbling sweetly and the propellors perfectly synched and enjoying the beautiful view of the coastal villages. Occasionally, I turned into a fjord for a better look at some feature. It wasn't the most efficient altitude, I should have been much higher but how often do these opportunities arise? They have to be taken. I love single-pilot flying and this was as good as it gets. Seven and a half hours later I landed at Norwich to clear Customs before refuelling and continuing to Gatwick.

* * * *

Le Mans was always a hectic weekend. Every June we would guarantee to pick up a passenger charter there for the famous 24-hour motor race. However, it was a very risky event from a flying point of view and after a few years, even Masey decided it wasn't worth the risk. Light aircraft, small jets and helicopters would descend on the little airfield from all corners of Europe and they would all be vying for a place in the very congested airspace. As flying into the airfield was strictly visual, it was a case of keeping a very good eye out and listening carefully on the single radio frequency for who was inbound and where they were. It was made worse by the fact that we never had the correct charts showing the reporting points for the arrival and departure. You could be guaranteed most years to be ramp-checked by the CAA at Le Mans - they pick their foreign venues carefully, naturally - and one thing they could be certain to ask for was evidence of a current chart. Luckily, one guy generally had an up-to-date one and you needed to quickly find out who this was. Then by agreement with everyone, this could then be discreetly handed between the pilots keeping one step ahead of the inspector as he moved around the UK-registered aircraft. Maybe they noticed it was always the same chart but they never mentioned it. The CAA have a habit of leaving some stones unturned when it suits them. We all had tales of near collisions in the Le Mans circuit and this is mine.

The weather is misty and the visibility is not too good. I arrive overhead the airfield but am too close in to land safely, so decide to do a climbing left-hand turn back to circuit height to position myself on a late downwind position. I radio my intentions and start the manoeuvre. I level off at 1,000ft above the airfield and start the turn onto finals for my approach to land on the runway. As I roll out on finals, directly above me, also on finals to the same runway another aircraft, a Cessna 310, appears out of nowhere, literally thirty feet above and ahead of me, close enough that I can hear the engines. He must have cut in ahead of me. Strange and random thoughts occur to you when this happens. First, there's the disbelief and then, before the adrenaline kicks in, you calmly notice little inconsequential details about the aircraft; the right engine is running a little too rich, the underbelly is dirty and it looks like an elevator static wick is missing. And then a few seconds later your heart starts thumping and you peel sharply away. I do exactly that and, hoping the passengers hadn't noticed, repositioned onto finals again and landed. Never a good experience.

Once safely on the ground, the trick was to inveigle yourself into one of the hospitality marquees, for example Mercedes, Jaguar or Audi, where gorgeous girls served champagne like water and the food was excellent. In the marquees you never actually saw the cars racing around the track, just heard them somewhere in the distance which was fine for me, having only a passing interest in motor racing. Wearing your pilot's uniform together with a good story about looking for one of your passengers was the preferred way to get entry into the hospitality enclosure and once you gained entry you stayed there. Most hosts seemed happy to have a uniformed pilot wandering about, they, astonishingly, thought it raised the tone. Where to sleep was another challenge though, as accommodation for miles around was booked months ahead and Masey never booked in advance. A lot of guys, myself included, often spent the night curled up in a sleeping bag in the back of the aircraft, waking up stiff, cold, hungover and hungry.

* * * *

Two aircraft, a Chieftain and a Titan and twelve passengers to Beauvais – that was the requirement on one particular Interflight charter. I was in the Chieftain, along with BC2 who had come along for the ride and Martyn was flying alone in the Titan. After being dropped off in Beauvais, the passengers wanted to be collected the next day from Pontoise, a town just to the north of Paris, to take them back to Gatwick. The plan was to reposition both aircraft from Beauvais to Pontoise. This all went fine; we dropped the passengers in Beauvais and received approval from ATC to do a formation takeoff, for a bit of fun, and then fly together the short distance to Pontoise.

We arrived at Pontoise just after ATC had gone home so the airfield was uncontrolled - effectively we had the place to ourselves. On the radio, I suggested to Martyn that we do a 'run and break' down the runway before peeling off downwind for a circuit to land. We agreed on a plan, I would go first and Martyn would follow twenty seconds later. I set up for a run-in with a gentle descent to build the speed up to around 180 kts. As I crossed the threshold of the runway, I was at around 200 kts and I dropped to around thirty feet and raced down the runway. It was exhilarating and we were all of the belief that you had to have fun in your flying. However, it didn't go entirely to plan.

At the end of the runway, there was a road with a line of poplars, French style, extending to the left and right of the runway threshold. As I tore down the runway, to my alarm I saw to my right a tall vehicle I hadn't seen, possibly a removals lorry, emerging from behind the poplars travelling along the road towards me. I was not much above the height of the lorry, close enough that the driver and I made eye contact. I can see his expression now, one of wide-eyed surprise as I flashed past the front of his cab. I don't know who was more surprised, him or me. Silly boy. When will you learn to always expect the unexpected?

* * * *

Gatwick ATC was good at mixing our piston operations with the faster jet traffic. Arrivals there would often require us to hold off south of the airport over Crawley before nipping in on a tight base leg to land, clear the runway quickly and get out of ATC's hair. As long as we were off the runway as quickly as possible, whether departing or arriving, ATC was happy to play the game in those days. On departure, an early turn was usually approved, again to get us away as quickly as possible. We all enjoyed this. An early right turn off Runway 26 meant taking off and immediately turning right as the gear was coming up. This brought us close to the control tower, sometimes very close. I think the sight and sound were enjoyed by the tower as much as we; a Chieftain at full power with the gear retracting as it flashed past must have looked and sounded spectacular.

Masey was good at offering crew jollies once a year or so. If the profits were healthy, we would close the company for a day, take two aircraft and head off to France for a decent lunch. It was always best not to be the designated driver for obvious reasons. Sitting sober at a restaurant table at Le Touquet or Deauville while all the others were getting drunk and enjoying a lovely meal was definitely the short straw. Martyn Bayley and I were the designated drivers one year, both of us flying Chieftains. We decided we would fly to Le Touquet at low level just for the hell of it.

A takeoff in sequence from Runway 26 at Gatwick and an early left turn had us away and heading for the coast in formation at 2000ft, Martyn just behind me to my right. Once over Newhaven, I swung left with Martyn tucked in close behind and we dropped down to 200ft together, flying fast over the grey water below the cliffs at Beachy Head before turning right for the Channel crossing. There is a golden rule when flying low level and that is to always trim the aircraft a little nose-up so you have to physically hold the aircraft down. That way if there is a sudden distraction, let's say you hit a seagull or become momentarily distracted, releasing forward pressure on the controls will cause the aircraft to climb safely away. No sudden surprises on this occasion luckily, although a little boat with three guys peacefully fishing mid-Channel was unexpected. I'm not sure who was more surprised, them or us, as we arrived seemingly out of nowhere and roared past in formation.

* * * *

The Interflight crew pub was the Six Bells in Horley, a 13th-century pub with very low ceilings right next to the church. For years this was also the pub of choice for all the airline crews at Gatwick and on Thursday nights in particular it was jammed to the doors with pilots and cabin crew, hot, sweaty and thick with cigarette smoke. It was the meeting place after work for anyone at Interflight who was still at the airport at around 6 pm, very much the after-hours 'office'. "Meet you at the Bells" was a familiar call.

After one particularly gruelling Nigerian trip on the Lear, I arranged to meet Masey at the Bells for a beer and a debrief of the trip. Martyn and I had been to Lagos, Kaduna and Sokoto. After the second beer and my accounts of bribing officials, the crappy hotels, the 'night fighters', the goats on the runways, the sudden airport closures etc., Masey said "How much did you use of the float?" My beer stops halfway to my mouth. Shit – the float! What had I done with it? It was customary to carry a lot of dollars on flights to Africa and other remote areas to pay for everything and generally 'facilitate' things. It's less common these days, but it's still a good idea as it's amazing what can be achieved once the mighty greenback makes an appearance. In those days, we usually carried $5-7,000 on African trips enough for hotels, meals, dashes and, if necessary, to buy some fuel. This was long before the days of reputable handling agents, fuel releases and pre-booked hotels all arranged on the internet before setting off. We used to just take the float and set off with a final instruction from Masey, "Do not break down!". We customarily kept the dollar float in a nondescript brown envelope in the captain's side pocket in the cockpit, deliberately ordinary and scruffy so it wouldn't attract attention if anyone glanced in. We jotted down any amounts we had used on a piece of paper so Masey could account for the spending at the end of the trip. But now, when Masey mentioned the float, I couldn't recall seeing it when I left the aircraft. I was dog-tired and had forgotten to check. "Of course, sorry, I left it in the aircraft. Let me go and get it now before I forget," I said downing my beer and secretly hoping against hope it was still in the usual place. Please God. Masey was a generous guy but $5000 is $5000.

I raced back to the GAT and got a lift out to the remote stand where we had parked the Lear overnight. Opening the door, I clambered into the cockpit. Using a torch, I searched everywhere but the envelope wasn't anywhere. I turned the cockpit upside down. Shit! I frantically racked my brain to think what might have happened. Think, think! Maybe it got accidentally thrown out with the rubbish in the hurry to clean up the aircraft after landing and get to the Six Bells? In this case, maybe it was in the two big black gash bags I had earlier heaved into one of the two big Biffa bins that were on the parking stand. I walked quickly across to the orange bin and lifted the lid. It reeked with the usual odour of rotting rubbish, oily rags and kerosene but I was too worried to care. Any one of the black bags could be the one I was looking for. I started to pull the bags out and rifle through them one by one desperately looking for the missing brown envelope.

Seconds later two unmarked cars arrived out of nowhere and skidded to a stop. I knew before the officers got out of the cars who they were. Customs officers and police. On the apron CCTV they had obviously seen me return to an aircraft that had recently returned from Nigeria and pull bags out of a nearby bin. How suspicious must that have looked? Naturally, I was retrieving a stash of drugs that I had brought into the country. It took some quick talking from me to convince the officers of my innocence and they stood watching me impassively as I returned to my task of rummaging through the bags in search of the dollar envelope. Finally, to my huge relief, I found one of our rubbish bags and I tore into it - and there was the envelope, covered in old food and coffee but I didn't care, it was all there. I pulled my cell phone from my back pocket and called Masey.

"Hi Simon, I've got the dollars, I'll drop them by the office in the morning," I said as calmly as possible. If only he knew.

* * * *

The Customs at Gatwick were notorious for being difficult. It was well known that, together with Luton Airport, Gatwick was a training airport for newly qualified customs officers who were zealous in their interpretation of the rules and seldom showed any discretion. I was on a medevac flight in the Hawker that landed at Gatwick late one evening. On board was a seriously ill patient who was being tended to by the excellent paramedic Doc McDermot who we will meet again in another tale. The patient was critical and needed hospital treatment without delay. As we taxied onto stand, I saw that the ambulance was waiting for us together with the Interflight handling team and Customs and Immigration. Excellent – so far so good, I thought. We shut down, opened the door and the officers entered the aircraft. The two immigration officers checked the passports and duly left when they were satisfied. The Customs officer, on the other hand, decided that now would be a good time to check the Doc's equipment, in particular his consignment of medicines.

Being a doctor and paramedic, Doc was carrying a range of controlled drugs including morphine for pain relief and these were listed on his manifest. Except there was an inconsistency – due to an oversight, one drug wasn't listed. The charming officer insisted that this had to be resolved before anyone could leave the aircraft. After several minutes of checking manifests and the Customs officer questioning the Doc as though he was a criminal, I exploded. "Look, for God's sake, this patient is in critical condition and in a lot of pain. Can't you at least let him leave in the ambulance while we sort this out? It's completely inhumane to hold him here!"

"No, I am afraid no one can disembark until we resolve this," he countered in the familiar po-faced manner of all Customs officers.

"OK, in that case, I would like to have a senior Customs officer attend, please," I responded.

This went down badly. I was aware of the consequences of crossing these little Hitlers but I also knew it was my prerogative to elevate my complaint. I was genuinely bloody angry – we had flown this patient at high speed and with great care only to be delayed by this petty bureaucracy on arrival. What's more, the Customs knew us and the Doc, we were not complete unknowns. Eventually, a senior officer arrived and after a further thirty minutes of pointless time-wasting and endless forms both Customs officers were satisfied – the Doc could leave with the patient.

* * * *

You get an interesting insight into the backdoor workings of governments in this business. In the early 1990s, we did a series of flights that had the smell of back-door payments about them that involved the South African, Spanish, French and UK governments. These flights involved positioning the Lear to Heathrow and meeting two passengers off the morning South African Airways flight from Johannesburg. We would park at the Heathrow GAT which in those days was located conveniently adjacent to Terminal 4. The SAA flight would disembark two hard-looking men from South African state security. They were solid muscle and looked as though they were wearing suits two sizes too small and would happily rip your arms off given half a chance, definitely not guys to mess with. They would leave the SAA 747 by the steps on the side of the air bridge, away from the disembarking passengers, and then be driven over to the GAT, skipping the usual UK Immigration procedures. They carried nothing between them but a slimline Samsonite briefcase. We would then depart and fly them down to Bilbao in northern Spain. There, joint Spanish and French police would meet them, and direct them into a waiting car with no passport checks. Two hours later they would return to Bilbao, minus the slimline briefcase. We would fly them back to LHR for the evening flight to Joburg, job done until the next time.

I am fairly certain what was in these Samsonites because I once tried to pick one up in the cabin. That might be thought of as risky given the less-than-friendly nature of the security agents but they probably knew no one would, or even could, run off with one of these cases. When I tried to lift it, it might as well have been welded to the floor; I thought the handle would come off in my hands. The fact that these guys walked with the case quite normally showed just how strong they were. There's only one thing that weighs that much in such a small volume and that's gold. Forget what you see in the movies where they lob gold ingots to each other as though they were house bricks – gold is very dense and immensely heavy. Masey had a theory that these flights involved backdoor South African gold payments to France maybe as payment for Mirage spares for the SAAF and I think he was probably right but who knows? They were certainly payments of some kind sanctioned by the three governments involved.

* * * *

For a couple of years, Interflight had a contract with an independent oil company called JKX Oil, based in Guildford. JKX were involved in wildcat drilling in various sites, mostly in Ukraine and Georgia. Masey was never convinced of their authenticity. He was certain that the company was set up to extract sizeable grants for exploration from the EU. He may have been correct as JKX never seemed to discover any oil or gas, wildcat sites are very expensive to operate and the executives always seemed to have a good time down route. I enjoyed the trips, partly as they reminded me of my days in the oil exploration business in the North Sea, only this time on land. The passengers were good company and we got to know them individually quite well and we would often be invited to dinners and nightclubs with their Ukrainian business partners which inevitably turned into big drinking sessions involving endless toasts and lots of vodka. The managing director had a different PA on each trip, usually a tall good-looking Ukrainian girl. We flew them regularly to Kyiv, Simferopol and Poltava in Ukraine and for a while operated a regular day return to Tbilisi, Georgia. The Tbilisi trips were long, tiring days. We used the Hawkers for these and at their speed, the sectors averaged 6:20 there and 6:40 back. Allowing a notional one hour on the ground (never achievable) it was just possible to make the duty times work on paper. Georgia at the time, 1993, was just coming out of a bitter civil war after its separation from the Soviet Union. The country was in chaos. There were munitions in the roads, some with unspent propellants still inside and with kids playing all over them, wrecked buildings, and burnt-out cars. Anything of value had been looted by gangs, even the copper wire from telegraph poles. A failed state by any definition. Tbilisi airport was functioning in a fashion but, on our first arrival there (luckily in good weather) we couldn't figure out why when flying the ILS localiser beam, we seemed to be approaching the runway at an angle. The Jeppesen charts made no reference to any offset and anyway a localiser has to be aligned within a maximum of 2 degrees of the runway. The offset was at least 10 degrees and angled towards the high ground that rose to 8,000ft to the northeast of the airfield. After landing, we asked the agent why this was and he explained with a shrug, "You know, captain, last week an Ilyushin….." he tailed off and made hand gestures that indicated it had skidded off the end of the 9,800ft runway. As it departed the runway, it had hit the localiser antenna and bent it out of alignment, but no one seemed to care much.

In those days flying to Russian and ex-Soviet airfields was a complicated juggling act of units. Altitudes were given in metres, not feet, altimeter settings were in millimetres of mercury, not millibars as is customary and ATC frequency changes depended on vertical, not lateral, distance. This meant that you changed radio frequency not as you climbed higher (as in most parts of the world) but as you got further from the departure airfield. As the first cleared altitude was typically 600m this meant you could be speeding along at 600m (2000ft) while trying to get a word in edgeways with ATC to get clearance to climb higher. This often put you below the safety altitude. Additionally, there were a lot of big military airfields littered about that didn't feature on any charts and as most airfields had the same orientation and staggered runway layout, it was easy to misidentify your destination. It was a lot to juggle at the end of a long flight. An ILS bent towards the high ground on approach was one other thing we could have happily done without so thank goodness for the good weather on this first trip that enabled us to get a good picture of the surrounding area. Affordable GPS was just coming in at the time and we had a handheld unit held on with a sucker on the captain's side window but it wasn't reliable due to the electrical heating of the window that affected reception. It was all a bit hit-and-miss.

The huge terminal building at Tbilisi airport was typically Soviet. The corridors were gloomy, lit with the occasional dim bulb every few yards and badly in need of another coat of the sickly pale green so favoured by the Soviets for their building interiors – and aircraft flight decks for some reason. The landing fee was paid through a hole in the wall in the airport offices to an old babushka wrapped in a scarf. In common with everywhere else in the former Soviet Union at the time, the cashier insisted not only to be paid in dollars, which was normal and fine, but in new dollar notes. Used and tatty dollar bills were not accepted. No amount of arguing would change this however hard we explained that it simply wasn't possible to get brand new notes every time. Probably even the President of the United States would be unable to guarantee new notes every time. And surely, we argued, minty fresh notes were more likely to be counterfeit? Nyet, captain! Every note had to be new and was individually and laboriously inspected for forgery under a UV light so the process of payment took a long time. The terminal lavatories were legendary. To this day they remain the benchmark for the worst I have ever encountered anywhere in the world, which - believe me - is saying something. The floor was covered in excrement. You had to enter on tiptoes and pray you didn't slip over.

After a few visits to the airport, I grew friendly with the ramp agent called Yuri who was also a co-pilot on a little Yak-40 airliner based at the airport. He was a young guy, ambitious and wanted to get out of the country and build a life for himself. Yuri's English was good and he loved to chat and improve his English further which I was happy to help him with. He also acted as our navigator to remote airfields near Tbilisi, such as Poti described later. "Captain, do you know the song 'Baker Street'?" he asked me on one trip. "Of course," I replied. "Please, can you bring this to me next time?"

As this made a refreshing change to the usual cynical request for dollars or whisky, I decided to get him a cassette of the album as a present. Besides, I had come to like him and his optimism. However, unfortunately just as I had bought the cassette, the contract came to an end and I never returned to Tbilisi. I posted it to him anyway together with my return address. I never expected it to arrive with only the following address: 'Yuri, Yak-40 Navigator, c/o Tbilisi Airport, Tbilisi, Republic of Georgia, CIS' but, to my amazement, it did and weeks later I got a scribbled note of thanks from him on the usual Soviet tissue paper.

He was so grateful and, better than that, he didn't include the usual request to keep in touch. On another occasion, I gave a pair of flip-flops from Woolworths to a guy in Zambia to replace his that were made out of old tyres and bits of rope. He nearly cried with happiness. We sometimes forget what we have and others don't in this world.

Occasionally we had to stay overnight in Tbilisi. The first time we wondered where we would end up, probably the usual rubbish hotel with threadbare curtains that never meet in the middle, black tea and stale bread for breakfast and a pervading smell of sweat and cabbage. But here was a pleasant surprise. Amid the rubble and mess of post-civil war Georgia, not far from the airport was the Metechi Palace Hotel a brand-new jewel of a hotel, built to western standards by the Austrian 'Marco Polo' hotels chain. It's now a Sheraton. Marco Polo hotels must have taken a gamble on things improving in Georgia which was a huge leap of faith at the time. It was a beacon of sanity amid all the chaos. On entry, you were greeted by a huge but empty atrium with coffee shops offering Viennese cakes, expensive boutiques, fresh flowers, external glass lifts and huge chandeliers. A first-world hotel, however it wasn't immune from the local culture. At the entrance to the hotel was a large sign depicting an automatic rifle with a red cross over it; all weapons had to be deposited with the concierge before passing through the X-ray machine and entering the hotel. Given that virtually all Georgian men have a tendency to banditry, that meant the concierge's office was equipped like a small armoury. The burly leather-jacketed locals were surprisingly compliant and watching them shrug off their weapons at the entrance was always interesting; Uzis, heavy calibre pistols, shotguns you name it – all were handed over the counter.

The power in the hotel was inclined to fail regularly so only a fool ever took the lifts and risked being stuck inside one for hours. But there was good food mostly and a decent bar on the top floor so overall it was happy days. On the first visit, being slaves to the rule most crew adopt, that you never stay just in the hotel and always explore, we walked into the city one evening and found a sign advertising a nightclub two floors below street level. We looked at each other and shrugged - looks perfect, let's go and take a look. Two bored girls pole dancing listlessly on the dance floor looked at us with the usual signs of predatory interest. You can never mask your Western origins and that means money. We took a seat in a booth and awaited events. Eventually, the waitress came over and we ordered drinks. As I looked around, I noticed that the back of the button-backed red velvet bench seat in the booth opposite was ripped open and taped off. We asked the waitress and she smiled apologetically and explained. A week earlier there had been a shooting at the club between rival mafia gangs and we were looking at the result.

The weather forecasting for Tbilisi was always hit and miss and one time we got badly caught out. The forecasted mist had turned into thick fog. Martyn and I arrived overhead and had a quick chat about what to do. There was no likelihood of an improvement for a while, so we decided to divert elsewhere. Our alternate airfield, on paper at least, was Yerevan in Armenia, 100 miles to the south. Not the best place to choose but options are thin on the ground in that part of the world. We were not in a position where we could hang around as we were operating on minimum fuel, so a decision had to be made quickly. Yerevan it was and we informed the JKX passengers that we would be diverting there, picking up some fuel and as soon as the weather cleared in Tbilisi we would return.

The flight to Yerevan was uneventful until we got the weather report for the airfield from the approach frequency. They were giving reports of heavy snow showers. Christ, where had that come from? Another reminder of the unpredictability of weather and forecasts in those days in that part of the world. We had no choice; we were committed as fuel was now critical. I flew the ILS and landed in heavy snow with visibility next to zero, probably 100 metres, well below our legal limit of 550 metres. Oh well, there was absolutely zero chance of being reported to any authority there and no one on the ground seemed the least bit concerned, they had other things to worry about. Armenia had recently suffered a devastating earthquake and the infrastructure, bad at the best of times in this poor country, was still non-existent. The local agent was helpful and apologetic about the lack of services and looking around you could see that the country was on its knees. I chatted with him with the usual pleasantries, then it was back to business. "We need fuel, please. Once the weather has cleared, we will depart for Tbilisi." "Fuel?" he replied, "Captain, there is no fuel. The earthquake…" he trailed off. Bloody hell. What on earth are we going to do now, I wondered?

"But captain, maybe we can help," he continued when he saw my crestfallen face. He then described his plan. A couple of hundred metres away in the corner of the apron was a parked TU-154 airliner that looked as though it hadn't flown for a while. If we positioned ourselves under its wing, he explained, he could arrange for us to take on some fuel from that aircraft using a funnel into our over-wing fuel caps. Martyn and I looked at each other. We didn't have many options so quickly agreed although we had some concerns. How long had the fuel been in the Tupolev? What about contamination? And possibly some strontium in the fuel tanks, often used as a jet fuel biocide to prevent fungus? Nasty stuff. Anyway, not having a better plan, we taxied the aircraft slowly through the slushy snow so that the over-wing refuelling cap of the left wing was exactly under the drooping wing of the Tupolev.

Two guys in overalls clambered onto our wing carrying a huge aluminium funnel which they positioned as best as they could over the over-wing fuelling caps on our aircraft. Then one of the guys reached up with a large screwdriver at arm's length and forced the fuel drain under the Tupolev wing to the open position. Immediately, a torrent of fuel gushed out of the Tupolev wing at a tremendous rate into the funnel. Due to the pronounced drooping of the Tupolev wing, the fuel pressure at the tips of the wing was significant. The two guys were trying to hold the funnel upright and direct the fuel into our wing tank but such was the force of the flow that most of it splashed all over the wing and onto the apron. I went inside and switched the aircraft battery on and monitored the fuel gauge for the left wing as it slowly increased in quantity. After a while, I figured that, once we had pumped the fuel across into the other wing to balance things out, we had enough fuel to fly back to Tbilisi although, with so much fuel around, I couldn't possibly risk starting the APU to start pumping until they had finished and we had the aircraft towed away. There was never any mention of payment but we had to dash them; they had gone to a huge effort to assist us and were absolutely drenched from head to toe in reeking jet fuel. I gave them $200 each from the aircraft float and a couple of bottles of scotch. They had saved the day and given us enough fuel to enable us to return to Tbilisi. What more can you ask of anyone? The amount we had 'borrowed' from the Tupolev probably wouldn't have even been noticed by the Tupolev crew given how much fuel it carries. And that was assuming the aircraft ever flew again which, judging by the look of it, didn't seem very likely.

* * * *

Simferopol in Crimea was another regular JKX destination. Designated an alternate aerodrome for the Russian 'Buran' space shuttle it boasted a very long 3700m north-south runway. Being quite close to the Sevastopol naval base just south of the airport, the area was sensitive and we had to be careful not to stray into any restricted areas. The airport was prone to fog and low clouds and it was on one such day that Masey and I were departing back to Gatwick. Cleared to backtrack the runway before turning round to takeoff, we taxied slowly down the huge runway. On the radio, we could hear ATC and another aircraft on the tower frequency but as it was in Russian or Ukrainian, we couldn't understand the conversation and so took no particular notice of it. The visibility was around 3000m and the cloud base was probably less than 100 ft so it was a somewhat murky day. We were about 600m from the end of the runway when suddenly out of the low cloud an aircraft, possibly an AN-24, with wheels down and landing flaps extended appeared heading straight for us. "Christ!" exclaimed Masey, simultaneously gunning the throttles to get out of the way of the aircraft that was certain to land on top of us. We were heading for the grass when we heard to roar of its engines as it passed overhead and away. Masey managed to brake before we ended up gardening and we stopped and looked at each other. "What the hell was that? Ask them what the fuck is going on!" A quick radio call to the tower and we got our answer. The AN-24 was doing practise ILS approaches and go-arounds on the runway we were backtracking but they hadn't felt it necessary to warn us.

Frequently, we would fly to Tbilisi and then, having cleared Customs and sometimes dropped a passenger or two there, reposition the aircraft to a little airfield at Poti, a small town on the coast of the Black Sea around 150 miles west of Tbilisi. Poti looked like a town in the aftermath of a chemical attack, with almost no one around and empty buildings everywhere, several without windows, curtains waving in the breeze. The beach was black with ash-coloured sand and was filthy, littered with rubbish. The airfield was small with no ATC, so we would always fly over the runway to assess it for pot-holes and stray dogs before committing to a landing. These flights required the carriage of a local navigator as they were internal flights, so we took Yuri, the pilot from Tbilisi mentioned earlier. Navigators were often required in the ex-Soviet Union CIS and were a mixed blessing. They were of course useful in talking to ATC but unfortunately also tried to interfere in the conduct of the flight. I would always explain that we can navigate our way anywhere in the world, we didn't need help in this, we only required them to talk to local ATC in their language, no more than that. They would sit on the jump seat, with their huge Russian peaked caps, drink our vodka and smoke vile Russian cigarettes. In those days it was required to have a Russian navigator even to fly to Moscow from the UK. Just to add insult to injury, the operator had the pleasure of paying for one of these guys to fly over to London from Russia for the trip.

Frank 'Bon' Bonfield, who was our lead Learjet pilot in the early days, due to his previous Learjet experience with a company called Jointair, was an ex-RAF Vulcan pilot, a truly top guy and a great pilot. I learned a lot from him as I cut my teeth on my first jet aircraft. His dry humour was a great antidote to tense moments that I invariably managed to create as, metaphorically, I hung onto the Lear's tail and found myself miles behind the aircraft for the first hundred hours or so. But one thing was guaranteed to make Bon fume and that was being told by a Russian how to get to Moscow. That was all he had ever trained for in the Vulcan during the Cold War with his megaton payload. "I don't need some bloody Russian telling me how to get to Moscow," he used to growl. "I can get there in any weather, in my sleep. Low level, high level, you name it, I can get there." Bon would sit hunched over the controls and refused to ever acknowledge the uniformed 'Ivan' sitting behind him. A few years later I showed Bon an article about the Vulcan in 'Aeroplane Monthly' magazine. This article showed in detail the exact mission plan for the Vulcan in case of hostilities – the profile, routeings, targets, diversions, contingencies the lot. Bon's face paled. "I don't believe it," he gasped, "that's exactly what we trained to do." What was once ultra-top-secret war planning could now be found in a magazine for £3.60. How times changed after the collapse of the Soviet Union and with it the Cold War.

I was flying with Bon in the Lear over Plovdiv, Bulgaria (this was back when all of Eastern Europe was still in the Soviet sphere) when we strayed off the airway centreline. This wasn't carelessness – there were no ground-based radio aids working that we could navigate with and the long-range navigation Omega VLF was useless as usual thanks to sunspot activity or 'lane-shift', or some other incomprehensible reason. We were dead-reckoning and hoping for the best. It was a clear day and we were at FL410. Suddenly, there was a strange noise. It sounded like heavy suitcases falling over in the cabin, a crumping, thudding sound. I glanced around. The passengers were dozing or looking out of the windows. Crump, crump… Just as I was about to ask Bon what he thought it was when he spoke, "Star shells," he growled. Sure enough, looking downwards as best as I could, there were small grey puffs of smoke approximately 10,000ft below us, blossoming periodically. It was the standard warning; you are straying into prohibited airspace. Time to get try and get back on the airway centreline so we altered heading quickly. Nothing was said on the radio by ATC, no warning to get back on track, nothing. Very Soviet.

* * * *

My initial Lear 35 course was in 1988 with Bon at FlightSafety in Tuscon, Arizona. As he was already rated and experienced on the aircraft, he was only doing a refresher whereas I was doing an initial course. This was the first time I had done a type rating in any structured way, up to this point it had all been self-study or, at best, looking at slides and listening to audio on some homemade course - often with the audio and visual completely out of sync just to make things more interesting. The course was excellent. It lasted three weeks, one week of 'chalk and talk' in the classroom followed by two weeks in the simulator. There were around eight of us on the course. On the first day, the ground instructor, a guy called Dave Duart, introduced himself. Like most of the instructors at FlightSafety, he was ex-military; they were generally good instructors, used to poor pay but happy to accept this for the excellent medical insurance FlightSafety provides. On day one of the course, Dave introduced himself and looked around the room, "OK, before we start, anyone in the classroom here got any jet experience?" We looked at one another. One guy hesitated a second then put his hand up and replied, "Yeah, I have some hours on the Citation." Dave ignored the student and after a few seconds, without batting an eye and with perfect timing, looked around and repeated, "So has anyone here got any jet experience?" to laughter from the rest of us. The Citation is an entry-level business jet often, unfairly, disparaged as the 'Slowtation'.

The Learjet was considered a proper jet and so it was – it was certified to Part 25 transport category standards, overpowered, fast, and climbed like a homesick angel. It even looked fast when parked. What more could you want? Dave was a good instructor always keeping an eye on the clock, military style and killing bullshit questions from some of the more eager students without hesitation. The same guy that boasted about his Cessna Citation experience asked, at five minutes to five in the afternoon, (itself a crime during any ground school when you're saturated with information and have had enough), "Sir, is there, like, an optimum speed for dumping fuel?" Dave looked at him for a second then turned away. "Nope."

The course was demanding for me, the aircraft was complicated compared to anything I had flown before but I devoured it. Finally, jet experience was coming my way. One of the instructors in the sim was a large character. He looked, walked and acted cowboy from his string tie to his crocodile skin boots – central casting for Marlboro Man. He chain-smoked all the time in the sim, ignoring the strict simulator rules. His face was heavily lined and his voice rasped from too many red-top cigarettes. Periodically, he would lean forward in the sim and drawl, reeeaal sloooow, "Right about now, y'aaall want to be setting your buuurgs," referring to the moveable plastic speed reference 'bugs' set on the outside of the airspeed dial.

On one of the two days off we had on the course Bon and I visited Davis-Monthan Air Force Base situated only five miles outside Tuscon. This is where the US military stores its surplus aircraft. In the bone-dry desert air of the Arizona desert, these aircraft are inhibited and covered in plastic in line upon line. It is an awesome sight, literally hundreds of aircraft that have been pensioned off from front line Air Force, Navy, Marine and National Guard service sit there in the sun. Most can be made fully serviceable in only a few weeks if an emergency requires it. There are more aircraft in storage here than in the combined air forces of several countries. Looking down from the surrounding hills onto the lines and lines of aircraft you get a true sense of the

Davis-Monthan Air Force Base

B-52 bombers being broken up

scale and power of the US military. At the time, some B-52 bombers were being cut up to comply with the recent SALT treaties. In the clear desert skies, their destruction would be easily verified by circling Russian spy satellites.

* * * *

Medical flights were the staple business on the Lear and to a lesser extent on the Hawkers because of its smaller entry door; unless they were 'walking wounded' it was difficult to manoeuvre a stretcher through the narrow opening on the Hawker without tipping, which didn't generally go down too well with the patient. These medical flights could be repatriations to the UK or vital organ transplant flights and I enjoyed flying all of them. I was very aware that I was helping someone live although occasionally on the repatriation flights, despite the paramedics' hard work, the patient died in flight. I had two inflight deaths over the years but for practical reasons, we had a tacit agreement with the medics that the patients always died on arrival back in the UK. The legal ramifications of dying while in foreign airspace would be too complicated and didn't change the outcome. A typical repatriation event would be a holidaymaker diving into too-shallow water onto rocks. Or even empty swimming pools after one too many. The insurance companies, generally Europ Assistance or Mondial, would weigh up the chance of the patient dying abroad (preferable, as it was cheaper) vs bringing them home. If the sums worked out, they would arrange for the paramedics and all the necessary equipment to fly in the aircraft to repatriate the patient. The paramedics were superb, very experienced in aeromedicine and full of black humour.

Organ transplant flights were another aspect of medical flights. These involved bringing vital organs such as the heart, lungs and kidneys, from a recently deceased person – often the victim of a road traffic accident – back to the UK for a suitable recipient. A Europe-wide database matched donors to recipients. We would fly a team of surgeons to somewhere in Europe where they would disappear for a few hours and then return to the aircraft with nothing more sophisticated than a picnic cool-box which contained the said organs resting on dry ice to keep them cool. I always had a horror of taking the cool box from the surgeons as they boarded, falling over my feet and spilling the gory contents all over the tarmac but, thank goodness, that never happened.

Annotating the flight plan with STS/HOSP (translated, 'Status: Hospital Flight') gave the flight highest priority from ATC meaning that you got direct routeings and mostly no speed restrictions. The organs' useful life was measured in only a few hours so, for example, on a flight back from Athens you really needed to hurry. Generally, we would land at Heathrow where an ambulance and police escort would be waiting to meet the aircraft to rush the surgeons and organs to the hospital. The time from extracting the organs in Athens to their arrival at the John Radcliffe Hospital in Oxford could be under five hours if things went perfectly and we tried to beat the record every time.

* * * *

I'm on a medevac flight to Liberia in West Africa. Flying with me is Mike Wennink, a freelance pilot who helps out from time to time. He is a very good pilot and nothing much fazes him. Masey used to joke that Mike could roll a cigarette and chat with a passenger behind him while flying a perfect ILS with one hand. Our destination is Monrovia, Liberia's capital, and the weather is awful. Try as we might, we can't dodge the late afternoon thunderstorms and if there's one thing Mike can't stand it's thunderstorms. Hunched down in the right seat with his eyes closed he occasionally pops his head up over the glare shield and every time he does so, there is a deafening clap of thunder and a brilliant flash of lightning made more menacing by the gathering darkness. I'm not exactly enjoying the conditions much either, but I have to laugh – Mike's timing is impeccably wrong. Head down, things are relatively calm. Head up and FLASH! BANG! We eventually land on a flooded runway in Monrovia, both of us relieved to be on the ground. I do a quick walk around the aircraft to see if we have taken a lightning strike we are unaware of. All's good but I am alarmed to see a panel on the left side of the rear empennage, beneath the engine, flapping loose. It's not structural and is a composite material of some sort. It's not ideal though and I motion to Mike, who is wandering around calming his nerves with a post-flight ciggie, to come and take a look. "Oh God," he laughs, waving his cigarette in his usual theatrical way. "Was that me?" I assure him this will be fine and anyway we don't really have an option stuck as we are in Liberia. No one is going to fix anything here. We always carried three things during our African trips to help get us home; a spare generator, a spare main wheel and rolls of speed tape. Today, it is the speed tape that saves the day. Together, Mike and I apply liberal amounts of tape to the loose panel. It looks unsightly but we reckon it will do the trick and the next day, after a fitful night's sleep in the airport hotel and with the patient on board, we fly home.

* * * *

One medevac repatriation in particular sticks in my mind as it involved a lot of complications. Masey got a call from the French government to quote for the repatriation of an oil worker from Luanda, Angola. This chap worked for Total the French oil company and had been involved in a road traffic accident. He had been hit in his Toyota Land Cruiser by a drunken Angolan soldier driving an army APC. The Land Cruiser is a tough vehicle but is no match for eight tonnes of solid steel. He was in a very bad way with multiple broken bones and marrow leaking into his bloodstream and needed urgent medical attention in France. The plan was to repatriate him ASAP to Paris for medical treatment and Masey was rubbing his hands - government contracts can always be priced at top dollar. Exactly why we got the job I don't know, maybe there were no French operators available at short notice. Anyway, Martyn and I left Gatwick with two paramedics and all their equipment, stopping twice on the way south at Agadir and Abidjan and arriving in Luanda at 5.00 am. It was raining but hot and very humid. Parking on a remote stand away from the main terminal building, we started to clean the aircraft, throwing out gash bags full of the catering we had eaten on the way down into a nearby drainage ditch, figuring that no one would notice.

Slowly I became aware of shadowy figures emerging out of the pre-dawn light. Before I knew it, a crowd of people were going through our rubbish searching for any food we had discarded. At least half of them were on crutches, a sobering reminder of the legacy of land mines that were everywhere in the country following the bitter civil war between UNITA and the MPLA. We secured the aircraft and made our way through the terminal building. It was poorly lit but we could make out the communist flags and signs erected everywhere by the Marxist government. The country, which is so rich in oil and gas, was in a desperate state. That night we all stayed in a safe house in town provided by Total. Martyn and I both slept badly with the air conditioning switching on and off all night, tossing and turning in the sticky air.

The next morning, we returned to the airport and started to prepare the aircraft for the long flight back to Paris. The ambulance, a no-frills flatbed Toyota, eventually arrived and we loaded the passenger on his stretcher into the aircraft. I could tell he was in a very bad way by looking at him and by the expression on 'Doc' McDermot's face. We have met Doc before in this story. He was a very experienced paramedic who worked freelance for Mondial Assistance and we regularly flew together. The other paramedic on the trip was Bridget, a diminutive nurse who was also very good and known to all and sundry as Bridget the Midget.

We set off northbound. The plan was to stop for fuel at Tamanrasset before continuing to Paris Le Bourget however, as we passed abeam Libreville, Doc came forward. "This chap is deteriorating fast. I would like him at a hospital as soon as possible. What are our options?" "Few," I told him, "this is Africa after all. I would suggest either Doula or Abidjan. Both are French and the hospitals should be as good as you get in West Africa. Abidjan would be my first choice. It's a big diversion from here though." "Yes, I agree, I was there six months ago, and the hospital is good. OK, let's do it", the Doc confirmed and we put plans in place to make the diversion, made easier by our HOSP status, although in those days you did pretty much what you wanted in Africa as ATC was rudimentary at best – very little radar and all clearances were procedural, mostly on crackly HF radio.

I called Masey on the HF to advise him of the change of plan and to ask him to advise Mondial so everything, all being well, would be ready on arrival in Abidjan. We started the left turn towards Abidjan and landed there two and a half hours later, where, as we taxied in, a modern, air-conditioned ambulance was waiting to receive the patient, a far cry from the flatbed in Luanda. Doc and Bridget went off with the ambulance to do the handover in the hospital and we refuelled the Lear and mooched around the apron waiting for their return.

The airport had a definite French feel to it; even the terminal building had tourist posters of Paris, Biarritz and the Cote d'Azur. The French have never really left Africa; countries like the Ivory Coast remain very much 'outre-mer' and under the French colonial thumb which is good news when flying in that region. Morocco, Algeria, Cote d'Ivoire, Gabon, and Cameroon all have good airports. Everything works pretty well in contrast to the former British colonies, like Ghana and especially Nigeria, where generally things have gone to hell in a handcart.

Here's an example of Abidjan's 'Frenchness'. As we were waiting for Doc and Bridget the Midget to return to the airport, a 747 freighter of UTA landed, cleared the runway and taxied slowly in to park next to us. Leaning against the Lear's tip tanks, we idly watched the unloading process then wandered over to take a closer look. The nose section lifted and a scissor jack loader rumbled into position belching diesel smoke and raised its hydraulic platform to the main cargo deck. We watched as four pallets of Evian water were offloaded and waited in expectation to see what the rest of the load might be but that was it, just the Evian. The scissor jack lowered and drove off and the crew closed the aircraft's nose section. After a final check of the aircraft, they left for the hotel. Clearly, for the French colonials, essential supplies.

UTA 747 freighter, stock photo

* * * *

Almaty, Kazakhstan 1992. Roy Cobb and I are in Alma-Ata, as it was known then, on a charter for three days. It's winter and bitterly cold. Roy and I leave our basic Soviet-style hotel that was all there was in those days and wander around the streets for a while looking for a bar or any kind of life. The city is deserted, the occasional car goes past on the wide, slushy boulevards and the streets are dimly lit. Gloomy and grim, nothing like the modern and booming Western-style city that exists now. Eventually, we find an open bar and go inside for some warmth and a drink. Everyone stares at us curiously, Europeans are a rare sight there in those days. It's warm and fuggy and a few people are sitting at sticky wooden tables. We get our drinks, hand over some single dollar bills and take the stairs to the basement where there are sounds of more life than at street level. After a few minutes, I am aware of a girl looking at us from across the room and after a while, she comes over. She is stunningly good-looking, with a dark Cleopatra-style haircut, slightly Asiatic, with high cheekbone features and piercing green eyes which, had this been the West, I would have put down to coloured contact lenses but not in 1990s Almaty. To this day, the most arresting face I have ever seen. In the King's Road, she would have been snapped up by any modelling agency before she had walked 100 yards. Roy and I start chatting to her trying to make it clear we are happy to be friendly but no more. She speaks good English which is unusual so there must be more to her than meets the eye, either a working girl or KGB. I look at Roy and he is transfixed, "Christ, I could leave home for this," he breathes into his beer.

After a while, we are joined by two men, a big bear of a man and a smaller sharp-faced guy who looks like Mac the Knife. "Please, can we sit?" the little guy asks, smiling but with cold, hard eyes. "Of course," I gesture to the spare chairs thinking that I'd rather they didn't as I have a bad feeling. Their English is also good and we soon discover why – they are both policemen. An hour passes and we exchange the usual common ground topics, English football, Margaret Thatcher etc, and they are getting drunker by the minute. I am thinking about how the hell we are going to extricate ourselves from this situation. We are in the basement of a bar with two drunk Kazakh detectives and a honey-trap beauty and no one would even know if we never reappeared. It's getting edgy as by this stage Mac the Knife is showing off with the pistol he has removed from his holster. He has it on the table spinning it around, drunkenly re-enacting the scene from 'The Deerhunter' his favourite movie and he's completely out of it. The big guy just watches us. Time to make a move.

"Mate, we need to get out of here now," I whisper to Roy. "I can see this getting out completely out of hand." "I'm with you, let's go" he replies. I look at my watch and start to make profuse apologies. "Sadly, we have to go. It was nice to meet you but we are very tired and must work tomorrow. Thank you, my friends." They smile drunkenly and start to insist that we meet up tomorrow but we shuffle away, towards the stairs and start climbing up, out of the basement. We weave our way through the ground-level bar and stumble outside. The freezing night air sobers us up quickly, it must be -10°C. One more wave goodbye in the general direction of the bar and we are gone. "Fuck, I'm glad to be out of there," I laugh nervously to Rob as I run to catch up with him. Rob is legging it down the street slipping and sliding over the icy pavements. "Me too," he says, "but that girl….."

* * * *

Odesa 1990. This was once a prosperous city on the Ukrainian coast until decades of Soviet centralisation had rendered it neglected and down at heel. The city is located in the northwest corner of the Black Sea to the west of the Crimea peninsular. As we land and taxi in, we can see the rundown terminal building and general rubbish and bins lying around. A couple of airport workers glance up but then don't give us a second look. A dog scratches itself in the sun. In the distance is a dilapidated AN-24 aircraft missing an engine. The airport has an air of general desertion and neglect, typical of the region.

I am on a trip with Brian Thompson and have just arrived from Madrid, empty, to collect some of the JKX Oil executives, to return to London. As Brian stays with the aircraft to supervise the refuelling, I wander over to the terminal building to pay the landing fee. There are two sets of double doors to enter the terminal with no indication of which side was best for the airport office, so I mentally flip a coin and choose the left set of doors. These close stiffly behind me and I am facing another set of swing doors. Putting my shoulder to these I push into the hall. Inside are abandoned check-in desks, old newspapers everywhere and the usual smell of old Russian buildings, a mix of sweat, diesel and urine. In the far corner of the hall, I detect movement. I freeze; there is a pack of dogs lying together on the floor, maybe ten to fifteen animals. The mixture of big dogs and small dogs and breeds together tells me one thing – these are dogs that are no longer domestic, they have been abandoned and have gone feral. They look hungry and mangy. The biggest dog, clearly the alpha, stares at me and stands up stiffly, the other dogs following his lead one by one. He starts to walk slowly over, never taking his eyes off me, growling quietly. I don't wait to see what is going to happen next. I bolt back through the swing doors and the other external set of doors and lay against them from the outside. I can hear the dogs growling and pawing only feet away but after a while, they lose interest and I suppose return to their corner. I moved across the front of the building and warily enter the second set of doors. Inside is a small office and the ground agent is sitting behind an old wooden desk. "You know you have wild dogs next door in the check-in hall? Dogs, crazy," I said pointing to my head, trying to get the point across and to sound as casual as I could while reaching inside my coat for the dollars. He looks at me, nods and shrugs and goes back to the papers he is preparing for our bill, a cigarette hanging from his lip.

* * * *

It's hard for pilots who now fly into Eastern Europe and the CIS regularly and are used to western standard hotels to appreciate how far things have come in thirty years. In Moscow, for example, in the late 1980s and early 1990s, there were no Holiday Inns, Marriotts or Westin hotels. There was just one hotel available to westerners, the infamous Hotel Rossiya which was the only hotel that the state-owned Intourist Bureau permitted tourists and businessmen, as 'guests of the Soviet Union', to stay at. Moscow was one of those cities where, if you moved in the right circles, you could live very well but for most people, residents and tourists alike, it was a struggle. Robert Maxwell's son Kevin told me it was one of his favourite cities in the world but, obviously, he moved in very different circles. The Hotel Rossiya was just off Red Square and designed so that there were only a few entrances and exits. This facilitated keeping tabs on the inmates – a good analogy as it had the atmosphere and smell of a prison. At one point the Rossiya was the world's biggest hotel with around 3,000 rooms. How to describe the experience of a stay there? It was depressing, to put it mildly, and required a stoic and grim sense of humour to survive. Each floor had its babushka wrapped in a shawl who reported on every coming and going and any other activity that might be deemed of interest to the authorities. The rooms were appalling, wood-panelled, dirty, gloomy and airless. We routinely took our own towels, soap and bath plugs together with cake, tea, coffee, UHT milk and a portable kettle so at least we could get a brew going. The carpets were disgusting, shiny and sticky to the extent that if you were lucky enough to get some threadbare towels supplied with the room you only used them to create a pathway to the bathroom.

Eating out was a challenge as the number of restaurants was very limited and all were universally terrible, tough meat and potato mostly. When Mcdonald's opened in Moscow in 1990 half of the queue that extended for hundreds of feet would comprise foreign tourists and businessmen desperate for food most of them wouldn't touch at home. Still, if that wasn't your kind of fun, then a look around the famous GUM department store made you realise that no matter which town you thought was bad in the West, by comparison it was positively Eldorado. Every shop under GUM's beautiful and ornate glass roof was bare of anything useful but still queues formed based solely on a rumour of new stock arriving. Maybe today, maybe tomorrow…

It was quite possible, although highly illegal, to change hard currency into Russian Roubles on the street at up to ten times the official rate. US dollars or the mighty Deutschmark were the preferred currencies with Sterling a distinct third. However, there wasn't much point as it simply wasn't possible to spend it. Firstly, Westerners stuck out like sore thumbs due to their good complexions, decent clothes and general demeanour and secondly, everyone knew that as a Westerner then you had hard currency so why would anyone accept Roubles from you? Especially Roubles that you probably obtained illegally; no one wanted to be entertained by the KGB at 3 am on a charge of committing a currency felony.

One interesting aspect of the collapse of the USSR was the de-centralisation of goods and services. Before about 1991, private jets were a rare sight in Russia and the CIS. Transiting through Mineralnye Vody in the Lear on the way back to Moscow, Masey and I refuelled and then had an interesting conversation with the Aeroflot agent there. Having obeyed the golden rule of refuelling and then negotiating how to pay for it, (this A. gives you options and B. ensures the agent doesn't abandon interest in you), I said to him, "OK, we pay now. How much for the fuel?" making the rubbing sign for money. He looked puzzled. "I have US dollars and want to pay for the fuel," I persisted. He still looked blank, so I showed him a couple of hundred bucks as a teaser and he finally twigged.

"Captain, please. I cannot take money, is not possible!" This was a novel response – turning down US dollars?

"Why not?" I said in exasperation as I wanted to pay and be on our way, "I have money."

"Is not possible. Is no account to pay money to," he said desperately and finally I understood. He had never encountered a jet before that wasn't state-run and therefore billed centrally. "You pay Aeroflot when you get to Vnukovo. I will arrange for this!" he smiled, mentioning the Moscow airport we were heading for and looking relieved. "OK, no problem," I agreed, thinking to myself that this will never happen and, sure enough, it didn't and so we got our fuel for free, only 3000 litres or so but, as they say, every little helps.

* * * *

Before the Berlin Wall came down, flying into Berlin, which was firmly in the Soviet zone, required flying down set corridors to access the three airports in the West Berlin sector: Tempelhof, Tegel and RAF Gatow. Access to the East Berlin airports in the Soviet sector such as Schönefeld was forbidden. These three twenty-mile-wide corridors were set up after the war to supply West Berlin and existed for decades after. In the corridors, the upper limit was 10,000ft – fine in 1947 in a piston airliner but not really suited to modern jet aircraft. We normally accessed the city via the central corridor as this was the shortest one, so it minimised the time spent at low altitude. For this reason, it was the most popular with airlines too; 10,000ft is no place to be in one of the 727s, BAC1-11s and DC-9s of the time. Only British, French, Soviet (occasionally Polish) and American airlines had this access to the city as the four occupying powers in Berlin. Flying to Berlin meant routeing to Hannover at normal altitudes and then dropping down to be below 10,000ft by the Hehlingen VOR for the 80 nm run down the corridor. The en route navigation charts warned that aircraft flying outside the corridors would be fired upon without warning– welcome to the friendly Democratic Republic of East Germany.

Tempelhof was an interesting airport. The terminal building was rebuilt in 1934 under the supervision of Albert Speer, Hitler's principal architect and it had a chilling atmosphere. True to Nazi form, it was built on a grand, curved scale and was so big that airliners could park out of the weather under its giant roof. It was a colossal structure, typical of the thousand-year thinking of the Third Reich. It was also famous as the main airport during the 1948 Berlin airlift. I collected Boris Becker there on a cold, wet day in 1990 and it was wonderful to be able to taxi directly into the roofed terminal and be in the dry out of the rain that was pelting down outside. The airport closed in October 2008, amid some controversy, after an appeal to keep it open failed and it is now a Berlin 'city park'.

Tegel, Tempelhof and Shönefeld have all been replaced by the new Berlin Brandenburg Airport that opened in 2020. The symbols of a divided Germany have finally been disposed of.

Berlin-Tempelhof Airport, showing the huge, covered terminal

* * * *

December 21st 1988. I'm taxiing to the GAT apron at Gatwick in one of the Titans having just landed from Aberdeen. It's dark, cold and drizzling, only four days before Christmas. A few yards away I can make out the figure of Bon at the Learjet moving quickly and wearing a thick jacket. The clamshell door is half open and he is tearing the engine and probe covers off. I shut down and walk over.

"What's going on, did you get a call out?" I ask him.

"Get in," Bon growls, "we are flying to Carlisle."

"Why?" I venture as Bon hands me the wet covers. "An aircraft has crashed near Lockerbie. Masey has called Martyn out but as you're here already, let's go. The ITN crew will be here in twenty minutes. I'll meet them if you prep the aircraft and call for the clearance."

I climb into the Lear and sit in the right seat trying to process what I had just heard. As I start the cockpit preparation checks, I realise that my planned night with a girlfriend at the Six Bells has just been hijacked.

And so began the horror of Pan Am Flight 103. Everybody knows where they were that night when the news broke, in the same way they did on the morning of 9/11 thirteen years later. The initial reports were of an aircraft crashing into a petrol station on the A74 at Lockerbie. There were no details available of what aircraft was involved other than it was an airliner, it was all very sketchy. Bad, but nothing as bad as what unfolded. Over the next few hours, the world learned that a Pan Am 747 named, in the Pan Am 'Clipper' tradition, "Clipper Maid of the Seas" under the command of Captain James MacQuarrie and carrying 243 passengers and 16 crew had been torn apart en route to New York by a terrorist bomb hidden in a cassette-radio player. Bodies, eighty tons of fuel, engines and very large pieces of fuselage, including the huge wing centre box, rained down on and around Lockerbie. News teams from all over Europe wanted to be there - and now, Carlisle Airport was a sleepy little airport in those days and was just ready to close for the night when Bon and I arrived. We were the first aircraft to land there that evening after the news of the crash broke but by the end of the night, every yard of tarmac was covered with parked aircraft. It's easy to see the reason why; Carlisle was the nearest

The forward section of the Clipper 'Maid of The Seas' lying on a Scottish hillside

Sherwood Crescent, Lockerbie showing the huge crater caused by the heavy wing section

The Pan Am 103 Memorial, Lockerbie

reasonably sized airport to Lockerbie, situated twenty miles southeast of the town. The only other airport option, Glasgow, is seventy miles further north.

Within thirty minutes of us arriving with our ITN crew, two unmarked C-130 Hercules arrived and some shadowy-looking people disembarked. SWAT teams possibly? This was, after all, a US-registered aircraft with 190 US citizens on board. Then more aircraft from all over Europe arrived, all carrying their news teams. This wasn't a ghoulish tabloid frenzy. I think everyone understood that this was huge, the worst aviation terrorist attack ever at that time and everyone wanted to make sense of the mess. It was a shocking event and this iconic picture of the cockpit section lying on its side on a Borders hillside will never be forgotten.

A few years later, I visited the town and went to the cemetery where there is a permanently floodlit memorial to the event with the names of all the passengers and crew carved into the granite stone. It was, by coincidence, a cold and foggy December evening like that on the evening of the catastrophe and this added to the atmosphere of the visit. Where the huge wing centre section crashed to the ground in Sherwood Crescent, demolishing three houses, was a significant gap and a large grassed-over crater. It was a sobering visit made more so as I reflected that my sister and her husband could easily have been on board. They were due to fly home to the Cayman Islands via New York for Christmas around that date and often flew with Pan Am.

* * * *

"Fancy a month in Yugoslavia?" Masey grinned at me in mid-December 1991.

"Maybe. What's it about?" I asked him and he explained. It seemed that the government of Montenegro had recently bought a Learjet to add to their Government flight department and wanted a TRE to teach them how to fly it. In for a penny, in for a pound, I thought - why not? It's all in a day's work and something different. "Tell me more," I said. "They have a Swedish contract pilot there at present but he can't do any more," Masey explained and I wondered what he means by that ambiguous statement – had the pilot had enough, if so why, or did he just have to get back to Sweden? "Don't worry, I'll swap you with Brian after a couple of weeks." I doubted that would ever happen knowing Masey but I agreed to go out to Titograd, (now Podgorica), the capital of Montenegro. I had nothing going on in my personal life and it sounded like a bit of an adventure and there was a decent per diem payment offered. So, after getting my pilot's licence validated for the Yugoslav aircraft registration, I set off.

I flew into Titograd in January 1992 with JAT Airways, the Yugoslav state carrier and then took a taxi downtown. What a dump the city was, derelict, Soviet, filthy. I checked into the same hotel that the Swedish pilot Olaf was staying in and met up with him the first evening at the bar where he was nursing a Slivovitz. Straightaway I suspected the problem; he had 'gone bush' and developed a liking to the local liquor a little too much. Slivovitz is a plum brandy produced in Serbia. Only Damson plums are used in its production but why anyone would be that specific is a bit of a mystery, it is pure fire water and tastes like paint stripper. Anyway, after chatting to Olaf for a while on the first evening we parted company and I went to bed.

It had been arranged that I would meet Dragan Popovic, the Government Flight Department's Chief Pilot at the hotel at 8 am after breakfast. My room was dark and the bed was damp. The curtains were standard Eastern European, in other words like tissue paper and not big enough to meet in the middle of the window so the room never got properly dark and I tossed and turned in the yellow light. I also had to get accustomed to the local culture. It seemed that my Montenegrin hosts were pyromaniacs and party lovers all rolled into one. I soon learnt that once they have had enough to drink they liked to set fire to any rubbish bins they could find (not hard in Titograd) and when over-refreshed shoot their weapons into the air just for fun, but on that first night I was wondering what the hell was going on and what I'd got myself into.

Dragan Popovic arrived at the hotel on time. He was a quietly spoken man with a goatee beard and I liked him straight away. We drive the five miles to the airport in his Russian-made jeep and we chatted about this and that. I was introduced to the guys in the hangar and took a look at the Learjet and the other aircraft of the Flight Department; two helicopters, a Bell 212 and a Bell 206 'Jet Ranger'. The Lear had been re-registered from its time in the US, where it had been owned by Goodfella Pizzas and now had its Yugoslav tail number, YU-BPY. I gave it a look over and checked the paperwork. At first glance, it looked in good shape, with good paint at least. This could mean a well-maintained aircraft or it could just be what's known in the industry as 'shine on shite'. However, a nice leather interior and tidy cockpit let me relax a little as these are better indicators of a well-looked-after aircraft. Dragan then offered me the choice of getting a taxi to and from the hotel each day or using one of the flight department's Zastavas – a gasping little car made in Serbia, part metal and part plastic and similar to the infamous Trabant. It was a truly terrible car that rattled and leaked and wouldn't, as they say in the car trade, pull the skin off a rice pudding. However, at least it gave me some freedom and independence while I was there, so I accepted it gracefully. I proudly took possession of the keys to my little yellow banger.

All the preliminaries done, it was time to meet the pilots I was to train. There were three of them, all helicopter pilots trained by the Yugoslav army, two of them instructors, lovely guys with a good sense of humour but I was not convinced that this background was so suitable. The Learjet is a demanding aircraft with the performance of a fighter and definitely not one I'd recommend cutting your teeth on as your first fixed-wing aircraft. They were experienced helicopter pilots, however, so I hoped they had a decent level of airmanship that I could build on. I went up with one of the instructors in the hefty Bell 212 on the first day and he was really good, making the helicopter dance to his tune. I spent a few hours with him in the 212 over the next few weeks trying to master the basics of flying a helicopter and soon discovered that this isn't so easy. As the rotor disk is a gyroscope it has a strong precession effect so every input that affects the tilt of the rotor disk has an effect elsewhere - pretty soon you are wobbling about all over the place. I may have been good in the Lear but this was his baby as I felt he was keen to show me. Helicopters are hard to master, however with the autopilot engaged, I found it flew pretty much like a fixed-wing aircraft. The 212 had an added advantage in that, as it was a two-engine version of the famous US Army Huey it sounded right with loud banging 'thwacks' from the rotors, pure Vietnam.

The daily run carrying Government officials involved a triangular route between Titograd, Sarajevo and Belgrade, a total distance of around 360 nm. This was before Sarajevo town centre became known the world over as a killing ground of sniper attacks and shelling. This busy route would make it a demanding day under any circumstances but having to watch them carefully and remove some of the wrong information and dubious practices they had picked up from Olaf made it especially hard work. One of their more alarming habits was never to land on the runway centreline; all of them would deliberately land with the left tip tank over the grass even on wide runways like Belgrade. I began to realise that this was just to wind me up so after a while I ignored the habit. My evenings were spent in the hotel or out with the guys savouring the very limited delights of the city and avoiding spent rounds falling from the sky. In the end, I did get swapped with Brian but not until I had done six weeks, not the promised two. By the time that came I'd had enough, the city in early spring was cold and depressing and there was precious little to do apart from flying. Shortly afterwards even that came to an end. With the bitter Balkan war in progress and because Montenegro was closely aligned with Serbia, the resulting US and EU sanctions meant that spare parts were impossible to get for either

The Montenegro Government Learjet YU-BPY

the Lear or the helicopters and the flight department was closed down. I brought a bottle of Slivovitz home but haven't opened it since. It still stands in my drinks cupboard to this day, a reminder of an interesting time.

* * * *

Lagos - what to say? The largest city in Africa was a frequent destination for us for medevac flights. It has a reputation among pilots as one of the worst destinations of all and for valid reasons. It's a broiling, teeming, sprawling mess of a city in permanent chaos with practically no working infrastructure. The city population doubled in size between the mid-1970s and the mid-1990s when it was 5-6 million with most people living in poverty. It's now over 14 million. Corruption and crime in Nigeria are the normal way of life and security is non-existent. The only thing it excels at is malaria hospitals. In Nigeria, they recognise the symptoms of malaria instantly, unlike in Europe where it is often passed off as flu, and they act quickly. If you get malaria, hope you are in

Nigeria, but for anything else hope you're not. That pretty much sums it up. The people of Lagos are not my favourite, tending to be aggressive and difficult, but I used to wonder if this is a result of the fetid climate that they live in. Was it nature or nurture? Port Harcourt, in the delta region, is the same. However, fly into Kano, Sokoto, Kaduna, Maiduguri, Jos or Abuja (the capital) and everyone is generally more friendly and helpful. Lagos is a treacle mine in the 100°F heat and 90% humidity – a sauna and totally draining.

It was a requirement to get PPR authority before flying to Nigeria. This meant sending a Telex with the flight details to the Nigerian Ministry of Aviation with all the flight details and, in theory, waiting for a positive reply. This could take days, if not weeks and obviously this system would never work for urgent medevac flights. So, we used to set off and 'wing it' as we neared the Nigerian border. The standard brusque demand from ATC of, "What is your clearance number?" would be replied with your birthdate with a few extra letters mixed in, or your Tesco Clubcard number – or anything else you could think of on the spur of the moment. And often this, aided by pretending to have radio difficulties, was sufficient, such was the inefficiency of everything in the country. Arriving in Lagos was always a bit nerve-wracking for several other reasons. You were generally low on fuel and power cuts were frequent, knocking out the ATC radio and runway lights without warning and, depending on the season and time of day, the weather could be really bad with heavy thunderstorms. On top of all this, the airport authority had the habit of announcing, out of the blue, that the airport was closed until further notice due to a VIP or 'presidential flight'. This would get everyone demanding answers at once. How long for? From what time? When is our expected approach time? etc etc. No one ever asked 'why?' as it was irrelevant and you were too busy with contingency plans. Anyway, ATC would remain oblivious to pleas to land from aircraft that were short of fuel. Everywhere in Nigeria is a long way from everywhere else and diversions are never welcome when flying on fumes.

Once you had landed your problems were far from over. In stultifying heat and humidity and generally dog-tired after a long flight with your shirt sticking to you like a warm rag, you would have to visit both civil and military officials, on opposite sides of the airfield and explain why you had arrived with no PPR. The fact that you were on an urgent medical flight made no difference at all.

It was expected to 'dash' the officers the right amount and in the correct order of importance and always present a goodwill present of 400 Marlboro and a bottle of Johnny Walker scotch. The skill was in working out who was in charge, for the first dash, so no one suffered a loss of face. Even just leaving the airport could take hours. On return, usually the next day, the process was followed in reverse but could take even longer. I had the company record of seven hours to get permission just to leave the country and that was seven hours spent before the long flight northbound. Getting airborne was a blessed relief. There's a saying amongst pilots that "Happiness is V2 out of Lagos" and it's true, you were on your way out of the swamp.

A trick the airport workers on the ramp played was to steal something from your aircraft, for example a link from the nosewheel steering assembly. This would then be offered back to you on departure for $500. And syphoning fuel from fuel tanks was commonplace. I met a Danish pilot there once and he told me of his particular incident. He landed in his Citation and left the aircraft for the night. The next day he noticed that the fuel quantity was indicating more than he arrived with. Strange, however he didn't think more of it. However, on takeoff, passing around 1500ft, both engines flamed out. Luckily it was daylight and he managed to glide the aircraft safely onto a highway that was under construction in the jungle. The reason he appeared to have more fuel on departure than he expected was that someone had drained his fuel and thoughtfully topped the tanks up with water. As the fuel probes measure liquid density, they recorded a higher figure of 'fuel' in the tanks, water being much denser than jet fuel. Ever since that event, he was rigorous in ensuring the over-wing fuel caps were locked tight and couldn't be opened - as I have also been ever since speaking to him. Yes, Nigeria was fun and games all right.

With that background to the lovely city of Lagos, I'll relate one event that was truly scary and could have ended badly. I am flying with Brian on a medevac flight to Lagos to collect an official who needs urgent medical treatment in London. As usual, as explained above, we didn't have any clearance number so we use our usual tricks at the border. We make it into Nigerian airspace OK, land at Lagos and make it through the airport without too much difficulty, maybe two or three hours only. We have taken the usual precautions of refuelling on arrival and parking the aircraft in such a way that we can taxi off any time we want, unimpeded – the two golden rules in Africa.

Outside the terminal building, the driver who was going to take us to the hotel on Victoria Island is waiting in an old Peugeot; the paramedics have gone off in a separate car. We are aware that there has recently been a change of government in the country. President Babangida has been removed and President Shonekan instated. The names are unimportant, what is more important is the fact that whenever there is a change at the top in Africa, all the familiar rules no longer apply. There are a few weeks of disruption before the new system of corruption takes hold and everyone knows once again where they stand. Anyway, we pile into the car and make our way through the airport car parks etc. and towards the main road into town, the driver skilfully dodging the potholes and stray dogs. The night is hot and the humid air envelops us like a hot towel. We are dog tired and have taken our uniform jackets and epaulettes off to look as inconspicuous as possible slumped in the back of the car, although we are aware that crew always stick out like a sore thumb. I wind down the window letting the breeze wash over me and with it the night smells of Lagos.

We approach the usual roadblock manned by armed police and soldiers and I get the dash of Marlboro and Johnny Walker (aka 'Johnny') ready to offer with the usual pleasantries and banter. So far so normal. As we get closer though I can see that the mood is different to usual. The police are more in the shadows, holding back and soldiers are manning the barrier, looking aggressive and edgy. The car stops and I pop my head out of the window. I can the that the soldiers are high on drink or drugs, their eyes red and wary. One of them has a bottle swinging loosely in his hand. I don't like what I see.

"Good evening, my friend, how are you? I have Johnny for you," I start with a smile, showing him the bottle. The sergeant looks at me with no expression but he's not friendly. Not at all. He shrugs his semi-automatic off his shoulder and rests the barrel on the car window, pointing in. It looks like an AK47 but I'm not sure and to be honest, when it's pointing at you, you don't care too much.

"No whisky, give me your dollars," he slurs, not taking his eyes off me. They always knew that crews were carrying dollars.

"I have Johnny for you and American cigarettes," I repeat. This usually works but not this time. Without a word, he turns away and motions our driver to turn off the road and down an unlit sandy dirt track. I can see our driver is very nervous and a nervous African, when there are guns about, is never good.

"I'm not giving this bastard any money," says Brian.

"Mate," I hiss back, "we will give them whatever they bloody want, this is no time for heroics. We could vanish here and never be seen again. Personally, I want to get home alive."

The driver pulls slowly off the main road and three of the soldiers follow us. I can see the driver is very nervous. I'm thinking fast. The sergeant prods the barrel into my chest and jerks his head. At the time I don't feel it much, such is the effect of adrenaline, but the gunsight is sharp and later it hurts like hell.

"Money captain." I'm aware that he could loose off half a dozen rounds into me by accident if not deliberately. Then the others would have to be killed too of course and a story concocted.

"My friend," I look into his eyes, bloodshot and dead, "we are here at the request of your new *President*." (I stress the word). I couldn't for the life of me remember the new president's name in the stress of the moment.

"His Excellency wishes us to fly his dear friend to London tomorrow. Tomorrow. I do not think it would be good if he heard of this happening to us this evening."

It's not true, the patient was nothing to do with the President, he would have used his own jets in any event but this guy would never know. I'm gambling on this working. My foot is shaking involuntarily and I am watching his face closely for his reaction. He just continues staring at me blankly for a few seconds, expressionless and then I see the cogs moving through the haze of drink and drugs.

"OK," he shrugs, waving the AK. "You go." motioning the driver back to the main road.

"Thank you," I say and manage a smile. "Please take the Johnny." I add a carton of Winston and press $500 into his wet hands, we're not on the main road yet. He tucks the wedge into his combat trousers pocket without looking. Experience with bribes tells him its approximate value. The driver backs up the car onto the road and we accelerate off. "I don't get paid enough for this shit," I say in an attempt to ease the tension. Brian remains silent, no longer so gung-ho. I know that Masey will have no problem absorbing the cost of the dash and would enjoy the story in the Six Bells, one thing he understood well enough was TIA – This Is Africa.

* * * *

Flying around Nigeria can have its lighter moments, however. Goats and shepherds can often be seen wandering across active runways or whole families living contentedly in wrecked aircraft on the edge of airports. On one trip, Brian and I are flying together again in the Learjet, this time to Sokoto in the north of the country, close to the border of Niger. It's a remote city about 240 miles west of Kano. Brian is Pilot Flying and I am in the right seat as Pilot Monitoring and working the radios etc. At top of descent, about 120 miles from the airfield, I call Sokoto up on their approach frequency to pass on our ETA and to get the runway in use, weather conditions etc. Usual stuff. No reply to my call so I try again a few minutes later, now in descent. Again nothing. OK, I think I'll try the Tower frequency and see if I can raise them instead, maybe they are only working one frequency. Nothing. By this time, we are only fifty miles out and so they should be hearing us perfectly.

"Sokoto Tower, this is Interflight 132, do you read?"

Again, a stony silence. Brian and I are more amused than concerned. At some point, they are certain to answer. As the traffic density in this region is very low, we are not duly concerned and are unlikely to be in anyone's way. We try 121.5 Mhz, the international frequency reserved for emergency calls, they must be monitoring this at least. Nothing. Then 123.45 Mhz, the international 'chat frequency', in case someone is nearby who could relay a message for us. Again, nothing. Now, with the field in sight, we decide to circle overhead to attract attention. We make a blind transmission on all frequencies alerting any aircraft in the vicinity of our intentions and our ETA overhead. After further repeated calls with no response, we decide to make a slow pass down the runway so we would be visible to anyone in the Tower and also to have a visual inspection of the runway. If it's unobstructed we decide we will go ahead and land anyway after the low pass. We make the pass flashing our landing lights and continuing to make repeated calls with no response and then land. As we taxi in, I can see a stream of five or six people walking out from the base of the Tower and walking purposely our way. Where did they come from? We shut down and open the door. It's blistering hot. One of the guys, clearly the boss, looks very angry.

"What do you think you are doing!" he shouts, glaring at me. "Whaa did you land without permission? What are you doing? This is not allowed!"

I explain that we tried every possible means to contact ATC for permission to land but were unable. So, we completed a standard ICAO Loss of Communications procedure and landed.

"Ah em going to report you! You will be arrested! I am the Chief of Facilities at the airport!"

Brian and I look around at the barren airport and then at each other and start laughing. Facilities? what facilities is he referring to exactly?

"Sure, go ahead," I say. "I completely agree, that is a very good idea."

I start to walk away and this enrages him even more and he moves across to stand in my way.

"Whaa do you abuse me in this fashion?" he shouts at me. "Ah am the boss here. You think I know fuck-nothing, but I tell you man I know fuck-all!"

That did it and Brian and I dissolved. As my parting shot, determined to have the last word, I say,

"How about next time you answer the radios, you goon. Try turning the bloody volume up so you can hear us!"

* * * *

Another medevac flight, this time to Aswan in southern Egypt. This is a huge stretch from Gatwick in the Learjet, a distance of approximately 2,400 nm, or around 200 nm - or 30 minutes flying - more than the book figures. This was going to take some planning. The winds were favourable on the day and using some clever fuel planning techniques and being savvy with the fuel flows we reckoned we could just make it – or at least give it a go. If it looked like we were running short of fuel, we could always divert on the way to either Cairo or Luxor. We had to be mindful that Aswan only has one runway so if it became blocked we would have a problem. So, before we got to abeam Luxor, we had to know it was safe to continue. As they are only 100 miles apart this would be no problem; a quick radio call ahead would do the trick.

Mike Wennink and I made the flight and landed safely at Aswan. Before landing, however, we decided to take a look at the enormous Aswan dam that bridges the river Nile by making an extended circuit. This turned out to be a big mistake. Although the tower did not comment on this, as we taxied in I could see a group of soldiers headed by an officer waiting to greet us.

"I don't like the look of this," I said to Mike. "What have we done wrong?"

We came to a halt, shut down and opened the door. The heat hit me. With an unmistakable air of authority, the officer came over and didn't look too pleased to see us. "Captain, come with me," he said. "You," he pointed at Mike, "stay here." As I followed the officer, I started to get concerned. Glancing back, I saw Mike and the medics waiting forlornly by the Learjet as half a dozen soldiers formed a cordon around it. The officer led me to a dusty concrete shed with a corrugated iron roof and motioned me inside. This was clearly his office, full of the usual military paraphernalia. A large fan was circulating the hot air and on the wall was a large-scale map of the airport and its surrounding area. A large area of the map to the east of the airport, over the dam, was shaded a dark pink and I developed a horrible feeling. He looked at me with a stony expression and jabbed a finger at the map. I noticed his clipped moustache and red beret, which made him look uncannily like Saddam Hussein.

"Captain, you have violated a Prohibited military area. Why is this? This is a military area and absolutely forbidden to overfly. This is a very serious offence. Explain to me."

Now I realised the problem and that we were in deep trouble. Violating prohibited areas is a serious issue everywhere in the world and especially in areas in the Middle East. They are published for good reasons, normally military, and here it was because of the strategic importance of the Aswan dam which we weren't aware of at the time. We were lucky not to have had warning shots fired at us. Or worse. In our excitement at having made this record-breaking flight, we had overlooked the prohibited area on our charts and blundered straight through it. The officer was clearly not amused and I had to think fast. I tried to look horrified which wasn't too hard to do as I had only to imagine the inside of an Egyptian jail or, worse, having to tell Masey that the Lear has been impounded.

"I am so sorry, Officer," I started. "We had no idea we were in a prohibited area. This was a genuine mistake. It will never happen again, I...."

The officer listened for a while then leant forward on his desk and looked at me coolly. He glanced down at my Rolex watch for a few seconds and for a while I thought he was going to ask me for it as a fine. His hand came up indicating that I should stop my waffling.

"Indeed. Come."

He gestured me to the door and we emerged into the blinding light of the day. As we approached the Lear, he barked an order and the soldiers jogged off into the distance. He looked into the cabin where Mike and the medics were sweating in the heat and then came outside again where only he and I were present.

"A payment is necessary. $500." I nodded and climbed quickly into the cockpit where we kept the aircraft dollar float. Peeling off five one-hundred dollar bills, I re-joined the officer outside and handed over the payment. He tucked it into his uniform top pocket with a practised air, turned and walked off.

"Thieving bastard," I muttered under my breath, but very relieved we has escaped more serious trouble. A few minutes later I climbed the crumbling concrete steps of the control tower to pay the landing fee and crossed paths with a rat the size of a small cat bolting down the steps. In the control tower, a man was curled up, sleeping on a pile of filthy old blankets. That was Aswan.

* * * *

Having a cast-iron stomach is a vital requirement when flying in remote areas as you never know the quality of the food you will be eating or even when you will get your next meal. In those days we survived on whatever we could get which was sometimes pretty dubious at times. But there were occasions when no matter how starving you were, discretion was the better part of valour when looking at local offerings. Martyn and I are in Port Harcourt about to set off northbound back to the UK with the usual fuel stop in Ghardaia, Algeria. We are both starving as the breakfast at the airport hotel was a while ago and had been awful and there was no prospect of any food for a long time. We grab a coffee at a cafe in the terminal building. The bar is dirty with a sticky old zinc counter to lean on and a few very old-looking rolls with God knows what fillings on a plate in the corner. Above the mirror at the back of the bar is a shelf with a plate of kebab meat skewers, attractively lit by an electric bulb. I can see Martyn eyeing these up hungrily.

"I'm going to have one," he says looking at me for confirmation.

"You must be totally, bloody mad," I respond, staring at him in disbelief. "They will be alive with germs, I mean look at them!"

We look at the offering and it looks like a textbook picture of exactly what not to eat when in a hot climate. Ever. Meat kebabs (pork even?), on a plate, in a hot environment gently warmed even more by an electric bulb. The whole thing screams "DON'T EAT ME!" Anyway, Martyn gets the girl, who is sitting on a stool sucking at the gap in her teeth, to pass over two of the kebabs and he starts to eat them guiltily.

"Don't blame me if you get the shits halfway home," I say.

The flight to Ghardaia is fine and Martyn clearly thinks he has got away with any adverse effects, but halfway through the final leg to Gatwick, things start to change.

"I feel bad," he says looking to me for sympathy.

"No shit?" I say looking across at him, relishing the irony of the comment. "I told you it was a bloody stupid idea to eat that minging kebab. God knows what it was or how long it had been there," I add showing the full extent of my sympathetic side. He is sweating a lot and holding his stomach, bent slightly forward.

"I'm going back," he says and that is the last I see of him for the flight. It's not the last I'm aware of him though, as the lav on the Lear is directly behind the cockpit and there is very little privacy indeed. He manages to crawl back into his seat for landing at Gatwick, looking awful. "Serves you right," I say gleefully.

* * * *

We are parked in Kano in Northern Nigeria. It's hot and hazy and Masey and I are waiting at the aircraft for the handling agent to collect us and take us to the hotel. There's a gusty wind blowing and the sand and grit start to stir and swirl around the apron and get into my eyes. The visibility has dropped even more and I look through squinted eyes into the wind. The haze has turned a funny brassy colour, curiously like before a snowstorm and then I notice in the distance a huge line of clouds. It's not like anything I have ever seen before and I watch for a while with an uneasy feeling; I can see that the clouds are billowing towards us.

Sandstorm!

"Simon, we need to get the covers on fast, it looks like a sandstorm is coming our way!"

He sticks his head out of the aircraft and looks in the direction of the wind. The clouds are on the ground and moving towards us fast lifting everything in their path, sand, dust, rubbish. I dive for the bag that contains our probe and engine covers and pull them out. Between us, Simon and I manage to get them on just as the storm hits us and we jump into the aircraft closing the clamshell doors behind us. We wait thirty minutes for the storm to pass and open the door. The air smells strange and there is a layer of sand an inch thick over everything including the aircraft. Luckily there has been no obvious damage to the aircraft that we can see, despite all the rubbish on the apron that had been blowing about as the storm passed. There's nothing more we could have done in the time available but I'm aware that what we have done may not be enough to fully protect the aircraft. The fine sand and dust have got everywhere and into places we didn't have time to protect; the static vents, the outflow valve, the underwing ducts, the engine vents, you name it. We are aware we may have some system abnormalities when we depart later but in the event we are lucky. Having carefully brushed off the sand from everywhere we could reach, the start-up, taxi and takeoff were normal.

* * * *

"Meet downstairs in 15?" Masey poses the usual rhetorical question. It is traditional to dump the bags and head out for a beer as soon as possible after checking into a hotel, especially after a long day's flying. We are in Nice and staying the night at the Beau Rivage hotel, a favourite crew hotel at the eastern end of the Promenade, near the old town.

An approaching desert sandstorm

"Sure, see you then," I respond as we head for the lifts.
Actually, tired as I was, I could kill a beer. In the 1890s, the hotel was the home of the playwright Anton Chekov, interestingly, but I doubt he ever felt as strange there as we did later that evening, unless he overdid the absinthe. I get to my room, throw my bag onto the bed, extract a pair of jeans and a shirt and head downstairs to meet Masey. We wander onto the promenade and find an open-air bar, full of people outside drinking at pavement tables, enjoying the warm evening. We order a couple of large Kronenbourg beers and chat about the day's flying and generally enjoy the view. Masey lights up a B&H.

"Fancy another?" he offers, gesturing to the empty glasses.

"Definitely, thanks," I respond, finally unwinding after the long day. He hobbles off to the bar in his characteristic pigeon-toed gait. He returns with the beers and we settle into the second drink. Halfway through I start to feel weary and struggling to concentrate. There's a slight buzzing in my ears. At the same time, Masey says,

"Do you feel OK?"

"I don't know," I reply, "I feel weird. You?" I am aware that my words are slurring and feel as though someone else is speaking, not me. I feel woozy and incredibly tired as though I have drunk eight pints. "There's something wrong with the beer don't touch it. Let's get back to the hotel," says Masey. We stand up unsteadily and start walking slowly back to the hotel. Every step is an effort but we make it and stagger across the lobby into the lifts. The front desk staff look at us strangely probably wondering how we had got into such a state only an hour after leaving the hotel.

"The bloody drinksh were shpiked, I'm schertain," Masey slurs as he staggers down the corridor to his room, bouncing off the walls. "Shee you in the morning."

I find my room and crash inside flopping face down onto the bed where I stayed, unmoving and fully dressed, for twelve hours, out for the count. The next morning we meet up for coffee. We have no obvious side effects, apart from a nagging headache, so we decide it's OK to fly back to Gatwick as planned although we should probably have been checked by a doctor. What had happened? Definitely, the drinks were spiked, there was no question of that, but why? Had Masey picked up the wrong drinks? Or were we the intended targets after all, to be mugged in some back street? Who knows, but we agreed it was a lucky escape as our wallets and watches and, most importantly, ourselves were still intact.

A few years later, a couple of TAG pilots had a similar experience in Hamburg but it didn't end so well. The guys were in the bar in the hotel, a decent hotel on the outskirts of the city when a young and attractive girl stopped at their table and started chatting. Things were going well, the girl was flirting and more drinks were ordered. The evening progressed well, and another girl joined them at their table. The next thing they remember was waking up in a hospital, bruised, befuddled and minus their wallets and watches. When they were released from the hospital a few days later and flown home by airline, as they were in no state to fly an aircraft, the DFO asked them into the office for their version of events. After hearing their story, he leant back, appraised them both for a few seconds and said,

"Come on guys, do you honestly think she would have been chatting you up? I mean, look at you."

* * * *

In November 1990 Brian and I were coming back empty to Gatwick after a medevac drop-off in Freetown, Sierra Leone. We were right on the limits of duty but as we were no longer a hospital flight, with the extra duty that permits, Brian and I could see that our planned refuelling stop in Tenerife was probably not going to happen. Due to earlier delays, we wouldn't make it without busting our duty time limits. So, with the lights of Tenerife out of sight but, metaphorically, twinkling and beckoning us on from 400 miles and an hour away, we decided to play safe and land somewhere on the way.

"What about here?" Brian asked, pointing on the chart to a place called Nouadhibou in Mauretania about a hundred miles ahead of us.

"Good as anywhere," I offered.

This turned out to be an interesting decision. On the approach to the northerly runway, we flew over the Bay of Nouadhibou which is home to one of the biggest ship cemeteries in the world which gave it a strange, out-of-world appearance. Hundreds of rusting hulks litter the bay, left there by shipowners who didn't want the expense of disposing of their ships legally. In exchange for some cash to the corrupt harbour officials, they have been allowed to abandon the hulks in the bay and on surrounding beaches where, eventually, they are broken up by the local ship scrappers or by natural forces. It's an extraordinary, ghostly sight.

The town is one of the poorest in Africa and the airport reflected this. Blowing sand covered most of the taxiways and part of the runway. In the blistering heat, a camel and its keeper were watching us from a distance; no one else was to be seen anywhere, no airport or Immigration officials, no one. Nothing marked the airport perimeter either, no fence or markings of any kind. Having cleared us to land, ATC seems to have gone home. We were on our own. After making the Learjet as secure and protected from the sand as possible and praying the aircraft would be safe overnight and we started to wonder if this plan was such a good idea after all. Satisfied we had done all we could, we wandered over to the airport hotel just across the road. As there was no fence of any sort this was an easy task. From a distance, the hotel looked promising, colonial style with a white castellated wall and what looked like a swimming pool in front of the building. However, as we got closer, we realised that our first impressions might have been a little skewed.

The 'swimming pool' was not filled with inviting, blue water but black rubbish bags which was clearly a playground for some large and evil-looking rats. Nice. The hotel looked as though it might have been comfortable in the French colonial era but was now derelict. We entered the slatted wooden door that we guessed led to the bare reception and banged the bell on the wooden counter. Eventually, an old man in a hooded blanket shuffled out and by conversing in pidgin French we managed to get two rooms for $20 each, which was daylight robbery under the circumstances. As this was obviously going to be a long night, we added a crate of Heineken and some bottles of Evian to the bill. Grabbing our keys, we wandered off and found our rooms. As I entered my room something struck me as odd. There was no air conditioning, no surprise there of course, but the window at least looked very clean from a distance. The desert night was as clear as if I was outside and as I threw my bag down and wandered over to look out, I could see why – there was no glass in the frame. I was looking directly across the black desert. I glanced into the shower room and saw what I thought from a distance was a rust mark in the sink; fair enough I didn't expect Western standards from this hotel. Except it wasn't rust; what greeted me there was an old turd. I shut the flimsy door and never ventured into the shower room again. That evening was spent in my room so I could keep an eye on my things, given the open window. The bed was an old horse-hair mattress with a rough blanket that reeked. Brian kept me company for a while and we drank enough of the Heineken to ensure we slept well. The next morning, we brushed our teeth in Heineken, tossed the keys onto the counter at reception and walked out of the hotel, past the swimming pool refuse, across the road and directly to the Learjet. To our relief, it looked exactly as we had left it. We breakfasted on some old bread rolls left from the day before, now stale and hard, and brewed up some tea before setting off for Tenerife only one hour away with just enough legal fuel reserves for the flight. One hour, two worlds.

Rusting hulks in the Bay of Nouadhibou

* * * *

The Greek islands in the late 80s and early 90s had no radar coverage and all the flights into the islands and overflying the airspace were under procedural control with pilots reporting their altitudes together with positions by range and distance from a beacon. This means that clearances and en route spacings were based on pilot position reports only, fine in remote areas like Africa but pretty scary around Greece in the summer months when the sky was full of aircraft loaded with holidaymakers coming and going to all the islands like so many bees around honey pots. I once heard an anonymous pilot on the radio call out in frustration as he was trying to get his descent clearance, "Can someone pleeeaase buy them a radar set for Christmas!" TCAS was only just being introduced but in those pre-TCAS days you just got used to building a 3D picture in your head of which aircraft were around you and building your own mental 'bubble'. TCAS is a fantastic tool and no one is nostalgic for the extra workload the mental gymnastics required, not me anyway.

With this background in mind, picture this. I landed in Kos on an air ambulance flight to collect a holidaymaker who likely has done something daft that probably involved alcohol somewhere in the story (diving into too-shallow water was a favourite). Kos is a quiet, pretty island in the Dodecanese but the airport is very busy during the peak holiday season, especially at certain times of the day. I needed to pay the landing fee which we often did in person as Masey seldom used a handling agent in order to keep the costs down. So, carrying my dollars and some drachmas for good measure, I walked across the apron to the little control tower, opened the door at the base of the tower and climbed the thirty or so steps to the top. As I got there, I saw the single controller talking fast, his hands clasped around his head and looking down at his desk. This was obviously one of the peak periods and he was concentrating hard with a mental picture in his head of all the aircraft under his responsibility that are either arriving or departing Kos or transiting his airspace overhead. The thought occurred to me – if I interrupt him he will lose the picture that it has probably taken him twenty minutes to build in his head and there could be carnage. He threw me a glance and put his hand up to request I keep quiet which I was going to do anyway. I was in awe of his ability to manage this workload single-handedly. Luckily, I wasn't in any particular hurry, we had got to Kos in good time and the medics had gone off to the hospital in the ambulance to retrieve the patient, so I kicked back and watched the goings on around the airport from the vantage point that all control towers provide. After thirty minutes the controller threw himself back in the chair, rubbed his temples, stretched and calmly said,

"Good afternoon, captain. How can I help you?" and we completed the transaction.

If the travelling public realised some of the things that go on in aviation, they would have every reason to be scared. It's a high-tech industry in so many areas but some aspects are not always as modern as is widely believed. In the North Atlantic and Pacific regions, for example, although aircraft and ATC now have sophisticated data-link systems for control, they still make use of HF radio as a backup and in other parts of the world HF is still the only reliable means of communication. Marconi himself would feel completely at home. As would Samuel Morse; radio beacons still identify themselves using the 'dits' and 'dahs' of Morse code.

* * * *

Although a lot of ambulance flights were planned a few days ahead - not being urgent, just requiring the planned repatriation of a patient who was stable in a local hospital - by their very nature, some of these flights were 'go nows'. This necessitated dropping everything and driving flat-out to Gatwick, generally getting to the airport at the same time as the paramedics. 'Go nows' could happen when the patient was in a hospital in a country where, after the attention of local doctors, their serious condition had become critical overnight. All the jet captains at Interflight had new company cars as a perk, decent ones too; a BMW 325i in my case. Hammering down the A217 from South London to Gatwick on a call-out was commonplace for me, so when I got pulled over by a motorcycle cop near Reigate one time, I wasn't surprised; it was only a matter of time before this happened. I always wore my uniform when I was in a hurry as I guessed it would level the gradient a bit when the policeman comes for his little chat at the window – all police tend to respond well to uniforms and on this occasion, I think it helped, as planned.

"Evening Sir. In a bit of a hurry are we?" he said with the usual sarcasm, eying me up cooly.

"Yes, officer. It's an emergency so I am in a bit of a hurry. Sorry." I emphasised the point by glancing at my watch.

"And what kind of emergency would that be then, Sir?" he said giving me a level stare.

"Well, I am the captain of an air ambulance flight which is due to takeoff for Athens in (I glance at my watch again for effect) one hour from now. It is urgent." The policeman stared at me for a few more seconds.

"I see, Sir. Just a minute." He walked off out of earshot and I saw him talking into his collar. "Right Sir, give me the address and follow me."

I told him I was going to the GAT at Gatwick and he nodded – to my surprise he knew where it is. He mounted his bike and on went 'the blues' and he shot off down the road with me in pursuit, with that comfortable feeling of, for once, being able to speed legally. And we did, believe me. When I arrived at the GAT, Masey was there waiting for me as I arrived with the motorcycle police escort, lights flashing.

"Bloody hell, that's one way to do it!" he grinned.

****

"Cleared direct TIGRA point, climb FL280 and contact Brindisi on 127.35." These were the last instructions from Athens Control as we approached the TIGRA reporting point on the Athens / Brindisi FIR boundary. It was August 1990 and Brian and I were on a daytime medevac flight from Corfu back to Manchester. We both agreed on the clearance and Brian repeated it back to Athens and wrote it down on the plog. We were in the Lear, in the climb and this was our usual hand-off between ATCCs - from Athens to Brindisi. We were expecting FL430 as our final cruising level, but for now we were cleared only to FL280 expecting Brindisi will clear us higher when we are radar identified by them. I was flying and Brian was the Pilot Monitoring. Brian was famous for being meticulous with his plog, every clearance and radio frequency change written down neatly in exact chronological order using, of all things, an ink fountain pen. As it should be with any plog, you could pick up one of Brian's and recreate the exact sequence of events for any entire flight years later if need be. As it turned out, this was a Godsend on this occasion. We were in cloud as we passed FL200 and then the clouds started to thin a little. As we were relatively light, our rate of climb was around 3000 feet/minute, pretty standard for the Lear. Passing FL240 the cloud cover thinned and I was astonished to see an aircraft very slightly ahead of us and to our left. It was an Iberia Boeing 727, no more than a hundred metres off to our left side and going the same direction.

"Christ!" I exclaimed, involuntarily as I see the 727. "What the fuck is he doing there!"

It was an impressive sight but not one that I wanted to indulge in too closely, particularly at 24,000ft and 300 kts. As I have mentioned before, strange thoughts go through your mind on these occasions before your reflex actions kick in. From my side, having a better view than Brian, I was curious to see that there was some oil streaking back on the number three engine cowling.

"We were definitely cleared to 280, weren't we?" I asked Brian tersely.

"Absolutely. We both heard it, I read it back and wrote it down," he replied. Then I instinctively turned to the right at the same time that the 727, the F/O obviously seeing us too as we close on him, turned left. We peeled a couple of miles apart and both started questioning ATC as to why we were within almost touching distance of each other. We spoke to Brindisi ATC as we crossed the FIR and they immediately gave standard separation between us and the 727. We guessed that they could see the lack of separation on their radar screens while we were under Athens ATC but were powerless to intervene until we were on their frequency. The next day we made the mandatory report to the CAA and we were assured that they would request the ATC tapes from both ATCCs but we learned months later that, guess what, these tapes had been 'lost' by Athens ATCC and were therefore unavailable. Proof enough for us of their mistake. As evidence of the clearance we had received, we were able to show the CAA a copy of Brian's meticulous plog. It's hard to believe this in these days of TCAS, the collision avoidance system, when you can see traffic that's close to you on an electronic display and receive aural advisory warnings. If we had not broken out of cloud when we did, we would never have even seen the 727, or he us. Worse still we could have collided. At times ignorance certainly is bliss.

* * * *

In 1988 Masey and I flew a charter for Mitsubishi around the Middle East in the Learjet. It was complicated for two main reasons; the first was that only one of the six Japanese passengers spoke any English and we were under strict instructions that all information for the party had to pass through him and him only. Talking to, or even making eye contact with, the main passenger, a senior Mitsubishi executive, was absolutely forbidden we were told. And the second reason was the itinerary. This had us visiting Egypt, Lebanon, Syria and Israel in six days. It would be hard to construct a more challenging group of countries than those from a diplomatic point of view but in the event, it all worked out OK with only a few minor hiccups. We were the first British aircraft cleared to land in Damascus for years following a break in diplomatic relations and, as far as we could tell, bearing in mind their Japanese inscrutability, the passengers were happy. The last stop was Athens and then home to Gatwick via Le Bourget in Paris.

On disembarkation at Gatwick, there was a great deal of Japanese protocol to endure, handshakes and bows (but not from the lead passenger, of course, who stared straight ahead, impassively) and then Masey and I were each handed a small, beautifully wrapped gift. By the size and heft I was, naturally, thinking along the lines of a Patek Philippe or Rolex as a corporate 'thank you' and as soon as the pax were out of sight I was tearing the paper off, eager to get at it. Imagine my astonishment and disappointment when I found out that the beautiful watch has somehow turned into something else – a plastic disposable camera, net worth around £5 at Boots. To this day I can't work out the message behind this. In my experience, all gifts from wealthy people convey a message of some sort, but what was the message behind these disposable cameras? On the face of it such a cheap gift was an insult and why they were presented to us so solemnly remains a mystery to me. Did we mess up somehow? Wouldn't it have been better to give nothing? Why all the ceremony? Baffling.

* * * *

May 1994 and the Cannes Film Festival is coming to an end. Martyn and I are at Nice Airport awaiting the arrival of Robert Redford to fly him back in the Lear to Gatwick. It's getting late and our 2230 departure time has slipped by an hour or so. Martyn and I have had a long day and are starting to get tired. We are crashed out in the cabin on the leather seats, not talking much. We have arranged for some ground power and the cabin lights are on to make the aircraft as welcoming as possible for the great actor's arrival.

Suddenly, we are aware of a fleet of cars approaching in the distance. This must be him at last. We stir ourselves, straighten our hair and ties, tuck our shirts in and stumble out into the night. The lead limo glides to a halt by the aircraft and two security guards step out to open the polished black doors while the accompanying paparazzi in the other cars jostle for position for the best shot. Out steps Mr Redford accompanied on either side by two beautiful models, covered in jewellery and projecting megawatt smiles all around. He effortlessly holds each girl around the waist and steers them to face the photographers for the obligatory photo shots, a scene I'm sure he has acted out a thousand times before. Flash guns pop (never mind our night vision) and the photos are completed – they would be great pictures, after all who doesn't like a movie star with beautiful girls next to a Learjet? He finally hugs the girls, kisses them each on the cheek in farewell and lets them sashay back to the limo as he steps into the Lear. The cars purr off across the apron as he slouches into the rear couch and closes his eyes.

"Jesus, I'm tired," he says, loosening his tie. I glance at him and can see that he suddenly appears years older than his 58 years now he's out of the glare of publicity. It's clearly been a long week and his age is catching up with him. But as long as it's required to play the part, he can still cut it. I'm impressed - that's star quality.

* * * *

The Learjet 35 was a wonderful aircraft. Born out of a Swiss-designed fighter aircraft it had legendary performance and showed its fighter heritage with crisp handling and even a drag chute for landing if the need ever arose. It was exhilarating to fly although something of a pain to operate. Small, with no APU or proper air conditioning and overwing refuelling it was a product of the 1960s. In hot climates on the ground you baked in the cockpit beneath the inch-thick windscreen as it wasn't until the engines were running that there was any air conditioning; the electric Freon A/C machine in the rear baggage bay was absolutely useless. The Lear is unquestionably a demanding jet. The high-speed end of the speed range was never a concern but the aircraft would bite if flown sloppily at the low-speed end of the speed envelope even with the modified 'Soft Flight' wing. The wing is thin and critical and the smallest blemish or collection of splatted bugs on the leading edge would cause the wing to stall aggressively and unpredictably.

Interflight contracted Northern Executive Aviation in Manchester for the Learjet maintenance. Even though NEA were direct competitors on the charter market (they also operated Learjets) they looked after us very well in spite of the endless but friendly abuse dished out from the guys in their Ops. We often flew the Lear from Manchester back to Gatwick in the late evenings following maintenance and it became customary to try and set a new record for the flight if the weather was good and ATC was quiet. Manchester airport to Gatwick with all the airways routeings is around 200 nm. To achieve the speed record, it was necessary to ask ATC at Manchester for an early left turn direct to the first waypoint on the way to Gatwick and a continuous high-speed climb to a lowish cruising level. On descent into Gatwick, we would ask for a visual onto a base leg to the runway. We routinely ignored speed controls and went flat out the whole way sometimes holding 300 kts to finals at Gatwick which required some frantic application of airbrake, gear and flaps to reduce speed for landing. For a while, I had the speed record from takeoff to touchdown of 34 minutes which meant an average speed of 353 kts – not bad.

For the Certificate of Airworthiness (C of A) renewal for the Learjet, it used to be necessary to complete an annual air test. This involved checking all the systems on the aircraft, hydraulics, bleed air, pressurisation, engine parameters, etc. As a TRE, I had CAA approval to do these flights. They were done to a set CAA schedule and normally took a couple of hours to complete as there was a lot to go through. You have to be careful during these test flights as you are looking at the normal and abnormal operation of all the systems and so good system knowledge and sound contingencies, in case it all goes wrong, are important.

One of the least favourite items on the test schedule was the stall test. The Lear, in common with most T-tail jet aircraft, has systems designed to warn the pilots of an impending stall (the stick shaker) and, in the event of such a stall, get them safely out of it (the stick pusher). The stick shaker would vibrate the control column strongly around 7-10 kts before the stall as a warning to increase speed. If nothing was done to prevent the stall at that point, then just before it occurred, the stick pusher would activate to throw the control column forwards violently. This happened with a force of about 60 lbs and the result was to push the nose of the aircraft downwards, immediately reducing the angle of attack and so un-stall the wing. The stick pusher is strong enough to snatch the control column out of your hands. Good systems designed to keep everyone safe. So why mess around with them you might ask? Well, the CAA in their infinite wisdom needed to know, on an annual basis, that the aircraft stick shaker and pusher still activated on schedule.

So, come the day, I am doing one of these C of A tests in the Lear. All the pressurisation, electrical, bleed system and gear tests have gone well with only a few write-ups to report after landing. I am with Martyn and we are at FL150 ready to perform the stall test. The first one on the schedule is to check the speed when the stick shaker activates. The first stall is in the 'clean' configuration, i.e. with no flaps extended and the gear retracted. I select the engine ignitions ON as added protection during the slow, nose-high flight, gently close the thrust levers and the aircraft slows as I hold the altitude. The stick shaker comes in at the correct speed and I lower the nose and add full thrust to recover to a safe speed. We configure for the tests with the gear extended and various degrees of flap extended and repeat the exercises. These work out fine too, right on schedule and so now for the full stall to the stick pusher. This one is crucial, so with the autopilot engaged and at a safe speed Martyn and I get our heads together and take our time to very carefully check the actual aircraft weight and C of G and come up with a figure from the AFM at which we can expect both the shaker and the pusher to activate. The speeds, in the clean configuration, are 106 kts for the shaker and 97 kts for the pusher. With these speeds in our heads, I set up for the stall. Engine ignitions ON, thrust levers idle, level flight, speed reducing at the recommended maximum of two knots/second, aircraft perfectly in balance etc, etc. At 106 kts the stick shaker starts rattling. That's good as it looks like our computations are correct. 105, 104, 103…the speed reduces, the shaker rattling all the time. 100..99..98..97… Nothing, no pusher. Then, as I am about to recover, at 95 kts all hell breaks loose.

The aircraft flicks violently to the left as the left wing stalls and the right wing rises and just at this point, the stick pusher kicks in slamming the control column forwards. Simultaneously, I apply full power and level the wings, watching as the rate of descent goes off the clock. The stick pusher and then the stick shaker stop and I regain control of the elevator but the speed is increasing rapidly in the descent with full power applied. I quickly close the thrust levers, extend the speed brakes and ease the aircraft out of the dive, very gently to avoid a secondary stall. We lost 5,000 feet in that manoeuvre. Martyn and I look at each other.

"I don't ever want to do that again," he says. "I think I need a change of underpants. Shall we say that everything works as it should?"

I agree and we have a nervous laugh. This stuff is for test pilots who are well-practised in the art not ordinary pilots. Curiously, the autopilot, which had been problematic for a while, not holding a heading or altitude very well, worked a lot better after that flick at the stall – maybe it jiggled a gyro or something, who knows.

* * * *

During the first Gulf War in 1990, we were busy shuttling ITN crews to and from Dhahran in Saudi Arabia. The military build-up at the airport ahead of the invasion of Iraq was staggering; it seemed that the entire US Military Air Command and National Guard transport fleets were there. However, we limited our time in Dhahran for obvious reasons as there was always the chance of a Scud attack from Iraq. The Scud was a 1950s Soviet-era missile in Saddam Hussein's arsenal that he launched into Israel from time to time to stir things up and threatened to launch into Saudi Arabia. Most broke up during descent being old and of poor build quality or were intercepted by missile defences so, although scaring the Israeli population, the Scuds were more of a nuisance than a proper threat. Fortunately, Saddam never equipped the Scuds with a gas or biological agent as he had threatened. Had that happened, things would have escalated badly.

Flights to Dhahran involved staying overnight however when you have been presented with a 'wine list' featuring fifteen different varieties of fruit juice at dinner when you are craving a beer, the attraction soon palls. We also had a few flights into Tel Aviv to extract very wealthy Israelis who, not unreasonably, wanted to get out of the country quickly. Tel Aviv airport was eerie with no aircraft to be seen apart from IAF electronic surveillance Boeing 707s parked on a distant ramp. All the El AL airline fleet had been dispersed to other airports around Europe and of course, there were no foreign airlines transiting through the airport, so it was like a ghost town. Interflight's insurance company loaded the hull premiums hugely for these flights - £20,000 per day excess was the going rate - although the risk of loss from an attack was slim. This excess was passed on directly to the passengers, of course, who didn't quibble the cost. It was a bit like the last plane out of Saigon – with no airline flights, we and a few other non-risk-averse operators were their only chance of escape. We took the gamble taking the view that Saddam wouldn't dare launch a serious missile attack on Tel Aviv and there was more chance of being struck by lightning than ending up under the sharp end of a Scud at the airport. Robert Moore, the well-known ITN correspondent, told us that he had it on good authority from his sources - and he had access to reliable sources - that the IAF had F-16s armed with nuclear weapons airborne 24 hours a day just in case. Had Saddam tried anything silly, parts of Iraq would have been vaporised within fifteen minutes. Thank God, it never escalated seriously and although the risks were small it was always good to collect the passengers and 'get out of Dodge'.

* * * *

Around the same time, we did a little bit of sub-hunting. It was reported that a Russian submarine was on the surface off Norway and on fire. The news channel ITN chartered the Lear to take a film crew to locate the sub and film it. Although we were told the sub's approximate position, it took a bit of finding but eventually we spotted it around a hundred miles off the west coast of Norway, stationary and wallowing in the swell. We started circling the smoking hulk so the film crew could get their shots through the window. As we rolled out of the turn at the end of the filming, we were bounced by a Royal Norwegian Air Force P-3 'Orion'. The Lockheed Orion is the military version of the Electra that Hunting Cargo operated and that I was to get to know quite well a few years later. The P-3 Orion is still used for maritime surveillance by several nations to this day. They were known to be fast and powerful aircraft and this was the first time that I witnessed it first-hand.

We were loitering at around 300 kts when the Orion bounced us, coming out of nowhere and storming past us in level flight as though we were standing still. And close – close enough that we could hear the heavy, throbbing beat of the four massive 4,300 shp Allison turboprops as it passed us. It pulled up and turned away, leaving four smokey trails behind.

* * * *

When Masey took the gamble to buy the Learjet he put everything he had into the purchase, including his house. It was a big step up from the King Airs and piston twins that he had been operating but with his usual canniness, he timed the purchase just right. It was the late 1980s and cash was king, flooding the economy after the City's 'Big Bang'. Demand for the Learjet was high from the start and we would often back-to-back trips. One crew would land and the

A Hunting Cargo Lockheed 'Electra', similar to a P-3 'Orion'

aircraft would be refuelled, turned around and depart again with another crew. It worked hard and made lots of money. However, to help fund the purchase Masey came up with an innovative scheme whereby private stakeholders were invited to invest money into the aircraft. The minimum stake was £5,000 with no upper limit. There would be no financial return but instead twice a year Masey would offer the investors the Lear free for a weekend to go wherever they wanted, depending on how much they had invested. In those days fuel was cheap so that cost was not much of a concern; all Masey had to allow for was the cost of the engine time and en route charges.

The first such jolly was to Marrakech in October 1988 and Martyn and I were the chosen crew to fly there for the night. It was a black-tie event for the passengers, so we thought why don't we fly in black tie too? Why the hell not - how often would we get this opportunity? So, eight of us, six passengers and two pilots all in evening dress, assembled on the chosen evening at the GAT at Gatwick for drinks and canapes. For Martyn and me sitting at 43,000 ft in black tie, bow ties and white scarfs on the way to Marrakech, it was a James Bond moment unlikely to ever be repeated. In the cabin, champagne was flowing and the party was already in full swing. On arrival at Marrakech, it took a while to convince the Immigration officials what was going on and that two of the assembled party were actually pilots. They looked at us suspiciously and carefully studied the General Declaration and then looked at us again. Martyn and I were listed on the Gen Dec as the crew, but clearly two pilots in evening dress were something outside their experience. Eventually, they must have realised that as the only two sober people in the party, we were just possibly the pilots. Satisfied, they handed our passports back and we left the terminal building and headed for the cars; I don't think they had ever encountered this kind of arrival before! Outside into the warm, scented evening air and two limos take us directly to the famous La Mamounia hotel for dinner. Magical.

* * * *

"What are you doing tomorrow?" Masey asks me rhetorically over a pint in the Six Bells. "Three guys to Malaga, wait a few hours then back." Sensing there was more to it than that I said, "OK. Is that it?"

"Well... no. They work for a debt collection agency and are going there to recover some assets." He watched me for my reaction and grinned. "If you get what I mean."

The next morning Brian and I are prepping the aircraft for the trip. BC2 comes over. "Have you seen these guys yet?" he asks. I tell him no. "Central casting for a hit squad," he laughs, "Wait and see." Sure enough, they are soon driven out to the aircraft in the van. There are three of them as we expected; a huge gorilla of a man with a face like a punchbag, six foot three and almost as wide; a hatchet-faced, alert little weasel and a Mr Nice. No baggage as such but the big guy is carrying a small grip. Pleasantries exchanged and safety briefing completed, we settle them on board and set off on the two-and-a-half-hour flight to Malaga. During the flight, I go back for a chat with Mr Nice who seems to be the lead passenger and the most approachable and I take all three of them in. Gorilla says nothing but studies the view from 41,000ft with a thousand-yard stare. The Weasel has cold eyes, is full of nervous energy, quick of movement and speaks in short bursts of conversation. And Mr Nice is charming, friendly

Interflight's Learjet 35A, G-CJET

and smiling and making all the right noises. We land at Malaga and taxi onto a stand. They disembark.

"We should be two to three hours, no more and then straight back to Gatwick as planned," beams Mr Nice and off they go. Sure enough, three hours later they return to the aircraft in the handling agent's car looking very different to when they left. All three are dishevelled with ties loose, shirts open wide and sleeves rolled up. It appears that something physical has definitely been going on. Mr Nice hefts the bag into the cabin and climbs in. "Right-o," he says, now a little less affable than on the way down as though he doesn't have to make an effort now, "Home, James and don't spare the horses," and he flops onto the rear bench seat with his feet on the soft leather of the seat opposite and closes his eyes. Normally I'd ask a passenger to take his feet off the seat but not on this occasion. Northbound, we call Masey on the HF. "How did it go?" he asks through the static.

"Fine," I respond, not going into details as HF is short-wave radio and open for the world to listen to. "Airborne at 1612, ETA Gatwick 1840."

"OK," says Masey not deterred in the least by the open frequency, "Can you get a cheque off them before you land? They haven't paid yet!"

"Roger," I reply, privately thinking I'll let him negotiate that one, there's no way I'm asking these guys for money. Obviously, this had been a private Masey deal and we didn't have the protection of going through a broker. In fact, I don't believe they ever paid but, probably in the interest of keeping his legs intact, Masey put that one down as a bad debt which I think was a good decision. I believe it was the only bad debt Interflight ever had.

* * * *

Martyn and I are on a night stop in Sofia, Bulgaria. It's wintertime and freezing cold with snow flurries and sleet and by 4.30 it's pitch dark. We check into the hotel and meet in the bar for a beer. "It's freezing outside but I spotted a nightclub-type restaurant just around the corner. Fancy trying it?" I ask Martyn. "Sure, why not,' he agreed, looking around, "better than staying in this dump." So, we head out, braving the foul weather. The club is standard Eastern European, dingy, over-furnished and thick with smoke. We find a table near the stage where some dancers are chatting among themselves, smoking, and waiting to start work. We order steak and fries and a bottle of red. The wine arrives and looks strangely familiar. I pick up the bottle, look at the label closely in the gloomy light and roar with laughter.

"Look at this!" I pass the bottle to Martyn.

"I don't believe it," he laughs. The bottle's label says, *'Specially Selected for Sainsbury's'*. Clearly a truck load of Bulgarian wine destined for Sainsbury's has been rerouted somewhat before crossing the border and somewhere in England a warehouse is expecting a consignment of wine that will never arrive. We raise a glass to the enterprising Bulgarian criminals.

* * * *

"Got a good one for you," Masey glances up from his desk through a curl of B&H smoke. It's April 1994.

"There's a rich New York stockbroker and his girlfriend coming to tour Europe. A guy called James Bullard. First stop Le Bourget, then Bologna and Venice. Pack for a few days. Looks like you and Johnboy for the trip, that OK?"

"Sure, I'm up for that," I tell him. John 'Johnboy' Eismark and I have shared many adventures together, so this sounds like it has the making of a great few days.

Over to Le Bourget in the Learjet two days later and, as I walk through the Transair terminal there, I spot Mr Bullard straightaway; 30-ish, trainers, slicked back hair, shades, a pasty complexion that tells of little fresh air and a long drape raincoat with a bottle of Jack Daniels in the inside pocket. It can only be him, a real Wall Street wolf.

"Jimmy Bullard", he offers his hand as I approach him, "Bologna right? Ya ready to go? We're picking up my girlfriend there."

"That's what I have, sir" I assure him.

"Call me Jimmy," he replies and I can tell that there won't be too many formalities on this trip.

We walk out to the Lear, I introduce Johnboy and we're away. In Bologna, I escort Bullard into the terminal building and we collect the girlfriend who's waiting by the information desk. Bullard's in an expansive mood, showing off.

"Where are you guys staying at in Venice?" I tell him we haven't got around to booking anywhere yet.

"OK, cool you're staying with us, we are staying at the goddam Gritti." Things are looking up. The next morning, I have breakfast on my balcony at the Gritti Palace, overlooking the Grand Canal, in the lovely spring sunshine. Johnboy and I meet up with Bullard mid-morning and I sense that all is not well. He looks terrible and keeps clutching his stomach with both hands, wincing.

"Goddam ulcer's killing me," he groans. Then he gives it to us straight. "You guys oughta know, me and the bitch split last night, she's going back home. So it's party time boys – where we gonna go, got any suggestions?"

That's a turn-up for the books. Johnboy and I exchange glances. A rich banker who wants to party and a blank itinerary – this won't happen again. Leaving Johnboy to offer some suggestions of where to go, I call Masey for advice.

"You can take him wherever he bloody well desires, Seychelles if he wants, just make sure there's a $50k deposit in the bank before every flight though!" Down to me, then. Thanks.

The next few days are crazy. Bullard parties in Amsterdam, Milan, back to Amsterdam, then Geneva. All the time I am chasing him for money and all the time his stock reply is, "Hey, it's coming, don't worry!" I want the money to arrive as this is turning out to be a fun week, so I'm happy to spend each day on the phone with Western Union on his behalf. In Milan, I explain that Johnboy and I are running out of clothes as we didn't expect to be away for so long and he peels off a wad of dollars,

"No problem, go get what you need".

In Amsterdam, we swap aircraft to the Hawker but even though Johnboy isn't rated on that aircraft and can't pilot it with me, Bullard insists he comes along as his guest for company. Masey eventually grounds the aircraft until more money is received and then at the very last-minute money is wired into the Interflight account and the next flight, to Geneva, is confirmed.

Meanwhile, Bullard is deteriorating every day. Without his girlfriend, he's in freefall. Every day he is on the phone shouting to his New York office,

"Tell my Dad to send more money NOW, goddammit!"

After each rant, he throws the receiver down onto the bed and clutches his stomach white-faced until the pain of the ulcer has receded, then he picks up the receiver and continues the call. With hours each day on the phone to New York, his hotel phone bills are astronomical and the hotel management wants to know how he'll be settling the bill. In between the calls he is swigging his bottle of Jack followed by pints of milk to keep his ulcer under control while he has one TV streaming New York stock prices and another running adult movies, both at full volume. It's an insane situation.

We finally say goodbye to Jimmy Bullard in Geneva but not before he has offered me and Johnboy a job flying for him in New York. That's another story.

* * * *

It's 4 am and Masey and I have landed in Cairo for our scheduled day stop. Nile Valley Aviation have met us on arrival and in their normal efficient way have catered to all the needs of the aircraft and dropped us off at the main terminal for us to pass through Immigration. We have arranged to meet them again on the land side of the terminal, once we have passed through Immigration and then they will drop us off at the airport Sheraton. Masey and I are dog-tired and just want to crash out in the hotel, it's been a long day. The concourse is quiet but, as ever at Cairo airport, is far from deserted; as usual assorted undesirables are sleeping on the floor and on benches. We make our way to the Immigration counter. There is only one officer on duty because of the time of day and after a while he stands up, yawning. He wanders over scratching his crotch and rubbing his stubble.

"Passports," he mumbles and we pass over our passports under the glass screen.

Masey is travelling on a temporary passport that he got at the local post office before we left having lost his proper passport somewhere. This was normal, he was forever losing passports, wallets, car keys etc. The officer looks at my passport and puts it to one side and then picks up Masey's thin, beige temporary passport. He obviously hasn't seen one of these before so after another glance at Masey he takes it back to his desk to examine it more closely. This takes a while and I'm starting to get a bad feeling.

"I hope this is going to work," I say to Masey.

"Of course it will, it's never a problem. I've done it loads of times before," he replies.

Another five minutes elapse before the officer comes back. Naturally, he is very busy at 4 am with just the two of us at his counter.

"This is not valid," he says. "Why not?" counters Masey, always the diplomat.

"Where is Egypt?" he says pointing to the list of countries that are listed in the passport as those that accept a temporary UK passport.

"Let me see?" says Masey. The officer slides the passport back under the glass and we take a look ourselves. Sure enough, Egypt isn't listed. I'm sure it was an oversight as practically every other country you could think of was listed – but not Egypt.

"Shit," says Masey, flatly. The officer gives a happy smile sensing that he has ruined our day.

"You must depart immediately." We explain that we can't as we are out of duty. "In this case, you must remain in the airport until you have rested," he grins evilly.

Happy now, he makes a phone call and five minutes later two armed guards arrive. Masey, all heart, turns to me,

"Look, you can go to the Sheraton and we'll meet up later tomorrow." But I decide to stay with him obeying the golden rule of never splitting a crew.

"You bloody owe me," I grumble.

So off we go with the guards to the Immigration detention centre, to all intents and purposes an airport prison. We get a cell each and an armed guard is posted outside the door to ensure we don't run off. Not only that, but to make sure we stay fully awake all night and fully enjoy all the facilities of the room, they bang on the door every thirty minutes. I look at the bed and wish that I had mastered the skill of levitation – the brown blanket is stained and stiff with dirt and I wouldn't have touched it with a barge pole. We spend a sleepless night looking at the welcoming lights of the nearby airport Sheraton through the bars of the windows. The next morning our attentive guards release us, tired and blearing and we head off in search of coffee and Nile Valley Aviation.

* * * *

Flight planning at Interflight was a little homemade. We pushed the aircraft hard and routinely achieved better than the book figures for range by using careful fuel-saving techniques. This in turn enabled us to accept trips other operators would turn down. Masey had his own views on fuel reserves - "we did this in BA" - and we often arrived at destination on fumes, just legal but no more. Sometimes even we couldn't get the trip to work on paper, the distance was just too great, so it wasn't unknown for us to 'lose' 100 miles on the handwritten plog. This is why Masey never wanted to use computerised flight plans; often the trips wouldn't be able to dispatch because the fuel calculations wouldn't work. The CAA never forced the company down the route of computerised plans, so we continued to get away with it.

One of the Hawkers that Masey had bought for a song was a very old -3B model, G-IFTC, that had been re-engined with Garrett 731 turbofans, actually a slightly more powerful version of the 731 engines fitted to the Lear. This was a terrific aircraft in many ways, as it had a great range which put Interflight into a niche market for charter. Masey and I, having delivered a nose leg assembly for an Airbus 310 to First Air in Ottawa, decided to put the Hawker to the test by flying directly from Ottawa to Gatwick, a distance of 3000 nm. This was stretching the Hawker's range quite a bit but Masey thought we could go for the record. The winds were favourable and the temperatures aloft colder than standard, so things were looking positive for the flight. If it didn't work out, we could always drop into Shannon which was exactly on our track. We were coming back empty, so how the return trip panned out in the event wasn't too important, as we didn't have passengers to worry about. The old Hawker had very little in the way of long-range navigation; in fact, practically nothing. Technically, it was far from legal for the North Atlantic but such triflings didn't worry Masey whose navigation skills, as a former flight navigator, were superb anyway. However, he brought along the company's portable Trimble GPS to back up our dead-reckoning and make sure we didn't get too lost.

Off we go. The flight progresses well and after two hours after takeoff from Ottawa we are coasting out about 150 nm SE of Goose Bay, as planned and two hours after that we are approaching longitude 30°W, traditionally the midpoint when crossing the North Atlantic. This meridian marks the point where you no longer speak to Gander ATC, which covers the western Atlantic and switch over to Shanwick ATC (Shannon/Prestwick) which covers the eastern Atlantic. I have just made the standard position report to Shanwick when the GPS goes blank. Masey is in the galley smoking a B&H and brewing up some tea.

"Simon," I call back, "the GPS has gone tits." He comes forward squinting through the cigarette smoke.

"Try cycling it." More in hope than expectation, I duly turn it off and then on again. Nothing, blank screen. "I think the batteries are dead," I say.

"OK don't, worry. I'll hook it up to the aircraft power," comes the reply.

Now I start to get concerned. I have every faith in Masey's technical knowledge and ability and there is nothing he likes more than lashing together a fix but buggering about with the aircraft's main 28v DC system mid-Atlantic with another 100 minutes to landfall in Ireland strikes me as rash. Masey disappears and comes back with a roll of wire and some insulation tape. The next thing, he is disassembling the seatbelt sign next to the main exit door to get to the live terminals.

"Simon, is this wise?" I offer. He looks at me, puzzled,

"Of course it's fine, why not?" he says and turns back to his work.

I sit there holding my breath thinking of the what-ifs and where I would go if it all goes dark, or worse, fumey. After five minutes Masey re-emerges with two ends of wire.

"Pass me the GPS." I hand it over. This is the moment of truth. He wraps the wires around the terminals and presses the power button and the Trimble comes to life again, hunting for a new satellite lock-on.

"See? No problem!" he announces with a grin and I start breathing again.

* * * *

Flying in Northern Canada can be a challenge. Not just because of the extreme remoteness of the northern part of the country and lack of suitable diversions, but also as a result of the huge magnetic variation because you are close to the magnetic North Pole. The magnetic North Pole is 250 miles from the geographical North Pole and its position is also constantly on the move.

Interflight's Hawker-3B Fan, G-IFTC

Unfortunately, and for purely historical reasons, aviation is wedded to magnetic north as its reference. The difference between true north and magnetic north is called 'variation'; in the UK it's only about 1° but in Canada it can be 25° or more and this can have strange effects. On a night flight from Churchill Falls westbound across Baffin Bay once, the effects were extreme and I had to work hard to keep my situational awareness. The wind was quite strong from the south and normally the aircraft would be heading into wind slightly to make good the desired track westwards, in exactly the same way you would head into the stream to get to the other bank if crossing a river in a boat; it's the same principle. However, because of the 25° of magnetic variation, we were actually heading away from the wind to make good the track. Mentally, this made no sense. I knew it was correct but it felt all wrong. Then we experienced a strong display of northern lights that gave me 'the leans' and I was convinced I was turning because the horizon no longer looked level. On such occasions, you really have to work to keep a sense of reality, especially when tired.

Northern lights

Canada also gets cold in winter, really cold, which sounds like stating the obvious but until you experience this level of cold it's hard to explain to anyone used to a European winter. It's the sort of numbing cold that we just don't get in Europe and I have only experienced elsewhere in Siberia and Kazakhstan. The sort of cold that hurts when you breathe, freezes your brain and welds any bare flesh to metal. So, when I took the wrong exit in the terminal at Iqaluit, in the Canadian Northwest Territories and found myself accidentally locked out of the building with no way back in, I started to get worried. It was very cold and windy and my new jacket from Marks & Spencer and my tissue-thin uniform trousers were quickly found to be completely useless. I felt naked from the waist down. I started shouting and banging on the thick sliding glass door but there was no one around.

"Hello? Hello? Hey! HEEEY!!"

My voice got carried away in the wind. Shit. What to do? Ten minutes went by and the weak sun was quickly disappearing over the horizon, not that it was producing any warmth but I knew that when it had gone it was going to get even colder. I was losing heat fast and was beginning to shiver uncontrollably. Across the apron, ice crystals blew over the frozen tarmac, little beads of ice.

Eventually, after 15 minutes or so, a ramp truck saw me hammering on the door and frantically looking around. The truck pulled up next to me, skidding slightly on the ice, the diesel pumping clouds of condensation from the exhaust into the frozen air. I yanked the door open and flopped inside where it was gloriously warm. Phew!

"Christ it's cold!" I said to the driver.

Or at least that's what I meant to say but I think what came out was "Croi ee cerld!" as my face was in a frozen rictus and my lips wouldn't move properly as though I had just gargled Novocain. My hands felt like blocks of ice and my feet seemed not to be attached to my body anymore. The driver stared at my clothes in disbelief and laughed. He was sitting in his warm cab, dressed in his goose-down parka looking for all the world like the Michelin Man.

"What is it with you British guys? Don't you ever wear coats?"

Iqaluit Airport in winter

I wouldn't make that mistake again. It's no coincidence that Airbus use Iqaluit for cold weather testing. The winter temperatures can easily drop to -35°C. It was probably -20°C on this occasion but with the wind chill effect it felt so, so much colder.

* * * *

One final story before we say goodbye to the Learjet. Martyn and I are flying G-CJET to St. Louis in February 1995 for some maintenance work prior to its sale. After seven years, Masey has decided it's time to move the aircraft on; the market has changed and larger cabin aircraft are now more popular. For Interflight, the days of the Lear are over. Gama Aviation is to be the new operator and it's time for us to say a fond farewell to our Learjet that had served us so well.

We are staging through Goose Bay in Newfoundland for a fuel stop on our way to St. Louis. It's only an hour and a half's flying time from Goose, so we haven't picked up too much fuel – enough to get there legally and no more. There's no point in making a present of fuel to the new owner after all. Goose Bay often has military aircraft transiting through and on this occasion, we are not disappointed; some RAF Tornados and RCAF F-18s are departing for a NATO exercise at the Canadian Forces base at Cold Lake, Alberta. They are waiting in a line at the runway hold on the opposite side of the airfield to us.

"Let's show the RAF what we can do," I suggest to Martyn. "and beat up the runway on takeoff. It's probably our last Lear takeoff after all." Martyn agrees, "Fine with me, go for it!"

We line up on runway 27 and I stand up the thrust levers to full thrust against the brakes. With brake release and at its light weight, the Lear surges forward down the 11,000ft runway, accelerating fast. At rotate speed, I lift the aircraft off the runway and immediately check forward to hold the aircraft close to the runway, no more than fifteen feet above the tarmac. The runway is passing beneath us in a blur and I can see the airfield perimeter fence approaching rapidly.

"Gear up, flap up" I call to Martyn and he reaches forward to the gear lever and the wheels tuck away. Up come the flaps too and the speed builds rapidly, 200, 250, 300 knots. At 350 knots indicated, the maximum speed allowed, I gently pull back on the yoke to establish a twenty-degree deck angle. The Lear rockets skywards into the blue with Martyn and I lying back in our seats. The rate of climb is phenomenal as we swap speed for performance. The altimeter is spinning like a top and a minute after takeoff we are passing through 10,000ft.

ATC calls us laconically.

"Thanks for the show, gentlemen. Contact Moncton Centre on 130.75. Good day."

AIR CONTRACTORS

I joined Hunting Cargo Airlines, which became Air Contractors (ACL), in January 1996 after ten years at Interflight. It was time to move on and I wanted to get on to bigger jets. At the time the ACL operated the Vickers Merchantman, which was the cargo version of the Vanguard and some Lockheed Electras. Just being introduced, was the Boeing 727 and I was employed as direct entry captain on this aircraft. All the aircraft were cargo variants contracted to DHL, UPS, TNT, FedEx etc, hence, once Hunting Cargo was sold off to a Belgium and South African consortium in 1998, the name changed to Air Contractors. Air Contractors eventually operated ten 727s and during the expansion, it was proposed to use some contract 727 pilots as the company was short of crew. Mexicana had some crews available and so they were hired on six-month contracts. There was a lot of grumbling about this with everyone coming up with their own stereotypes of Mexicans; lazy, bandits, unkempt, being a little too fond of siestas under sombreros, etc etc. "I'm not flying with any bloody Mexican," was the general refrain being heard in the crew rooms before their arrival. When these guys arrived, however, we were in for a shock and everyone had to eat their words. Not only were they very good pilots and highly experienced on the 727, (some had 8,000 hours on the 727 alone as it was all they had flown since initial flight school), they were great guys too. They could really fly the 727, there was no doubt about that and they taught us all a lot about the aircraft. These guys lived in Mexico but were paid US airline salaries in dollars so in fact it was they who were slumming it by coming to Europe; in Mexico they lived like kings. They came to Europe for a variety of reasons but mostly they were crazy about European football. One F/O was even a trained opera singer who sang like Pavarotti. He preferred to fly rather than earn fortunes singing opera. Takes all sorts, I suppose.

My conversion to the 727 is the usual four-week slog, two weeks of classroom 'chalk and talk' followed by two weeks in the simulator. Come the day of the initial rating Skill Test to see if we could put into practice all we had learned and dazzle the examiner with our proficiency, me and a new F/O arrive at the simulator building for the test. Hunting Cargo had the habit of employing all kinds of unsuitable and random people who had managed to convince the company that they were competent and our examiner, an Australian called Ted Ortez, was a prime example. Where they found him, God alone knows. We listen as he starts his brief for the all-important test.

"G'day, gentlemen, today you are going to demonstrate that you can fly the 727 to a decent standard but I have to tell you now that one of you is likely to fail."

He pauses for dramatic effect. What? The F/O and I look at each other. Did we just hear that? I laugh nervously, convinced that this must be some down-under joke but he looks back deadpan. Well, this is new and I make a mental note – this bastard may just be serious. I have been flying for too long to be intimidated by that kind of crap and am determined to show him that even though I was new to the 727 I can fly an aircraft, which is what happens and me and the other chap pass with no problem.

The 727 is a three-engined jet that can carry up to twenty-four tonnes of cargo after conversion to a freighter. But they were old aircraft by the time we got them, many of them had already had many years in airline service. They were ex-American Airlines, Delta and Korean Airlines and they had tens of thousands of hours of airframe life. One was reputed to be the aircraft that Boeing chose to convert from a -100 Series to the longer -200 series in 1967. Over its approximately thirty-year life, this aircraft was allegedly nudging 60,000 hours on the airframe. More significantly, like most of the 727s we operated, it had a very high number of cycles, i.e. the number of times it had taken off, pressurised and landed again. (This is what wears airframes the most, as the Hawaiian airline Aloha Airlines found out in April 1988 when one of their Boeing 737s ended up as a cabriolet when the roof blew off).

This particular aircraft used to flex at a certain pressure differential, around 2 psi, as the hull pressurised on climb out. The fuselage skin right behind the flight deck, having flexed, would snap back suddenly – what's known as 'oil canning'. No matter how much I was expecting it, the sharp CRACK as the skin popped back into shape always made me jump out of my skin mostly because of concerns we all had about the cargo door. The 727s Air Contractors operated had been converted to freighters on the cheap and didn't have shoot bolts to fully secure the large cargo door that was fitted on the forward left side of the aircraft. Such bolts, if we had had them, would have slid from the cargo door into the airframe securing the door completely. It would be impossible for the door to open in flight. As it was, the whole door, on our conversions, was only held at the top by hinges and the bottom by a simple torque tube activated electrically. This arrangement left the middle of the door unsecured and I always had an image in my mind of it bulging slightly with the pressurisation although I tried to put this out of my mind – some things are best not thought about. Hence my disquiet with loud cracking sounds in flight. Because of the lack of shoot bolts, the CAA wouldn't have this conversion on the UK register and so they were operated under an Irish AOC instead. On the instrument panel in front of the pilots, duplicated on the flight engineer's panel, was a large red CARGO DOOR light that illuminated if the door opened even fractionally in flight. This light was designed to get your full attention. And it did.

Flying out of Lyon in the early hours, northbound to Brussels, we were at around 10,000ft in the climb when the CARGO DOOR light illuminated in front of me. My heart skipped and I swung around to the flight engineer behind me. He was under training and being supervised by John Spencer, a very experienced F/E and trainer who was sitting behind me in the cockpit's fourth seat. The climb checks had been completed and John was slumped in his seat relaxing but keeping an eye on the trainee on the panel. But the instant he saw the light on the engineer's panel and before I said a word, he moved like lightning and reached across to the panel to knock off both air conditioning packs and so take air pressure off the inside of the aircraft and, most importantly, the cargo door.

Despite this quick action, the warning light stubbornly remained illuminated and, after a quick discussion with John and the F/O as to the best course of action, I declared an emergency to ATC, the only time I have ever done this for real. I requested a diversion to Geneva just a short distance over the hills to the east and the nearest airport open at that time of night. With the door light still illuminated we were in an unknown condition and I was afraid that, if the fault was genuine and the door opened fully, this could make the aircraft uncontrollable with unpredictable consequences. Although aircraft have successfully landed in this condition in the past, I didn't want to risk trying it. With proper shoot bolts, I would have been far less worried as the door physically couldn't have opened and I would have asked John to go and take a visual look. But as it was, I wanted everyone firmly strapped in. Geneva ATC was superb and gave us priority to land in either direction on their single runway. We were on the ground there within twenty minutes and as we taxied in off the runway the light extinguished. Maintenance at Jet Aviation Geneva later confirmed it was, as suspected, just a faulty microswitch.

The only other incident I had in the two and a half years on the 727, before I moved to the much larger Airbus 300, was an engine fire warning. We were flying southbound in the cruise from Copenhagen to Cologne on a cold winter's night when we got a fire warning on the centre engine. I glanced back at the engineer. He was a very good training engineer and knew the 727 like the back of his hand, tremendously knowledgeable. I won't name him as, unfortunately, he also liked a wee dram from time to time. On some days the flight deck would smell like a distillery but we all took the view that he was safer in that known and steady condition than sober and going cold turkey. At any rate, I had every confidence in him, he never appeared under the influence, the mark of a true alcoholic I suppose. Just as I called for the engine fire checklist, the bell stopped. Then it started again. Then stopped. We exchanged glances. The fire detection 'loops' could be shorting out electrically as a result of a fault – or a real fire might be giving the same effect by burning through the loops.

"I'd be inclined to shut it down," I suggested and he agreed.

"OK, Engine Fire checklist, please," I said and the engineer and the F/O ran through the checklist. Two minutes later the engine was shut down and secured. The two-engined landing at Cologne was firmer than usual without the thrust of the third engine but strange – every engine failure practice in the simulator was always a side engine to make things more demanding and never the centre engine.

Most of the crews at Air Contractors were large characters, particularly the flight engineers, exclusively ex-RAF or ex-airline including two from the BA

Concorde fleet. The Chief Flight Engineer, Geoff Manning, was a big man who didn't suffer fools gladly and was idolised and mimicked by everyone. His first loves were steam engines and large quantities of beer but he was serious when it came to work and had a huge engineering knowledge. His pragmatic approach to work and men was shown in his company 'Notice to Crew' memos, easily the best I have ever read, witty and absolutely to the point.

Werner Werdenberg, a tall German-Swiss, was one of the funniest guys I have ever known as long as you appreciated his acid wit and obeyed his drinking rules. He could never "eat on an empty stomach" which meant several beers before lunch and "Ein fur der Strasse" afterwards was mandatory. He was a Marmite character - you either loved him or loathed him. I was in the first camp. Ask anyone who ever flew the Boeing 707 about Werner and they would almost certainly know him; he was definitely not one of those "I think I know him" characters. One first officer, had lost his medical and couldn't fly as a pilot any longer, so Werner was tasked with re-training him as a Flight Engineer. One day Werner noticed this character using a flight deck emergency torch to complete the pre-flight external check. This is a thoughtless move as these torches are for emergency use only and should be left in place and fully charged. This was the last straw for Werner who didn't like him anyway. He shouted at him,

"You are ze absolute vanker, isn't it! As long as I have ze hole in ze arse you vill never be ze flight engineer!"

Dave Farthing was an absolute gentleman, ex-BA, always immaculately dressed in a belted raincoat, polished shoes and a cap. Chris Jervis, an ex-Navy man who had served on the carrier HMS Ark Royal. A Cheshire man to his bones, he could drink heroic quantities of beer but be stone-cold sober a few hours later and ate curries that took the glaze off the plate. Al Barnett, a lovely guy, ex-RAF Nimrod F/E who was probably the worst car driver I have ever been with, but later became a taxi driver in Eastbourne. Ron Hodgson was a Lancashire man to his core and a joy to fly with as he could brighten up any crew at 3 am with his positive and happy demeanour. His main sport was taking the mickey out of Germans to their face. He had broken the peak of his uniform hat like a guardsman and had replaced the ACL cap badge with a Russian hammer and sickle badge. I had bought the badge in Red Square years before and I gave it to Ron and he was very proud of it. The conversation with our German friends would go something like this:

"Eee," Ron would say to the young TNT loading supervisor in Dusseldorf, with his head thrown back to look under the hat brim, always with a smiley but puzzled expression on his mobile face, "So, this lad Hitler, he wasn't actually a German was he?"

"Yeees, this is true," said the supervisor warily after a pause, looking for a trap. "He was, in fact, Austrian." With this, Ron would offer a huge and disarming grin and guffaw loudly,

"Ah, well then lad, that's all right then isn't it? I often wondered. He was a right bugger though, wasn't he? Fancy a cuppa tea, lad?"

Ron would only drink leaf tea with first pickings leaves – tea bag 'builders tea' was a heresy to him. "Dioxins, lad, dioxins," he would caution, serious for once. I was in a taxi one evening in Cologne with Ron and, sensing a chance for some fun, he asked the driver if we could drive to the airport via the old, historic part of town.

"Zer is no old part of ze town," the taxi driver said sourly. "It was all bombed by you, ze Eeenglish. Apart from ze railway station."

As we drove past the station it was all lit up under the long glass roof with bright lights and Ron, after an appropriate pause and with a big grin on his face, exclaimed,

"Well, how the fuck did they miss that?"

Don Burton was another character, an ex-Heavylift Airlines F/E on the Boeing 707 and the Shorts 'Belfast' transport, aka 'The Slug'. The Belfast was a huge 100-ton turboprop dating from the early 1960s designed to transport troops over to West Germany in the event the Soviet Red Army got ambitious and started crossing the German plains. It had a flight deck the size of a dance hall and behind this was a galley area. Heavylift used to fly The Slug across the Atlantic to French Guyana for Aerospatiale carrying their rocket payloads and Don was allegedly very proud of his cooking abilities in the galley behind the flight deck during these long flights. An ex-Heavylift captain with ACL told me a different story, however. "Don't believe that crap Don comes out with about his cooking," he said. "The muck he produced was completely inedible." Without fail, Don's stock phrase when crossing the UK coast inbound to

East Midlands or Stansted, was, "A green and pleasant land, too good for ---s," as he peered forward through the windscreen, baseball cap pulled low over his eyes. The derogative term varied daily. Don was at his best in the simulator. When practising engine failures on takeoff, the bread and butter of simulator training and as the aircraft clawed its way aloft on the remaining engine, he would slowly lean forward with the checklist and announce to the captain,

"Right, who's flying it, you or the boy?"

The 'boy' in the right seat was often a 20,000 hour veteran pilot, no longer a captain due to age, but this didn't matter to Don. To him, anyone in the right seat was 'the boy' and that's all there was to it. Eating out with Don was entertaining. He always favoured the same dish if it was on the menu.

"I'll have spag bol," he said. "I don't want nuffing foreign."

"Don," I used to remind him, "that is foreign. It's an Italian dish." and I would always get the same response.

"No, mate. Spag bol, decent grub."

Although they weren't pilots, all of the flight engineers were good aviators who kept a close eye on the idiots in front of them who might try to do them harm in the early hours of the morning. They would often remind us that their job was akin to being a stagecoach driver – they were obliged to watch two arseholes all night long. Anyone who hasn't flown a three-man crew has missed out, it is easily the best and safest operation. Especially during abnormal or emergency situations. One pilot is assigned to do nothing but fly the aircraft while the other pilot and the F/E, armed with the checklist, get their heads together to sort the problem out between them. In main airline operations, the use of flight engineers ended with increasingly automated aircraft introduced from the 1980s onwards. A lot of F/Es saw operations like ACL, Heavylift and other cargo operators as a stay of execution and a few more years of work before retirement. ACL employed a lot of pilots and flight engineers who were nearing the end of their flying careers. It was possible to construct a crew with a combined age of three days short of 190 years; a captain one day under sixty and the F/O and F/E each one day under sixty-five. But more importantly, that total could mean more than 120 years of flying experience between them. A lot of them had all flown the older three-man jets such as Comets, 707s, 727s, 747s, TriStars, A300s, DC-8s, DC-10s and Concorde, not to mention DC4s, DC6s and Lockheed Electras. Lots and lots of experience.

Two funny stories illustrate the experience of the F/Es. I was flying jump seat one time positioning back to Brussels to go home when we got a call on the radio from ATC, relayed from the company, to return to Stockholm for some reason. Being too heavy to land back immediately, it was clear we would have to dump some fuel first to lose weight. The captain, known to be a little weak and inclined to flap (he was known as 'Thrush' as he was considered an irritating part of a lady's anatomy), turned around to the F/E Ron Hodgson.

"We are too heavy to return, we'll have to dump some fuel!" Ron looked at him with his usual grin hooked over each ear.

"Don't be a c---, lad," he replied in his laconic Mancunian accent. "I've already done it!"

On another occasion, Wally Ross, a very experienced 727 engineer, was in the jump seat positioning somewhere, which we did a lot, on an American airline called Kitty Hawk Aircargo that was subcontracted to DHL in Europe for a while. Kitty Hawk operated 727s like us and was what is known in the US as a 'supplemental' airline. Supplementals can work overseas but, other than the fact that they are US-registered aircraft with US crews, the FAA turn a blind eye to them in some areas, especially with regard to duty times. They weren't too popular with us as we saw them as Americans treating Europe as their backyard, as usual, and poaching European jobs; it was inconceivable that European crews would ever be allowed to operate in the same way in the US.

Some of the guys on these Kitty Hawk 727s were not very experienced and were trying to build time to get into the major airlines back home, which I suppose is fair enough. The young F/E on the panel had got himself into a proper muddle with the fuel distribution and the aircraft was getting dangerously out of balance with the wrong amount of fuel in each tank group. The autopilot kept disconnecting as a result due to the fuel imbalance. He had been guilty of the crime of 'recreational crossfeeding' ie tinkering unnecessarily with the fuel quantities in each tank by switching fuel pumps on or off. On the thirsty JT8 engines, this could get out of hand quickly and was never recommended especially as the imbalance limit on the 727 between the left and right tank groups was a measly 1000 lbs. That took very little time to achieve with the old

JT8 that drank fuel like crazy. Worse, he didn't know how to correct the situation and was starting to sweat. Wally watched this development with a wry interest and after a while put his paper down and slowly leant across the cockpit and tapped him on the shoulder.

"Listen to me, lad." The F/E looked around a look of relief on his face.

"Remember - always turn something on before turning something off. I'm sure they taught you that in ground school?" The young lad nodded quickly.

"Right then. Switch the Group 1 tank pumps ON, open the crossfeed, turn the Group 2 pumps OFF and watch the gauges like a bloody hawk." Within two minutes the fuel equilibrium was restored and Wally picked up his paper again.

* * * *

Flying cargo aircraft has its own challenges due to the dangerous materials often carried. Climbing out of Cologne in the Airbus on a wet and gloomy night on our way to Stockholm, first one and then a string of red smoke warning lights illuminate as we are passing 3000ft. Don Burton, the F/E and I exchange worried looks. The highly sensitive smoke detectors on the main cargo deck have sensed a change in air composition and sent warnings to the smoke detector lights on the flight engineer's panel. I experience the tingle of adrenaline. I know from the NOTOC that on this flight, not unusually, we are carrying some qualities of flammable liquids and a small quantity of oxidizers. So, this could be a genuine emergency, or it just could be the wet ULDs misting slightly as the main deck warmed. Before I declare an emergency, return to the airport and trigger a full-scale response from the services at Cologne, I turn to Don.

"Don, can you go back and take a look? Let me know what you see." Don unstraps and moves quickly through the flight deck door, across the small passenger and galley area and switches on the main deck lights. Looking through the plastic window of the forward barrier netting he can't see anything past the forward ULDs but craning his neck upwards can just see that their tops are misting in the air conditioning – no guarantee that there is no smoke anywhere else but it gives some weight to our hope that this is all the warnings signify. As he returns to the flight deck to tell me, one by one the smoke warning lights extinguish. We all relax.

"Thank fuck," says Don and I agree. Smoke and fire on any aircraft is the worst situation and the likelihood of experiencing this on a cargo aircraft given the quantities and mix of sometimes hazardous material they carry is that much greater. It can have devastating consequences; in 2010 a fully serviceable Boeing 747 operated by UPS departed Dubai and crashed twenty-five minutes later with an incapacitated crew and burnt control runs due to onboard fire and smoke.

* * * *

One of the more interesting aspects of ACL was the horse flights. Ireland is renowned for horse breeding, so it was no surprise that there was a demand for these flights to another centre of equine excellence, Deauville in France. The flights were generally on a Saturday from either Dublin or Cork. We were aware that the value of the horses equalled or probably outweighed the value of the old 727s; they were worth literally millions and none of us wanted to be responsible for a horse stampeding and breaking a leg. The onboard groom carried a 'humane killer' gun that was safe to use onboard and, as a last resort, this would shoot a bolt into the horse's head to put it down. The horses, usually three or four, boarded up a shallow ramp into the aircraft through the large cargo door and were gently coaxed into makeshift stables that kept them safe and protected the cargo deck from any corrosive urine. As they boarded, the stallions fretted and whinnied, their eyes rolling in apprehension at this strange and scary environment. You could see that these beautiful animals were both very highly strung and very valuable.

Once they were settled and calmed down, we would close up, start engines and taxi off, planning the taxi far ahead to minimise even the gentlest braking. Takeoffs needed a long runway and gentle application of thrust to keep the acceleration low. It was important to fly with extraordinary care and smoothness to keep these prima donna darlings happy and calm, so the climb-out and descents were flown at very low deck angles and power changes made incrementally and very slowly. The landings too had to be smooth but this wasn't hard to achieve in the 727 even for me; it was very easy to land well. Luckily all my horse flights were successful but they were always nerve-wracking to say the least.

* * * *

The loaders at East Midlands weren't the brightest guys on the block but then it's unlikely that shift work at 3 am on a cold and wet airport ramp is ever going to attract the best of the local gene pool. I am departing the airport for Dublin on the DHL run in the early hours one winter's night. The freight bins are loaded, the dispatcher has brought the paperwork and the aircraft is closed up and ready to depart. "Eurotrans 489, can you contact your Operations please?" ATC calls. I acknowledge, hand the radio to the F/O and call Ops on my cellphone. "Evening, Mark. Can you hold the pushback for a couple of minutes, we have some last-minute priority freight to load before you go", the Dispatcher informs me. No problem. After a few minutes, I see the annunciator light come on indicating that the forward belly hold door has been opened and shortly afterwards I hear the 'thump' as it's closed again and the light extinguishes. We push back and are on our way. Shortly after takeoff, ATC informs us that several parcels have been found on the runway by the runway inspection car. Not just parcels but the high-priority parcels we had delayed departure for. It turned out that some of the loaders had placed parcels inside the undercarriage gear doors, mistaking this area with its light on as a cargo hold. Why they also opened the forward belly door, goodness knows. Maybe it looked too much like a hold to possibly be a hold. Anyway, when we selected the wheels up after takeoff, the gear doors opened and it rained precious parcels all the way down the runway. DHL – 'Drop It, Hide It, Lose It' as we used to say.

* * * *

ACL benefited from some interesting guys - guys who wouldn't fit the demographic of passenger airlines. Craig was a Welsh chap with tiny, battered wire-framed glasses. He was quiet and kept himself to himself. I did his initial type rating course on the A300 and during the course, he happened to mention that he had spent a lot of time in N'Djamena in Chad. Strange I thought, not many people do that. He had an interesting air about him but I couldn't put my finger on it. A few months later over a beer, he told me the reason for his time

Typical Boeing 727 cargo door without shoot bolts. Stock photo

A 727 Flight Engineer's panel – the fuel system is centre left, cargo door light top centre. Stock photo

in Chad; he had spent four years in the French Foreign Legion, the infamous 'Legion Etrangere'. "Why?" I had to ask. "Simple. I thought it was the best way to escape from Wales," was the reply. Fair enough, to each his own.

One day we are in the crew bus driving through Budapest from the airport to the hotel after our night's work. Craig is gazing out of the window. Suddenly he sits up and cranes his neck around as the bus drives along the road. I follow his gaze and see an insignia over a non-descript doorway.

"That's a Legion Club, I'd recognise it anywhere. I'm going there at lunchtime."

Great, I thought, that's the last I'll see of him. However, to my surprise and relief, he did show up on time for pick-up in the evening, looking reflective. "How was it?", I asked him. "Bloody great," was his reply. "Just like the old days. There was a guy there I knew from Niger. They asked me if I wanted to join up again". "Well?", I asked. "I just might", he replied thoughtfully, "It's better than flying nights for the rest of my life".

* * * *

Pat Morgan was one of the Irish first officers on the 727 in the early days of ACL. Pat was a good pilot but an absolute liability in a bar. I first met him in a pub in Dublin where he was sitting in the corner nursing a large glass of water and was staring at me fixedly. I assumed he'd had his fill and was rehydrating.

"Pat not drinking?" I asked someone. "Pat? You're joking!" was the reply, "He's on the gin".

Pat would start the evening with a few pints and then move on to neat gin. After a few glasses of the mother's ruin, he had the habit of staring at people, generally the wrong sort of people. This generally led to a fight given the sort of bars we often frequented, such as our Brussels favourites, the Sports Bar and Hermann's. Hermann's was run by - you're ahead of me - Hermann who was a German guy with a manic look known to us, obviously, as 'Hermann the German'. His bar was down a flight of stairs below street level and a real dive but the beer was cheap and he was open all hours; he never seemed to sleep. One evening Pat picked the wrong guy to stare at and inevitably a fight started. Two huge bouncers grabbed Pat and dragged him up the stairs into the street.

"Pat," I goaded him the next day, "It's traditional to get thrown down the stairs into the gutter, not up the bloody stairs! What happened, anyway?"

"Oi didn't like the way the fecker was looking at me", was the reply.

Another pilot, Al Bampton who was an ex-Royal Brunei captain now first officer due to his age, became over-refreshed at Hermann's one evening and started to throw Hermann Nazi salutes when refused more beer. This ended the same way and the last I saw of Al was him being frog-marched up and out of the premises by the same bouncers with his legs not touching the floor.

* * * *

And now to Howard (his name changed as I have nothing good to say about him). This character was a thoroughly unpleasant captain who flew with Hunting Cargo and then ACL for a lot longer than he ever should have. All of us in the company could only assume that he had photos of someone in management. I flew with him a few times when he completed some of my line training on the 727 (somewhat perfunctory as I learned very little useful from him about the aircraft) and took an instant dislike to him. He was arrogant, vain and had very little airmanship, that indefinable quality that most pilots develop over years of flying. During my line training, he played his favourite trick of deliberately mis-setting the cleared level in the altitude alert window to see if the other guy spotted it or not – criminal stupidity. When he was on the Vickers 'Merchantman' he enjoyed short-changing his crews out of their per diem expenses. In those days, before I joined, the guys were paid in traveller's cheques by the captain at the end of each flying day for expenses, meals etc. This seemed a quaint and old-fashioned payment method at first but there was method in the company's madness as they were untraceable by the Inland Revenue. Anyway, this character used to play the old trick of double folding some, not all, of the cheques so that what appeared to be, say, £100 being thumbed and handed over by him to the crew member was actually only £60 or £80. He was diddling his crew and then flatly denying it when confronted.

I mentioned his lack of airmanship and vanity and this incident illustrates both well. On a takeoff from Cologne one night he struck the hydraulic tail skid at the back of the 727 by rotating too quickly on takeoff. When the F/E, on his

Me and Amanda, Cologne, 1997

post-flight check after the first sector, saw that the tail skid was missing its red paint on the ablative metal - sure evidence that the aircraft tail had scrapped the runway - he flatly refused to admit it and flew another three sectors that night. This was an absolute no-no as Boeing deemed this a 'land as soon as practicable' event because of possible damage to the rear pressure bulkhead if the strike was severe. An engineering inspection was mandatory because if this pressure bulkhead failed in flight, the weight of air in the fuselage suddenly escaping could blow the tail section off, as tragically happened to the JAL 747 in August 1985. This alone was a sackable offence in my view but no, the company continued to let him fly and, incredibly, continue as a trainer. It was also his task to monitor our noise performance on the 727 fleet at various noise-sensitive airports (more of which below) and he used to revel in calling you up to tell you how badly you had done the night before at a certain airport, although he was no better than anyone else at achieving the required noise levels.

But, worst of all, he had also slept with the underage teenage daughter of one of the 727 first officers. This guy, not unreasonably, literally wanted to kill him and as a prelude of worse things undoubtedly to come, threw him through the plate glass door of the Palazzo Hotel in Bergamo after an explosive row, shattering glass everywhere. It took a few of us to explain to ACL Crewing not to ever again pair these two together as a crew. But Howard eventually got his comeuppance. He was driving to work in Brussels one evening when he was forced off the road by another car and given a sound beating which had him off work for several weeks. No one ever admitted anything but I'm sure this wasn't a chance mugging. He had made enough enemies over the years that there would be a line a hundred yards long of people wanting to get even.

You get the picture. In short, an absolute creep.

* * * *

The 727 was a very noisy aircraft due to its early-generation Pratt & Whitney JT8 engines. To meet Stage 3 noise requirements, FedEx in the US, which had a huge 727 fleet, had come up with a plan to meet the regulations. This involved limiting the maximum takeoff weight to 177,600 lbs and fitting the lower-powered JT8-7 engine with a reduced 14,000 lbs of thrust and a modified exhaust duct. Added to this was a complicated takeoff profile that included a two-stage thrust cutback and a climb-out at minimum manoeuvring speed to 3000ft. In our view, all this did was spread the noise around more as it took longer to climb up and away from the airport but we were obliged to stick with it and, on a good day if it was cold and there was no temperature inversion, you might get away with it. STAGE THREE (referencing the ICAO noise abatement rules) was painted in big letters on the engine cowlings, but I don't think that fooled anyone for a minute.

In order to get the required rest days in any given week, the Irish Aviation Authority insisted that we had thirty-six hours clear of duty somewhere in the DHL network during our eight days on. The way the schedules worked out, one of the suitable cities was Helsinki and rather than stay there for the 36 hours, some of the single guys made trips across to St. Petersburg where the girls were great looking and freely available. Rod Anyan, a confirmed bachelor everyone thought, was a New Zealander who made this trip a few times and eventually ended up marrying a gorgeous and educated Russian girl who he took back to London. Rod was also renowned for his love of good food. He was a keen windsurfer who liked to eat well and often. "You can't run a first-class engine on cheap fuel" was his stock phrase.

Unfortunately, this isn't always possible when flying nights but most captains usually managed to jolly him along enough that he would last until breakfast at the hotel at the end of the night's work. However, one night in Nuremberg on the 727 when flying on the DHL network, Rod dug his heels in. Like the rest of us, he had been unable to eat at the hotel in Bergamo before we started duty (Italians just don't understand eating at 6 pm and the hotel kitchens were firmly closed) and now there was a delay to the loading of the freight.

"Mate," he said to me in his strong Kiwi accent, "I have got to eat something."

"Don't you have a sandwich or something to keep you going?" I asked in hope more than expectation.

"Nah, mate, bugger all."

"OK," I offered, "if you've got to eat, you've got to eat. Go into the terminal and get something. Remember our revised off blocks time is 2140 now, so be back at 2130 latest, OK? Don't be late for God's sake." Rod agreed and left the cockpit. "Thanks, mate."

It was one of my first trips with the company and although I certainly didn't want to be late departing, I wanted to be known as a captain that would stick up for his crew. At the end of the day, not eating properly is a flight safety issue and one of the ongoing gripes with DHL was the lack of access to food during our ten-hour night duty. Maybe this would help to highlight the issue.

Soon afterwards the DHL ramp agent came on board and informed me that they would start loading shortly and would we be on time for our revised off-block time – or maybe even early?

"And verr is ze ozzer pilot?" he asked, looking in surprise at the vacant seat in the cockpit.

"Oh, he has just gone to get a sandwich, he'll be back any moment. Don't worry," I smiled at him. The agent pointedly looked at his watch and left.

"But you know, all ze cafes in the terminal are shut at zis time," was his parting comment.

At 2120 I was getting anxious - there was no sign of Rod. The ramp agent was also asking where he was. The tug was hooked up and the tug driver was plugged in on the ground intercom and calling me. "Ground to cockpit, we are connected, the steering bypass pin is installed and we are ready to push anytime". I suggested the ramp agent send someone into the terminal quickly and try and find him. Which he did. Rod was found, not in any old cheap café, but in the main airport restaurant finishing off a big steak and fries with a glass of Perrier to wash it down. By the time we got him sat in his seat in the aircraft, the doors closed and the steps removed, we were two minutes late for pushback, right on the limit with DHL before big penalties were imposed.

"Rod, I didn't mean you to have a bloody steak!" I fumed.

"Mate, there was nothing else open. And you can't run a first-class engine on cheap fuel."

* * * *

"What was that, did you see it?" Don Burton, the F/E, suddenly leans forward and points ahead of us. I had seen it too in the corner of my eye, a momentary flash in the distance. I look up from the plog.

"I don't know, a meteorite maybe?" I venture and glance down again.

"No way, it was much too big!"

"Lightning then?" offers Paul Springthorpe the F/O. No, we agree there was

An Air Contractors Boeing 727

A TNT Boeing 727 operated by Air Contractors, showing the cargo door

-168-

no such activity forecast that night. We are puzzled and chat about it for a bit then let the subject drop and continue northbound to land at Brussels. In the crew room, the news is starting to filter through and we learn that what we had witnessed was the horrific mid-air collision of the DHL 757, named 'City of Manama' and a Russian TU-154 belonging to Bashkirian Airlines over Uberlingen, in southern Germany. Somehow through a mixture of ATC controller overload, as a result of staff shortages, and incorrect reactions to the TCAS (the collision avoidance system fitted to both aircraft) the two aircraft had collided in mid-air killing all 71 people aboard both aircraft. This included, tragically, 45 school kids on board the Russian airliner on a school trip to Barcelona. To add to the tragedy, one of the children's fathers confronted the controller at his home near Zurich eighteen months later and killed him in revenge for the death of his wife and two children.

It was July 1st 2002 and the evening had started for us in Rome and we had completed the first leg of the evening to Bergamo, an airport in northern Italy close to the Alps and a major DHL hub. Paul, Don and I were in the A300 and in the distance further down the ramp, I could see the familiar 'City of Manama' 757 also loading the bins like us. They had landed from Bahrain earlier in the evening and were ready to depart ahead of us, all exactly as scheduled. Loaded and closed up we taxied out to the active runway and, as we did so, I watched the 757 as 'Eurotrans 611' started its takeoff roll on its way, like us, to Brussels. Ten minutes later we too were airborne and following the 757 but about sixty to seventy miles behind it and that's why the flash of the explosion was bright but not so much so. It's one of the ironies of GPS (or probably GLONASS in the Russian aircraft's case, a similar system) that the superb accuracy of these systems guarantees accuracy to within a wingspan when flying along an airway and so a collision was inevitable. Twenty years earlier there would have been a good chance that the aircraft would have been sufficiently offset from the airway centreline to miss each other. This was a shocking accident that shook up the airline world and led to some improved TCAS software and training. Sometimes progress exacts a terrible toll.

The two aircraft involved in the collision over Uberlingen

* * * *

One of our routes from Brussels in the 727 in the late 1990s had us overnighting in Belfast. At the time, we were staying downtown in the Europa Hotel which has two claims to fame; one is President Clinton stayed there twice during the peace process in 1995 (and I once occupied the same room as he had) and the other is that it is the most bombed hotel in Europe – damaged an estimated thirty-three times between 1970 and 1994. It must be one of the ugliest hotels in Western Europe, probably because with each rebuild minimum effort was spent as it was likely to be redesigned by the IRA again before long.

ACL had a contract with a private hire car company for crew pickup at 6.30 each evening for transport to the Aldergrove Airport for the start of our night's work. On one occasion we are waiting for the car and it doesn't show up. Belfast being Belfast at the time, all manner of things could have caused the driver to decide against coming into town. At 6.40 we can't wait any longer and I realise we will have to get another cab to take us to the airport or we will be late. The only option, at this last minute, is to take a black cab. Black cabs aren't the best choice in Belfast as they are run by the criminal gangs either part of, or connected to, the IRA but I can see no other option at short notice. I flag down a passing cab and we pile in with our bags. The driver is silent but I can see him checking us out in the rear-view mirror. The three of us are sitting on the back seat making small talk but after a while, we fall silent. We exchange glances; all of us are getting increasingly uneasy about this journey as the driver takes a very different route to the airport than we are used to, through the heavily Catholic West Belfast, his home turf. I stare out of the window as we drive through slum estate after slum estate. It is truly an eye-opener and the history of the Catholics being denied decent jobs in Belfast is evident during this drive. The poverty and crime are clear to see and I feel that everyone is staring at us as we drive along, as we are so obviously not locals. Eventually, the driver climbs up the hill to the motorway and we are back in familiar territory. It's with relief that we arrive at the airport, which as always is like a military compound; walls topped with razor wire, police and army armoured vehicles, powerful arc lights, soldiers looking tense and watchful and several vehicle security checks before getting to the terminal. And always, in the distance, the sound of helicopters.

* * * *

In 1998 ACL started to introduce the Airbus A300 freighter on all the routes and to phase out the old 727s. To this end, we all, in stages, went to Miami to do the four-week conversion course with Continental Airlines. The A300 was the first wide-body twin-engined airliner in the world and was also, until the Boeing 777 came along, the world's biggest twin-engined aircraft. It was a very good freighter as it was reasonably cheap to operate, built like the proverbial (so could absorb the knocks associated with cargo) and could carry around forty-two tonnes of freight. The twelve A300s ACL operated were ex-Carnival Airlines, Olympic Airlines and Egyptair and converted to freighters by either British Aerospace or Deutsche Aerospace by strengthening the floor, adding rollers and slotting in a new cargo door fuselage section – this time a proper job with 'shoot bolts', unlike our old 727s.

The simulator Continental leased was run by Pan Am, sadly long since defunct as the pioneering airline it once was, but still running as a training organisation. Crews on the conversion course stayed in the Holiday Inn on the NE corner of Miami airport for the duration of the course. Knowing ACL, it was probably the cheapest hotel they could find, in a rough area and not a place to venture out after dark although, being crew, that didn't put us off at all. At Werner's command, it was mandatory to call in at Mike's Bar on the way back to the hotel for a quick beer or two and then walk back to the hotel along the unlit road. Mike's Bar was an Irish bar and a real dive, set back from the road, down a dimly lit lane. We never got mugged probably because even the muggers thought we were either absolutely daft or a police plant.

The Holiday Inn wasn't even a proper Holiday Inn, just a franchise staffed with undesirable characters most of whom couldn't even speak any English. Even the hotel Manager was suspect - one of the captains gave him his traveller's cheques to put in the hotel safe only to be told they were missing when he asked for them back two days later. The hotel was also filthy. After breakfast one morning, we were about to pile into the hire car and set off for the training school when Don Burton, one of the F/Es, said,

"Hang on a minute chaps. I need to go back to my room, I have forgotten my sim pass." He disappeared and returned five minutes later white-faced.

"You won't believe this. When I get back to my room, housekeeping is stripping my bed. The bloody mattress is crawling with bugs and lice."

Amanda came out to visit towards the end of the course and I used to let her take the hire car once she had dropped us off at the training centre each day. She was four months pregnant with Henry at the time but keen to have a look around and do some shopping etc., rather than stay in the hotel all day. She got lost one day when returning to the hotel and took a wrong turn off the freeway, ending up in the Cuban quarter. Fortunately, a police patrol car, noticing that her car had tourist rental plates and that she was heading for a dangerous area, followed her as she took the turn. At the first traffic lights, they flashed her and pulled her over. One of the cops sauntered over to her car, hand on his pistol, bent down and spoke through the window.

"Ma'am, lock your doors, follow us closely and do not under any circumstances stop at any traffic lights. If they are red, just follow us close behind. Even we don't patrol in this area," he said.

* * * *

My bedside phone rang and I reached over to pick it up. Dave Heath my F/O was on the other end.

"Turn the TV on," he said.

"Piss off, Dave. I'm in bed. What time is it anyway?" I replied.

"Never mind. Turn the TV on," he repeated. And so began 9/11 for me.

We were in the Dorint hotel in Freising, a small town not far from Munich airport, at the end of the night's work. Having checked into the hotel and had a couple of beers over a late breakfast, we crashed for the day. So far, so normal. Dave's phone call woke me at around 2 pm and normality ended. I switched the TV on and watched as the terrible events of the day unfolded live on air. I watched the aircraft hit the twin towers, smashing into the buildings on that beautiful September morning; the confused TV anchormen trying to make sense of it all; the panicking crowds in Manhattan; the billowing clouds of dust and the final collapse of the towers. Truly a terrible day and one that everyone remembers where they were when it happened - like Kennedy's assassination or the Challenger space shuttle explosion. Although we usually slept in as long as possible on these day stops ahead of the night's flying it was impossible on this day; like millions of others, I watched the TV, transfixed and unable to tear myself away from the unfolding events.

When we got to the airport for the evening's work, the security was intense and all three of us were subdued and tired from not getting enough sleep. Suddenly life was different; the atmosphere everywhere was one of threat and danger. That evening we transited through East Midlands Airport. In the crew room, all the talk was of the attacks and how this was going to affect us as a cargo airline and I began to wonder – how much of the cargo that we carry is properly screened and vetted? Just how easy would it be to hide explosives in a ULD and bring us down? Can we rely on bombed cargo aircraft not having the headline impact of a bombed passenger aircraft and so not worth targeting – or not? An airliner bombing had happened only thirteen years earlier at Lockerbie and that now seemed minor in comparison.

We changed aircraft at East Midlands for the run through to Shannon where the night's work ended. Shannon airport was an incredible sight, packed with mostly American airliners, Delta, TWA, United, American, Northwest, you name it. 747s, DC-10s, Airbuses, L1011s, all types of aircraft. All aircraft flying either in the US or inbound to the US had been ordered by the FAA to land at the nearest suitable airport. US airspace was in lockdown. For a lot of aircraft on the Atlantic run, at that time of day westbound from Europe to the US, the nearest suitable airport was Shannon. A lot of fuel was dumped that morning as aircraft reduced weight to land so prematurely. The ramp was jam-packed, an amazing sight but for all the wrong reasons.

* * * *

Flying for a cargo airline has its advantages and taking passengers along is one of them. Happily, cargo airlines are exempt from the locked cockpit door requirement that was introduced to all passenger jets after 9/11 so passengers could sit in our flight decks without restriction. On the French Post/FedEx routes we routinely took families from Paris to Ajaccio in Corsica for their summer holidays. As long as they had some connection to a French Post employee (sometimes I suspect a pretty loose connection) the company allowed them to travel for free. Mum, Dad and maybe a couple of kids with buckets and spades would board at the last minute before the doors closed and sit either in the four passenger seats behind the flight deck or in the flight deck itself, whichever they preferred.

On one flight, a young couple was taking advantage of this amicable arrangement. They board the aircraft in Paris, as usual, and decide to sit in the passenger area just behind the flight deck where there were four or five seats. Halfway into the flight and, fancying a cup of tea, I turn around to Chris Jervis, the F/E that evening.

"Any chance of a brew, Chris?"

He leaves his panel and walks back to the galley to the hot cup. Seconds later he's back, shutting the cockpit door firmly behind him.

"Bloody hell, shipmate,'" he splutters, "they are bloody at it back there! She's…you know..…"

I'd never thought it was possible to shock Chris being an ex-Navy man but he was clearly taken aback. I roared with laughter.

"Good for them, why not? Anyway, more importantly, where's my brew?" It was only a forty-minute flight from Paris to Marseilles but they had decided to take the opportunity in the dark to join the mile-high club never expecting interruptions - especially from a flight engineer.

I decided that it would be fun for Henry to come along on a flight one night. He was six at the time so old enough to enjoy the experience. The principal French Post/FedEx line started in Dublin before routeing to Ajaccio via Stansted, Paris and Marseilles. The two companies worked in partnership so the Dublin-Stansted-Paris sector was a FedEx run and the Paris-Marseilles-Ajaccio sectors were for French Post. With approval for Henry to come along on the flight from ACL's Chief Pilot Con Murphy, Henry and I flew on Ryanair to Dublin for me to start my week's work. Amanda would collect Henry in Stansted and they would drive home together while I carried on to Paris.

After a night in the Dublin airport hotel, we made our way through security nice and early so I could show Henry around the aircraft. Later the other crew members, Werner and Paul, arrived and with Henry safely sitting in the centre jump seat with a good view of everything, we set off. It was a beautiful clear night and you could see for miles but the long day and the excitement were proving too much for Henry. Just before landing into Stansted, he was nodding forward into his straps, fast asleep.

* * * *

The final few years with ACL were spent flying on contract for French Post/FedEx in the Airbus A300. The end of one of the routes we flew on this contract ended in Ajaccio in Corsica, as mentioned above. We stayed in the lovely Sofitel resort a few miles down the coast from the airport and had use of a little French Post van to run around in. We would arrive at the hotel at around 6.30 am, sleep a few hours, get up for lunch and then have an afternoon siesta before driving to the airport for the night's work.

Corsica is a lovely island with the best beaches in the Mediterranean but its reputation as a bandit island is well justified. The Corsicans see themselves as different to the French, who they view as an occupying force. You could say they have always been troublesome; Napoleon himself was Corsican. Their dislike of French authority is evidenced by road signs that are holed with shotgun blasts, re-written in the Corsican language (which has a heavy Tuscan and Sardinian influence) and the occasional bombed post office - not encouraging news for us as crews of a French Post aircraft! We had half a dozen favourite restaurants for lunch, one of which was a small place overlooking the beach about two miles down the coast from the hotel. Over the time we were on this route, we got to know the guys in this restaurant and they looked after us well. One day the three of us turned up as usual and noticed several black limousines parked outside in the small car park next to the beach. Unusual, we thought. Anyway, undeterred, we walked up the stairs to the restaurant and I pushed the front door to open it as usual. Strangely, it was locked but we could see there were several people seated at the tables inside, all big and in dark suits and dark glasses who ignored the figure of me staring in. It was like a scene from 'The Godfather'. The 'maitre de' spotted me with my face pressed to the glass and walked towards the door. He looked uncomfortable.

"Monsieur," he whispered as he opened the door, "I am sorry but the restaurant is closed today….."

Henry on his Airbus trip

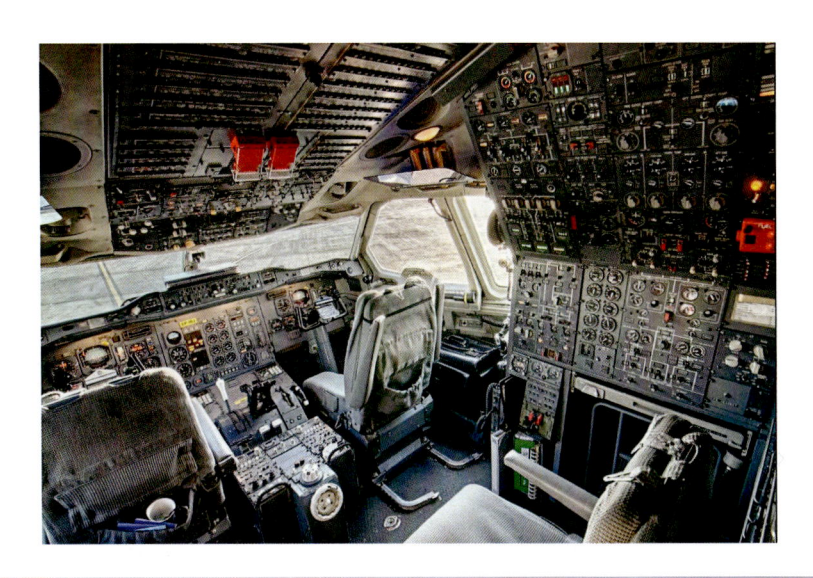

A300 flight deck and a French Post A300 in Ajaccio, F/E Chris Jervis beneath

He shrugged and looked meaningfully over his shoulder as his voice trailed off. He didn't need to explain – we could take a hint. This looked like a meeting of the Families and the restaurant was closed for a working lunch. Time to try another of our favourite spots.

BP

It was time to move on from ACL. Ten years of flying nights were starting to take its toll and I was finding that the twelve-hour change in sleep pattern that was required every eight days meant that I couldn't sleep properly either at work or at home. I was getting tired and aware that working nights was not a healthy existence. So, as much as I was enjoying the flying with ACL, when I got an opportunity to go back to my first love of corporate flying, this time flying for the oil giant BP, I grabbed it with both hands. Airline flying is fine but by its nature is relatively undemanding and doesn't stretch one's thinking. Our biggest decisions at ACL generally revolved around which restaurant to go to for lunch. Such is airline flying; time to get back to flying that demanded more of me.

Lord Browne, the chairman of BP, had use of a Gulfstream GV that the company had inherited from Amoco when the two companies merged in 1998 (at $48bn, it was at the time the world's biggest merger ever). The aircraft was in mint condition and Lord Browne absolutely loved it. Like a lot of top-level businessmen, it represented a haven of peace and tranquillity away from the demands of everyday corporate life and, like other CEOs, you could see him visibly relax as he boarded the aircraft. He loved fine wine, fine food and expensive cigars and we ensured we were well-stocked with them all. Our brief was to source the catering from the best restaurants in whichever city we flew to, so naturally we ate very well too as we always made it our task to track down the nearest Michelin-starred restaurant. After years of eating stale sandwiches stuffed into my flight bag and drinking disgusting aircraft tea, now I was eating sushi and fillet steak at 45,000ft.

The GV is a long-range, 6500 nm jet. Ours was well equipped with a full crew rest area and a hot water shower for Lord Browne. London to Los Angeles or Singapore was possible and we flew to both and everywhere in between.

A lot of the flights were to the US, typically Chicago, New York, Houston and Alaska. Oman, Borneo, Beijing and Dubai were other frequent destinations. Lord Browne had an interest in the famous Staglin vineyard in Napa Valley, so we visited there from time to time which was no particular hardship, as Napa offers some of the prettiest countryside in California.

We visited some more remote places too. One such place was Biak in Indonesia, where BP had some offshore oil and gas interests. Frans Kaisiepo International Airport had a well-maintained 11,500ft east-west runway with an ILS on one end. It was kept operational as a refuelling stop for Garuda the national airline and also, I'm guessing, for the Indonesian Air Force. That's as far as familiar western technology went in Biak, however. After landing and putting the aircraft to bed for the night, we asked the local BP agent about the accommodation. It turned out that there was a safe house where we could sleep but we were warned not to go into the nearest town at night as this was a lawless region, plagued with mosquitos and not safe after dark. So naturally, in the tradition of all crews, we planned to get a lift into town as soon as possible. 'Town' is a generous term for what was a collection of wooden houses and dirt roads. The other captain with me was Terry, the lead pilot of the operation and the engineer/steward the excellent Nigel Wall. BP wanted to carry an engineer (known in the industry as a 'flying spanner') on all flights to take care of the aircraft. Coming from a world of somewhat different flight engineers, I was amazed that Terry could find two engineers that could both maintain the aircraft and also conduct a first-class service in the cabin. Nigel, and the other engineer Stuart Barrow, were excellent at both tasks; Lord Browne got on well with them in the cabin, trusted them and they were both very experienced Gulfstream engineers. Terry was known as 'Techno Terry' as he always carried two or three Blackberrys everywhere he went and prided himself on being connected all the time on any network. This place was a challenge, however.

"I can't get a signal," he said in puzzlement on the way to the wooden lodge accommodation that would be our accommodation for the night, waving his Blackberry around in the bus in a desperate attempt to find service.

"Terry," Nigel said at last, exasperated, "they have barely seen the bloody wheel here, never mind having a cellphone service!"

BP's Gulfstream V, VP-BEP

It was true. Walking around near our lodge house before we set off to the town, we looked at the locals who lived like Neolithic man, barefoot, dressed in loincloths, living in huts made from palm leaves and cooking in iron pots on an open fire. It was like going back 5,000 years apart from some plastic utensils. They stared at us with curiosity and friendly, toothless grins. We hitched a lift into town after sunset, ignoring the dire warnings from the agent. It was hot and humid and, he was right, the mosquitos were out in force. The town was rough and the atmosphere not too friendly. Not to be deterred we found a bar, signified by a single neon strip that said 'BAR' and walked in. Being a seasoned crew, we didn't miss this subtle clue. Inside was a dirt floor with a crude wooden bar at one end and maybe twenty local men drinking bottled beer served from crates behind the bar. Understandably, it went quiet as we walked in, as strangers were a rare sight in this town. The men stared at us as we walked to the bar. I bought a crate of Amstel as it seemed simpler to point to a crate and hand over $20 rather than get involved in a small order. Warm beers in hand, Nigel and I had a look around while Terry was heads-down still trying to get a signal on his phone. I had to give him full marks for trying. We noticed some of the men going through a bead curtain at the back of the bar and then coming back a short while after with stupid grins on their faces.

"What's going on back there?" Nigel asked.

"No idea," I replied, "Why don't you go and find out?"

Nigel put his beer down on the bar. "OK, I'm off," he said and went through the curtain. Two minutes later he came back shaking with laughter.

"There's a bloody brothel back there with the ugliest mooses I have ever seen! Absolute fucking gorillas!" He glanced along the filthy wooden bar, a worried look on his face.

"Hey, hang on a minute, who's pinched my beer?" I pointed to a tiny wizened old man, who was sitting on the filthy floor, grinning from ear to ear, pointing and laughing at Nigel.

"I think it's him." In his hand, he had a bottle of Amstel that he hadn't had minutes before. He must have swiped it from the bar when we weren't looking.

"Bloody typical," fumed Nigel, "I turn my back for two minutes and a sodding pygmy steals my beer!"

* * * *

This wonderful job came to an end when the new CEO, Tony Hayward, decided to sell the aircraft and use NetJets for their corporate transportation needs. This decision was in part due to an expensive incident with the aircraft at Biggin Hill. One of the handling agent's less-than-clever minions was pushing the aircraft up a slight incline using a tug and tow bar that weren't up to the task. The aircraft was around a quarter full of fuel so weighed about 60,000 lbs. As the tug strained against the load, suddenly the tow bar shear pin broke and the tug careered forwards and then sideways into the aircraft, the sharp metal roof over the cab puncturing the fuselage of the Gulfstream, right through the pressure hull. It could have been still worse as the tug driver, in desperation, threw a heavy rubber chock under the main wheels in an attempt to stop the aircraft rolling. The chock compressed under the weight of the empty aircraft and pinged clear, luckily sideways – had it pinged upwards it could have punctured the wing tank and there would have been an uncontrollable fuel leak too. After a damage assessment by Gulfstream and a metal plate fitted over the fuselage hole, we ferried the aircraft to the Gulfstream factory in Savannah where it stayed for three months undergoing extensive repairs. Despite insurance, the final repair bill was huge and BP decided to sell the aircraft.

The family, with VP-BEP, at Farnborough

TAG AVIATION

So ended a couple of years of great flying but, as often happens, one door closing opens another. I was lucky to be offered the position of Chief Pilot with TAG Aviation early in 2008 and started there that April. Unfortunately, 2008 was the start of the worldwide financial crisis and my priority as CP was to try and keep pilots in jobs as owners either sold their jets or the banks repossessed them. Consequently, I didn't have a TAG aircraft assigned to me until October 2009 but during these eighteen months I did some freelance flying wherever I could so as to keep current on the jets I was rated on at the time, the Gulfstream V and 550.

One company that offered me some flying was International Jet Club, who operated several Gulfstream 550s for private owners and, like TAG, was also based at Farnborough. I got a call from the Ops Manager there one day, whom I knew from Interflight days, to see if I could crew a 550 for three days' flying to the Caribbean. This was to be with a pal of mine, Colin Darrah, so I was very happy to accept. Colin is a first-rate guy, one of the best in the business, relaxed, humorous, open and far ahead of the game. On this flight, we were flying privately for the aircraft owner and so we didn't have the duty time protection of a commercial operation. The owner was an Irish billionaire whose business interests included cellular networks throughout the Caribbean and Pacific. He lived in Dublin and liked to travel a lot during the week but be home to his family at weekends and so was a great owner to fly for. Although he worked his crew hard, it was mostly Mondays to Fridays with weekends off.

Colin and I positioned the Gulfstream over to Dublin for the flight the following day to Tegucigalpa in Honduras. Tegucigalpa is a notoriously demanding airport, in the mountains 3300ft above sea level and rated as one of the most dangerous in the world. The landing to the northerly runway is tricky and requires very good terrain awareness and speed control off a curved arrival. Although improved in recent years, the final approach, onto a shortish 6,600ft runway, was over a ridge of high ground which was cleared by only 100ft or so with local kids waving and filming. After clearing the ridge, it was necessary to drop down onto the runway without gaining extra speed. It required careful flying (and still does) and in the day was a popular hit on YouTube. For some reason, neither of us had slept well at all in Dublin the night before the flight so we both started the day tired. Tiredness and fatigue are very insidious and can be hazardous in this business. Managing your rest is the biggest challenge in long-range flying; crack that and it's easy enough, otherwise it's a struggle. This story is a good example of fatigue.

The flight to Tegucigalpa, with Colin flying (as he knew Tegucigalpa well), was around ten hours and uneventful. Fortunately, the weather was fine, a little misty but good enough for a visual approach and we negotiated the famous ridge and landed safely. Tired but OK. The owner then dropped a bombshell.

Tegucigalpa Airport showing the famous ridge just before the runway

"Lads," he said in his Dublin lilt, "I need you to plan for a flight to Trinidad. I need about three hours here then we'll go, OK?" and off he went. Colin and I looked at each other wearily – we had been expecting to stop in Tegucigalpa. I did the usual mental flight plan; Trinidad (Port of Spain) had to be another three hours or so. When the owner left, we went back to the cockpit and ran a quick plan on the FMS. It came out at 3:15 hours. God, this was going to end up being a very long day! We left the APU running and tried to nap in the aircraft for a bit while the owner was away but not with much success, both of us were overtired and restless and the airport was noisy.

True to his word, the owner arrived three hours later and we started up and set off for Port of Spain with me in the left seat this time. Towards the end of the flight, we were getting really tired. Colin looked across at me.

"Mate, I'm knackered. Can I suggest we get this aircraft on the ground as soon as we can?" I agreed, we were both running out of mental capacity to deal with any extra workload, should that arise.

The night was clear and the air smooth, so I increased the speed to 0.87m. I felt like I had a tight band around my head and my vision was gritty and bleary. Worse the sun was coming up through a lemon-coloured sky which, for me anyway, always makes me feel more tired not more alert. I was thinking through a fog. We asked our flight attendant, Ali, to sit on the jump seat to keep an eye on us and feed us coffee, water or tell jokes; anything to keep us alert. Three hours and eighteen minutes later we landed in Trinidad, after a straight-in approach as we were the only movement in the early hours. We taxied to the parking stand, shut down and the owner disembarked.

"Thanks, lads, I appreciate it. We'll be leaving the day after tomorrow. Have dinner on me tonight," and with that, he slipped us 100 Euros each.

He was aware we were dog-tired and the gesture was nice. By the time we left for the hotel, having tidied up and secured the aircraft, the total 'on duty' time, after the fitful night in Dublin, was over nineteen hours but over forty hours since we had slept properly.

I did one more flight for this owner which involved flying by airline to Singapore to pick up a trip following a crew swap. This was a fabulous trip, taking in Papua New Guinea, the Solomon Islands, Tonga, New Caledonia, Vanuatu, Fiji, the Cook Islands and ending up in Tahiti. It was a tiring trip done at the owner's usual breakneck speed with minimum rest in each place, as well as crossing the International Date Line which is very disorientating. This trip was my first experience of the Pacific and its immense size. The last sector was from Tahiti to Vancouver, for the next crew swap. This took nine hours all of which was over water with no land in sight. Once you have flown the Pacific you never look at the Atlantic in the same way again.

* * * *

Occasionally the Home Office has someone in their care, courtesy of HM Prison Service, that they are more than keen to expel from the UK. In August 2013 TAG accepted a charter on my Falcon 7X to repatriate a 'lifer' in Wakefield Prison to his home country, Surinam. The Home Office had approached KLM which was the only airline with a twice-weekly service to the capital Paramaribo, because of the Dutch colonial connection, but they didn't want to get involved when they heard more about the prisoner, so the Home Office approached TAG. This prisoner was bad. We found out he had killed someone outside a nightclub in London and while in Wakefield, (which is a high-security Category A prison for the real nasties who are deemed 'highly dangerous'; ie murderers, rapists and the like), he had tried to kill a prison officer with the favoured weapon of the con; a plastic toilet brush, melted, fashioned into a point and allowed to harden again. Wakefield Prison is known in prison circles as 'Monster Mansion' and has been home to a lot of household names over the years, truly a house of horrors.

"How do you feel about this?" I asked my friend Pascal Balin who was to fly with me as co-captain.

"Phhh," he gave a Gallic shrug, "I do not know. He could be a crazy bastard, you know." My thoughts exactly.

The Home Office told us that the prisoner would be shackled the whole way across to Paramaribo and would be escorted by four security guards. There would also be a Home Office representative and a medic with a sedative in case the prisoner got excited. What can possibly go wrong?

"Here's my ideas," I said to Pascal. "I suggest that we go through the aircraft and remove anything that could possibly be used as a weapon. Especially in the rear toilet. Basically, remove everything and move the first aid kit and fire extinguishers forward."

Pascal nodded. "I think we should take a male flight attendant also," he remarked which seemed a good idea. It would be just our luck that this guy got amorous mid-ocean. Mark Hollands-Martel, TAG's Head of Cabin Services and known to all as Mark H-M, agreed to come along as the F/A. He was a very experienced guy, so I knew we were in good hands down the back.

The day of the flight arrived and we met the lady from the Home Office, the medic and the security guards at Farnborough.

"So, what will happen when we get to Paramaribo?" I asked her out of curiosity, after the initial pleasantries.

"Oh, don't worry, it's all been arranged. The Surinamese authorities will meet us on arrival to escort the prisoner away," she reassured me. Fair enough. The security guards were big, tough-looking guys and I wondered who was scarier, these guys or the prisoner himself, anyway we would find out soon enough.

Off we went to Leeds-Bradford Airport, which was the closest airport to Wakefield, about fourteen miles by road. We parked in the corner of the east apron and awaited events. Soon we were aware of a police helicopter overhead and then police cars arrived on the apron. Shortly afterwards the prison van with blacked-out windows drove onto the apron, complete with a motorcycle escort, and pulled up close to the aircraft. We were impressed, this guy was getting the treatment all right, and the police were obviously taking no chances. The four security guards had a conflab with the police officers and were drawing up a plan as to how they would manage the transfer of the prisoner. The helicopter was still buzzing overhead and by now quite a crowd had assembled at the wire security fence and was watching events closely. I guessed that there had been some coverage in the local media.

Finally, the moment arrived and we got a close look at our VIP passenger and companion for the next ten hours or so. The rear doors to the police van opened and he stepped out. He was a burly black guy, probably seventeen stone. He was wearing an orange jumpsuit and was handcuffed, had his feet shackled together and was also padlocked to two prison officers. We made direct eye contact and he smiled slightly; I felt a shiver. With some shuffling, he managed to make it up the steps and into the aircraft where the four security guards walked him to the rear of the aircraft and onto the right-side divan as agreed. There were to be two guards opposite on the other divan and one on either side of him and he would remain shackled for the whole of the flight.

"What happens when he wants to use the toilet in flight?" was one of my questions at the briefing we had together before leaving Farnborough.

"Don't worry we will accompany him into the toilet, he will never be on his own."

Let's hope so, I thought having seen him; I didn't want this guy breaking loose down the back mid-Atlantic. Anyway, with everyone settled on board, we closed up, started engines and departed. I imagined the prison officers we left behind at the airport were pleased to see the back of him, although there were probably plenty more like him back at Monster Mansion.

The flight was around nine hours and uneventful. The prisoner was good as gold, seemingly enjoying himself. I realised that he was perhaps not 'the full picnic' which somehow made him all the more sinister. However, at the start of the approach into Paramaribo's Zandery airport, when we extended the slat/flaps to the Slat/Flap 1 position, we got a CAS showing that the inboard slats had failed to extend. Not a big deal for landing with a little extra speed but a no-go for departure. I was reminded of the last thing Barry, our maintenance Fleet Manager, had said before we left Farnborough, half joking, "Do not break down!" You can imagine the content of my phone call to Barry with the news we were AOG. It was a nightmare to get the Dassault engineers to Paramaribo with the spare part but that's another story.

We landed and taxied to the ramp. I had seldom seen such a sleepy airport. It was situated in the middle of the equatorial jungle about twenty-eight miles south of the capital. Nothing was moving in the damp heat. ATC seemed asleep and uninterested in us now we had landed so we taxied to where we thought was a good spot and shut down. The prisoner had been allowed to change during the flight into jeans and a tee shirt and was sitting quietly in his seat, like a good boy. Mark H-M opened the main door and the jungle heat hit us. I deplaned and took a look around – so where was the promised reception committee? There was no one taking any interest in our arrival. In the distance, there was a bored airport security man scratching his backside but no one else was in sight.

"So, what do we do now? Where is everyone?" I asked the lady from the Home Office.

She looked confused and a little embarrassed, clearly there had been a breakdown in communication somewhere. There was no sign of the promised reception committee of Surinamese officials. It was good to see and no surprise, that even at supposedly high Government level there are cock-ups too.

"Well," she said hesitantly, "I suppose he can go. He's done his time and he's back on home territory, so our job is done."

The prisoner walked down the steps and hesitated, seemingly uncertain of what to do next. He made a great show of thanking us for the flight (how many cons get a flight home by private jet?), smiled broadly and shook our hands, offered bear hugs and said he wanted to keep in touch with everyone. So, naturally, I gave him Pascal's email address. The last I saw of him was a lone figure loping across the deserted apron to freedom in a new T-shirt and trainers and clutching a small rucksack with his worldly possessions. I suspected it wouldn't be long before he was arrested again, knowing his previous behaviour.

The prisoner, centre, with minders and Pascal, right, in Paramaribo

* * * *

The Falcon 7X we used for this flight was first and foremost a charter aircraft and the preceding story was just one of several charters we undertook. I managed the aircraft for four years overall. It was owned by a very wealthy Saudi family who, it seems, had bought it almost as an afterthought, an addition to their fleet of other aircraft. Having bought it, they gave it to TAG to manage and earn money by chartering. They weren't interested in using the aircraft for themselves other than maybe twice a year when they wanted to fly from Riyadh to Casablanca return, probably just to see that we were looking after their asset as much as anything else. The result of this was that we had some great charter trips, to the Caribbean, Africa and the USA sometimes for a week or two. It was almost always south or west, seldom east or north which suited us just fine.

One of the most important clients that TAG had was the giant Japan Tobacco International and we picked up several charters for this company to Tanzania, Uganda, South Africa, Mozambique and other tobacco-growing regions in Africa. The Japanese executives were hard-drinking guys who also enjoyed their tobacco products in the cabin. We were continually impressed at the amount of whisky they could down and still function enough to attend meetings. Had any of us drunk that amount, we'd have been wrecked for days.

So, to an unusual experience in Joburg. We had seen from the Gen Dec that the lead passenger had his birthday in a couple of days so we decided, as the aircraft was out of whisky anyway, to restock with some special whisky as a birthday gift for him – all in the interests of client relationships etc. Nick, Frankie (the flight attendant) and I were staying at the Michelangelo Hotel in downtown Joburg and asked the concierge for the best place to go to get some decent whisky.

"I know the place. I'll arrange for a bus for you, leave it to me. Is 2 pm ok for you?" asks the concierge. Sure, why not, so at two o'clock we head to the hotel car park and pile into the dented Nissan minivan and head off. We have no idea where we are going not knowing the local area but I can see that the area isn't that good even by Joburg standards. And it gets worse. We look at each other.

"Where the hell is he taking us?" asks Frankie nervously.

"I have no idea, let's see," I venture. And then I see on my phone map that we are in Soweto, the rough and notorious township to the west of Joburg's city centre. A few minutes later the driver pulls up outside a Makro liquor outlet.

We look at each other. "Jeez, look at this lot," says Nick.

He is looking out of the window at the guards posted outside the store, all armed with pump action shotguns, baseball caps and flak jackets. The store itself is surrounded by barbed wire and grills. This is a different world. We get out of the van and enter the store. Inside there is a middle-aged white South African woman who turns out to be the store manager. "What are you guys doing here?" she asks in astonishment, "I haven't had any white guys in here for a while!" We look around and sure enough, the shop and the area outside is full of local black guys. We explain what we are looking for, i.e. fine whiskey, and she takes us to a cabinet that is heavily barred and padlocked. Inside is an amazing selection of very expensive Scotch and Japanese whiskeys – actually the best selection I have ever seen with prices to match at £200-300 a bottle. The hotel concierge was right after all. We select a couple of vintage Suntory single malts and a 50-year-old Glenfiddich and move towards the checkout to pay. The manager accompanies us. "I'll authorise them to buy these," she says to the cashier as he looks at us suspiciously. There is another security guard also armed with a pump action shotgun at the till watching everyone carefully. The atmosphere is less than friendly so we pay quickly, say goodbye to the manager and move outside swiftly to the relative safety of the minivan, moving quickly through the crowds with the bottles hidden under a coat. We pile back into the van and slam the door shut. "Back to the Michelangelo, please! Quick as you can," I say to the driver and we grind off up the hill.

Falcon 7X at Farnborough

* * * *

    In May 2011, I am on a charter trip to India. I am with flying with Graeme Pollard and Louise Barton who is a freelance F/A for the ten days. It's an amazing trip taking in Dehli, Jaipur, Varanasi and Udaipur. India is an incredible country, frustrating and beautiful in equal measure but nowhere else hits the senses in the same way. Loud colours, smells, teeming crowds and terrible poverty mix with luxury and extreme wealth. It's a country that cannot be described adequately in words; it must be visited to be experienced properly.

    We land in the 7X at Udaipur airport, Rajasthan, in the early evening and park the aircraft on the main ramp. It's a sleepy airport. There is one Boeing 737 belonging to a local airline parked next to us and not much else. With the handling agent, I escort the two passengers, a wealthy Italian couple, through the new terminal building, see them into their taxi and return to the aircraft to help with the tidying up. After a long flight, it always takes at least one hour to sort out the cabin, complete the post-flight items and generally husband the aircraft. Eventually, we are finished and, leaving the aircraft properly chocked and with the brakes off as is customary, we set off for the hotel. I leave the big green "BRAKES OFF" sign in the cockpit window so there is no doubt to anyone that the parking brake is released so that in an emergency the aircraft could be towed to another position. We have booked rooms at the Lake Palace hotel, surely one of the most beautiful hotels in the world, a marble palace set in the middle of Lake Pichola. We spend two nights there and it is everything we expected, a fabulous experience.

    On the third day, we return to the airport in the morning for the flight to Varanasi. The following day, we would be heading back to Cuneo in northwest Italy. With the help of the handling agent, we navigate our way through the usual bureaucracy in the terminal and make our way airside. I look at the aircraft in the distance and stop dead. The aircraft is parked, where we left it three days previously, but I can see there are no chocks in place under the wheels. My blood turns to ice.

    "What has happened to the chocks! Where are they? How long has the aircraft been without chocks?" I shout at the agent.

The fabulous Lake Palace Hotel, Udaipur

The aircraft is completely unprotected and, worse, is on a slight gradient on the ramp that I hadn't noticed previously. The slightest disturbance from a gust of wind or jet blast and eighteen tonnes of empty aircraft would start moving and once underway nothing would stop it. $50m of Dassault high technology would end up in the ditch.

"Where are the bloody chocks?" I yell again at the agent. "Get some - now!"

The agent reverts to the default Indian defensive position, obsequious and head shaking.

"I am sorry, sir. I am wanting to assist you but we have no more chocks, sir. I am only having chocks for one aircraft, isn't it?"

I look at a NetJets Gulfstream that is parked next to us. Its chocks look suspiciously like the ones we had placed under our wheels – if the airport only has one set of chocks then either that crew or the agent must have pinched them from us.

"Those are our chocks on the Gulfstream! Are you telling me you took ours away and gave them to that crew? You knew we had released the brakes and there's a sign in the bloody window to tell you for fuck's sake! Get a piece of wood then, anything."

I'm yelling at him because I'm nervous. I'd be happy to use his head as a chock at this stage. After all, it's my signature in the Tech Log so I am 100% responsible for the safety of the aircraft no matter whose fault it might be. I think about opening the main door to get access to the cockpit to reset the brakes but decide against it - what if even that slight disturbance sets the aircraft moving? The agent shakes his head in Indian affirmation and runs off. Two minutes later he is back with two pieces of 4x4 wood. I check them carefully for nails then place them either side of the main wheels. I can start breathing again, the aircraft is safe.

* * * *

A similar event happened to me in the Learjet in Prague years before. We had landed and taxied to a remote parking area reserved for private aircraft and were spending the usual hour or so tidying up the aircraft and putting the engine and probes covers on. From a distance, but not up close, you could see that the ground fell away very slightly behind the aircraft towards a drainage ditch. The only chocks the handling agent had available were small wooden nosewheel chocks and these were in place before the parking brake was released. As is normal practice, we dumped all the hydraulic pressure before closing the aircraft up. I had completed my final walk round and was about to get in the crew van when I noticed that the chock behind the nose wheel had shifted somehow and was no longer holding the nose wheel in place. Was it my imagination or was the aircraft very, very slowly creeping backwards? I wasn't about to wait to find out. It is amazing how quickly you can move when your adrenaline is pumping. As with the incident at Udaipur, I had visions of the aircraft sitting nose high in the ditch if I didn't act immediately. I dropped everything, leapt to the main door, unlocked it and opened both halves of the clamshell door. I threw myself into the cockpit, simultaneously flicking on both the batteries and the auxiliary hydraulic pump and stood on the brakes. Unfortunately, it took a few seconds for hydraulic pressure to build again but eventually the brakes bit. The nose of the aircraft lifted slightly as it came to a halt then I set the parking brake and breathed a huge sigh of relief.

* * * *

August 2017. After a few days in Battle Creek, Michigan, where the Falcon has been on maintenance with Duncan Aviation, we have arrived in Las Vegas for a couple of days as the passengers enjoy the delights of the city. Rising late in the morning, I meet my crew for breakfast and afterwards leave the hotel for a walk and to get some fresh air, such as it is in Vegas in the summer heat. It's blistering hot in the sun but it's good to get away from our casino hotel, The Cosmopolitan, that is heaving with tourists and slot machines zombies. After a while, I take a turning onto The Strip and walk west past the famous landmarks - Caesar's Palace, The Bellagio and The Tropicana. Opposite the Luxor hotel there is a large empty arena with hoardings advertising the upcoming 'Route 91 Harvest' music festival and some big names in country music. I walk into the plot through one of the open entry gates and wander around, just killing time. A little way away is the Mandalay Bay hotel shining like a bar of gold. How would I know that four weeks later from a room on the corner of the 32nd floor of the hotel a gunman called Stephen Paddock, holed up with twenty-three semi-automatic weapons and packets of ammunition, will shoot dead fifty-one festival goers and injure countless others in the very spot where I am now standing?

* * * *

"The flight will take about an hour and I'm going to fly at low level. This is a flight where you will definitely want to watch out of the window!"

It's December 2010 and I am flying Amanda, Henry and Eleanor from Male, the main island in the Maldives, to Gan, a small island 310 miles south, right at the southern end of the Maldives island chain. I have just operated a charter flight with four passengers from Paris to Male where they are going to spend the two weeks over Christmas and New Year. Thanks to staff travel with British Airways, Amanda and the kids are coming out to join me which is wonderful. Parking is not available in Male due to the congestion over Christmas and New Year, so it's required to position the aircraft to Gan. This is usual; Male airport gets incredibly busy over this period and if you don't reserve parking months early you always have to reposition elsewhere, typically Gan or somewhere in Sri Lanka. The owners of the aircraft, a Falcon 7X owned by the BG Group, have kindly given me permission for Amanda and the kids to come along with me on this repositioning flight rather than have to take an airline flight to Gan. They arrived in Male on the daily British Airways service around an hour before our arrival from Paris and are waiting for me in the handling agent's office, tired but very excited. Perfect timing. Despite a last-minute uncertainty of the charter due to permit delays, Amanda and I decided the day before that we should take the gamble and they should set off on the BA flight anyway. If the charter cancelled at the last minute, as can happen, and I never make it to Male – well, there are worse places to be stranded for a night before flying back home.

Again, I believe that you have to take opportunities when you can. How many times would I get the opportunity to fly my family in a Falcon across the Indian Ocean? I am determined that they will remember this flight forever so rather than fly at 30,000ft for the flight, I ask TAG Operations to file a flight plan low down, only 10,000ft. Not an efficient altitude but so worth it; the view of the islands from this height is absolutely stunning. The flight to Gan is wonderful and everything I told the family it would be. The Maldive Islands chain is surely one of the few natural landscapes in the world that looks as good in real life as it does on a travel agent's website. From above, the sea has the purest shades of blue from light turquoise to azure to deep, deep blue and scattered everywhere are islands of white sand, some with resorts on and some without. It is so colourful it looks like a colour-enhanced photograph. As we fly south, we pass over one island, miles from any other, with dazzling sand and a diameter of probably a hundred feet. Sometime, years ago, a solitary coconut washed ashore and now, right in the middle of this island is a solitary palm tree. Pure Robinson Crusoe.

* * * *

For the two years we had it under management, I was the CAM on a Gulfstream 550 based in Muscat. The aircraft was made available by the owner

Maldives, with the family, December 2010

for charter and in this role it was a busy aircraft and earned both TAG and the owner good money. Most of the flights were charter flights, just the way I like it; they are much more varied than owner flights which tend to be repetitive, flying to the same old destinations time after time. Charter flights bring challenges and new destinations which I always enjoyed and was one of my reasons for leaving airline life.

In December one year we picked up a lovely charter to St. Lucia for the Christmas and New Year period - December 22nd to January 3rd. Nothing new by way of a destination but perfect for Christmas and New Year. My crew for the trip was Pete McGowan and Frankie Lombardi. Pete was a recently retired

British Airways 757/767 Fleet Captain and all-round good guy. At the time he was flying for the Royal Flight in Bahrain and freelancing for TAG from time to time. Frankie and I had worked together for years on another TAG aircraft. We were a good crew and I was really looking forward to the trip.

Amanda immediately looked into getting British Airways staff travel for her, Henry and Eleanor to fly out and join me and she managed to get seats out on the same day as my flight. Wonderful! Not only that, but the departure time for the BA flight from Gatwick was almost the same as my planned departure time from Farnborough: 1030. If it worked out, we would be paralleling each other over the Atlantic all the way to St. Lucia.

I left our house at 7 am to drive to Farnborough. It was a cold, wet December morning miserable in every sense and as I said goodbye to my family I wondered if this would all really work out as planned. Would our flight cancel at the last minute? It can happen. Would we leave on time? Often passengers are delayed. Would the BA flight leave on time? Would Amanda and the kids even get on the flight? There were so many variables at play.

Arriving at Farnborough at 8 am would give me and my crew two and a half hours to prep the aircraft for the flight. To some people this sounds like a lot of time but it's standard for a long-range flight. There is a lot to do. I like to be fully ready at least thirty minutes before the scheduled departure time and then relax with a coffee. That gives a clear two hours to refuel, load and check the flight plan, sort the cabin, the flight attendant to load the catering and the crew to have their briefing. And that's if the weather is good – in cold weather at least another hour is needed for de-icing etc. You can see, two hours goes by very quickly.

Luckily on this day the six passengers are on time, the bags are loaded and start clearance obtained. We release the brakes at exactly 1030 and as we taxi out, I wonder – are Amanda and the kids leaving on time too with British Airways? We takeoff into a low, grey murk and head west. We obtain our oceanic clearance, coast out over Ireland and start the long oceanic leg to St. Lucia. I am listening out for Amanda's BA flight on the radio but don't hear anything, so I decide to make a blind transmission on the radio on the common 'chat' frequency that's used between aircraft on the North Atlantic.

"Speedbird 2159 this is Golf Sierra Foxtrot, do you read?"

Nothing. I try again and still nothing. I decide to wait for a while before transmitting again. Assuming we left at the same time and from airports close to each other, we can't be that far apart as we fly at the same speed and are going basically the same direction - albeit the BA flight would be on the NAT Tracks to St. Lucia whereas we are flying a more direct route. At 30° West, traditionally the half-way point on the North Atlantic routeings, I try again.

"Speedbird 2159 this is G-SF, do you read?" This time, after a few seconds, I get a faint, crackly, reply. "G-SF, this is Speedbird 2159, go ahead." Bingo, I've made contact!

"Speedbird 2159, G-SF, we are routeing Farnborough to St. Lucia. We just checked 30W at FL 430. I have a request."

"Go ahead," comes the reply.

"I believe you have my wife on board. Her name is Amanda Blois-Brooke and she is travelling with our children. Any chance we could have a quick chat?"

"Standby."

I know what the crew are thinking – they will have to summon the Purser, check if Amanda is on board, get her to the flight deck, against all the rules even though she is a BA employee and then show her how to use a headset and speak to me. Hassle but it's a quiet phase of flight and hopefully they will go along with it if they are decent guys. And they do as five minutes later I hear.

"G-SF I have Amanda for you. Go ahead."

Fantastic! It worked and we have a brief and slightly stilted chat, aware that every aircraft within two hundred miles will be able to listen in to our chat on this open frequency. After a few minutes we say our goodbyes; I thank the BA crew for their cooperation and sign off.

Five hours later I arrive with Pete and Frankie at the hotel in St. Lucia and there in the lobby are Amanda, Henry and Els waiting for me. I had last seen them thirteen hours earlier at our front door during the early hours of a dismal December morning and now we are all together again in warm sunshine having chatted by radio on the way over the Atlantic. How many things had to slot together to get that to work? A unique experience unlikely ever to be repeated.

* * * *

2020. The year of COVID-19. Within a short time into the new year, life as everyone knew it changed in ways unimaginable only weeks before. The virus - which everyone assumed was another SARS and would stay in the Far East - spread rapidly around the world. The virus affected the global aviation industry in a way that was unprecedented, worse even than 9/11. Passenger demand fell off a cliff as populations were ordered to stay at home, airlines put entire fleets into long-term storage and airports closed. Thousands of aircraft sat on aprons and taxiways all over the world awaiting an increase in demand. A silence descended on the world. The sky was bereft of aircraft and contrails and the resulting quiet symbolised the damaging effect on the industry and the colossal cost to countries whose economies were now running 20% below normal levels and who were running up huge debts to support ailing industries.

The business aviation limped on but the flying was reduced by a huge margin as demand for charter flights fell away and owners found fewer and fewer countries that would accept their aircraft. Their travel options shrank quickly. A lot of crews were furloughed by their owners or asked to accept large pay cuts and their aircraft were put into storage. Luckily on the private Falcon 7X I was managing at the time, we escaped these draconian cuts and we kept flight-ready throughout. We managed to accomplish some flights during this period.

In April the family owners requested a flight to collect boxes of medication from Germany and drop some of the consignment off in Geneva for some family members there, before returning to Farnborough with the remaining stock. With country borders closed to road traffic, using their aircraft was the only option. Ceri Williams and I were the rostered crew for the flight and we met at Farnborough at 8.30 am for a chat and coffee before the 10 am departure time. The airport was in near shutdown with only six to seven movements expected for the whole day – and we accounted for two of those. There was a dreamlike stillness to everything; it was a strange and oddly distracting atmosphere. We had decided to operate without a flight attendant, just the two of us, in order to maintain some isolation and reduce unnecessary close contact with others.

The medication was being prepared by a specialist clinic. We departed

Farnborough on time and set course for Baden-Baden the nearest airport to the hospital. The flight over was quiet with air traffic levels at a fraction of normal European levels. Usually, you would see aircraft everywhere, either physically or by their distant contrails; on that day we saw one aircraft way off in the distance. We arrived at a deserted Baden-Baden airport and taxied to the FBO to collect the packages. The police and handling agent were all masked to the full and formalities were kept to the minimum. I collected the boxes, threw them into the cabin, closed the door and we started engines for the short hop to Geneva.

Geneva is normally a very busy airport situated at the southern end of Lake Geneva in the foothills of the Alps. In normal circumstances there is either a landing or departure every ninety seconds and fifteen million passengers a year pass through the airport. We had another eerily quiet flight across from Baden-Baden and were cleared to land miles out on final approach as there was literally no other traffic. For the hour we were on the ground sorting out which parts of the consignment needed to be offloaded we saw just one other aircraft movement where normally there would be forty. An unworldly still hung over the airport with Swiss and easyJet aircraft lined up parked, their engines wrapped in plastic for storage.

The flight back to the UK was the same as the outbound flight. Not an aircraft in sight and ATC almost silent apart from clearing us on direct routeings that we would never normally be granted. We were quiet, lost in our own thoughts.

"Have you noticed how smooth the air is?" Ceri asked me after a while as we continue westwards.

I looked out of the window at the blue sky and nodded. He was right, the air was like silk. Chance, or because of the reduced traffic? At the time, no one knew how this crisis would pan out. However, at the time of writing, the travel industry is almost back to pre-pandemic levels and air traffic, in Europe at least, is back to normal levels. The Covid pandemic was a strange and unsettling time, happily now consigned to history.

TIGER MOTH

The Tiger Moth is a training aircraft that was used by the RAF for basic instruction during the 1930s. Nearly 9,000 were built and flown in the UK and Empire countries. It was the principal trainer for all aircrew pilots up to and during the Second World War. After the war there was a huge surplus of these aircraft, many of which were literally burned – rumours abound of serviceable Tigers being available for as little as £25 in 1945. The Tiger Moth was developed in 1931 from the Gipsy Moth which was known for the long-distance flights made famous by the likes of Amy Johnson and Francis Chichester. So, in design, the Tiger dated from the 1920s and flew like it – terrible ailerons but very effective rudder and elevators. With only 145 hp, a lot of drag from the bracing wires and a large wing area, it can be a handful close to the ground and even when taxiing in.

Tail wheel aircraft are often referred to as 'tail draggers' but in the case of the Tiger with just a metal tail skid and no wheel brakes that's exactly true, it simply drags its tail along the ground to stop. Like all tail draggers it demands full attention all the time; as the saying goes, a flight is never over in a Tiger until the aircraft has come to a complete stop and the engine is switched off. Because the centre of gravity is behind the wheels in a tail dragger, the natural tendency is for the aircraft to swap ends on the ground. This tendency increases as the aircraft slows down and directional control is lost which is why you see tail draggers waggling their rudders furiously during the final stages of the landing roll, even those with the luxury of wheel brakes. In summary, the Tiger is easy to fly but demanding to fly well.

Being a basic aircraft nearly ninety years old in design, the engine required hand swinging to start. The safest way to do this requires two pilots one in the aircraft with the other outside swinging the prop. The pilot sitting in the aircraft controls the procedure letting the other know when the fuel is on, the throttle set and the magnetos switched on. The pilot's call of "Fuel on, throttle set, switches on" for starting, once an engine has been primed, has been the standard litany with hand-swung engines for a hundred years. However, flying mostly alone, I developed a system whereby I could start the engine solo but this required great care and double-checking everything especially when cold and tired at the end of a day (me, not the engine).

Charles Lindberg writing about his early days flying the mail in the 1920s describes it this way. To appreciate a Tiger, you need a sense of history and as you can see from his account of starting the engine, nothing has changed much:

"It's really a stunt for one man and a very dangerous stunt if he doesn't watch himself. The trick of handling a propeller is to make your muscles pull away from it. If you lean against a blade, on contact you're asking for some broken bones. I chock the wheels, tie the stick back with my safety belt, check switches, give the engine three primer shots, retard spark, close throttle, run back to the propeller, catch one blade with my left hand, scrape over frozen ground with my moccasins as I pull a cylinder through compression. One... two...three...four blades through. Leave the fifth sixty degrees below horizontal. Back to the cockpit. Throttle one half inch open. Switches on. Back to the propeller, ten feet to the right side. Got to watch this. Grip the blade, throw my weight against it, angle forward to clear its bone shattering strength....let go....catch balance ....back for another try. There's a 'ping' this time....the blade moves forward...stops as I trip away.......No action on the third blade. On the fourth she hits – one cylinder, two and the engine catches. I stumble as the blade jumps from my hand. I scramble around the wing to my cockpit, ease on throttle. A roar from the engine, she's safe now. I unsnap the belt from the stick and climb into the pilot's seat."

The Tiger Moth is a leveller of egos and any Tiger Moth pilot who tells you that they have never had a hairy moment in the aircraft is a teller of falsehoods. I've certainly had a few and what follows is one that raised my pulse rate more than a little. Many years ago, I was flying my first Tiger, G-ANDE, to Northrepps Airfield in North Norfolk, for the annual airshow. Northrepps has moved location now but at the time was a 490m strip cut out of a wheat field and orientated north-south, a lovely rural setting not far from Cromer. The so-called control office was an old Edwardian bathing hut and next to that was an old Portakabin which was the domain of the airstrip owner, Chris Gurney. Chris was wheelchair-bound having been smashed up in a Tiger Moth accident when the pilot, the son of a local MP, decided to try and slow roll the aircraft at low altitude. As others have discovered over the years, this is seldom a good idea.

Chris was a huge character and always to be found in the Portakabin working the air-ground radio and surrounded by cans of beer and discarded packets of Winston cigarettes.

On the day in question there is a noticeable southerly breeze, maybe 10 kts, blowing straight up the north-south runway. The strip has a significant upslope when landing to the north – officially 1.8% but I doubt it was ever surveyed and I would put it at a lot more, maybe 3-4%. I arrive overhead and do a mental calculation. I know the wind is southerly but that means landing downhill and accepting the slope. Alternatively, should I land with the wind behind me but upslope to help with stopping bearing in mind the Tiger has no brakes? My gut feeling is to land uphill accepting the breeze behind me and I set up for an approach for the northerly runway.

I make a 'wheeler' landing and touchdown as slowly as possible, the automatic wing slats fully extended. So far so good. I can sense the ground speed is higher than my airspeed but I am expecting this with the wind behind me. The tail comes down and now the fun begins. The aircraft is now presenting its large wing area to the prevailing tailwind and is not slowing down at all even though I am travelling up a significant slope. It soon becomes apparent that, if I do nothing, I will run off the end of the runway where there is quite a tall hedge with a lane behind it. I have two choices, either deliberately ground loop the Tiger to stop quickly on the runway, but this has risks of damaging the wings, or go around for another attempt. I make an instant decision and apply full power for another go. The engine picks up cleanly but out of the corner of my eye, I can see the airspeed remains only just indicating off the stop so below the stalling speed. With the hedge fast approaching, I am fully committed and at the last possible moment, I have no option but to very, very gently tease the stick back. Too firm a pull would surely stall the wing. A last glance at the ASI confirms that I have barely any airspeed. Somehow and to this day I am not sure how, I just clear the hedge at the end of the runway, the wing slats still fully extended, the Tiger only just controllable and on the very edge of a stall. Maybe the slight wind travelling up the slope helped to lift me a little, who knows? Keeping the nose down I regain speed and climb away my heart racing. Nearby was an airstrip at Gunton Park, loosely defined between the park's oak trees, so I decide to land there and compose myself.

My Tiger Moth G-AOZH

Henry and Eleanor with 'ZH', August 2005

I land, switch off, clamber out of the cockpit still shaking and sit on the walkway of the wing. After a few minutes, I fish out my cell phone and give Chris a call in the Northrepps Control hut.

"Bloody hell, that was close!" he laughs. I can hear him take a drag on his Winston. "What the hell happened? I thought you were going to pile into the hedge!"

So did I but I don't tell him so. I explain, trying to make light of it but my voice probably betraying me due to the adrenaline still coursing through my body.

"I tell you what," Chris says. "Have another go. I'll get a couple of the lads to meet you half-way down the strip when you land. Land downhill, into wind and they will be there to grab the wing and slow you down if necessary."

Ten minutes later, I am overhead Northrepps again this time landing to the south; downhill but into wind. Chris has two guys on the strip to help me slow down should I need it but I don't; I stop comfortably in 2/3 the runway length and the guys on each wingtip swing the Tiger around to backtrack up the runway. Looking back on it, I imagine that the only lift I had on the go-around was from the propeller wash over this inboard section of the wing. There was clearly very little over the main section of the wings as reflected by the ASI reading. If the engine had not picked up instantly it would have been another story.

What did I learn from this? Firstly, gut feelings are useful but sadly aren't always correct. And secondly, it's better to be lucky than good.

* * * *

My first exposure to the Tiger was through my friend Nick Probett who ran Chauffair, a jet charter company based at Farnborough. Nick bought a lovely Tiger, G-ANEL, in 1988 which was an original 1940 de Havilland example (most were built in the UK under licence by Morris Motors). Nick showed me the basics and then let me solo in it which was generous of him.

Over the course of a few wine-fuelled evenings, we decided it would be a good idea to get another Tiger and base the two at Redhill Aerodrome doing so-called 'trial lessons' under Chauffair's AOC – the most legal way you could do such things. After some hunting around we bought G-ANDE in 1990. This aircraft was what is called a 'bitsa' - it had bits off this aircraft and bits off that aircraft to make one whole one. Its only original feature was probably the registration. I bought it in pieces from Ben Borsberry who had it kept in his barn pending restoration and on a cold spring day, with a couple of friends to help, I drove a large van to meet Ben at his barn at Kidmore End to collect the bits.

G-ANDE was a somewhat infamous Tiger. In May 1977 at the annual Biggin Hill airshow it was in a formation with two other Tigers coming in to land when a helicopter lifted off beneath it; the helicopter rotors sliced the Tiger's undercarriage clean off. Tragically, the helicopter crashed onto a parked Cessna 150 and all aboard the helicopter were killed but G-ANDE managed to belly land safely on the grass and the two occupants were uninjured.

We gave the job of restoring the bits of G-ANDE to create a 'new' Tiger to a company at Chilbolton airfield in Hampshire who is best kept nameless. They promised to complete the task for a fixed price but naturally things always cost more than anticipated and towards the end of the project they were forced to cut corners to keep on budget. Unfortunately, as the engine was the last item to be worked on, it suffered most from the skimping. This was a bag of nails from day one with excessive oil consumption and continual magneto problems. Eventually the company went bust and we managed to get the aircraft flown out just before the receivers came in to seize all its assets, but that's another story.

Nick and I set up a company called 'The Vintage Aeroplane Company Ltd.' to run these two Tigers from Redhill and all the costs, fuel and maintenance, went through Chauffair's books – when you are running a fleet of business jets, the cost of running a couple of Tiger Moths as well is insignificant so for a couple of years I enjoyed free flying, which was pretty nice. G-ANEL was painted red and G-ANDE blue, both with silver wings and both looking like the authentic 'flying club' style of the 1930s. Because we were on a full-blown AOC (probably the first time this had ever been done with Tiger Moths) we were able to apply for an A-B flight permission rather than the more common A-A the CAA generally allowed for light aircraft. A-A means you have to land back at the same airfield that you took off from; A-B means you can fly to other airfields and so opens up a lot more possibilities for work.

In July 1993, at the time the Channel Tunnel was being constructed, Nick took a call from NHK, the Japanese Broadcasting Corporation, who wanted to fly in a Tiger Moth over the green fields of Kent and the white cliffs of Dover before including the terminal construction site at Folkestone as a short documentary for Japanese TV. In other words, they wanted a corny glimpse of

The Vintage Aeroplane Company's Tiger Moths, G-ANDE and G-ANEL

'Ye Olde England' juxtaposed with a big new engineering project. Nick gave me a call,

"What do you think? NHK will have a few bob - how shall we charge this one?"

I thought for a moment. If they didn't use us there was no one else who could do it legally in a Tiger and they'd have to use a helicopter.

"Why don't we charge them the same as a helicopter and then add a 10% margin for extras? Cash, naturally. We should charge from Redhill to Headcorn, do the flight and then return to Redhill. We can always negotiate down if necessary, but I doubt they'll bother," I suggested.

"Yep, I like it," Nick replied. I'll get some prices from helicopter operators and we can match the price. It's for this Saturday. Can you do the flight as I'm tied up? The weather looks OK."

The going rate for a Jet Ranger helicopter at the time averaged around £500 an hour so Nick came up with a figure of £1500 for the flight, a ridiculous amount of money at the time for two and a half hour's flying in a Tiger Moth but, as predicted, the TV company didn't question it. The Saturday arrives, the weather gods keep their promise and I set off in G-ANDE for Headcorn, a small grass airfield near Tenterden in Kent mostly covered in grazing sheep, where Nick has agreed to meet with the TV crew. It is perfect for the planned flight, lovely countryside and not far from Folkestone. As I taxi off the runway to the parking area, I see the group of Japanese chaps waiting patiently, all in a line, for my arrival. I shut down, hop out and walk over to meet them. As one, they bow to nearly waist level which shows a huge respect to me. I'm slightly embarrassed. Japanese are an unfamiliar sight at Headcorn and a few people are watching with interest. The lead Japanese gentleman bows again and passes me a brown paper envelope. I don't count it; it feels reassuringly thick and Japanese have too much honour to pull a fast one. I tuck it safely into my flying jacket.

I identify the cameraman who will fly with me and we start chatting in broken English, me doing the safety brief, which he probably doesn't understand a word of but he nods courteously, and going through the suggested itinerary on the chart. I then get him ready to sit in the front cockpit but before he gets in, to my surprise, he reaches for a bandana to tie around his forehead. In he gets and I pop his goggles on and do a sudden doubletake – he looks for all the world like a Kamikaze pilot; leather jacket, the bandana tied tightly around his head and wearing goggles. It's central casting for Pearl Harbour and I don't know whether to laugh or run away. One of his colleagues passes him the big Sony video camera which is far too big to manage in the small cockpit so he is able to point it in one direction only, out the right side of the cockpit. I make a note to allow for this as we fly along. I hope fervently that he doesn't drop it onto the wing at any point.

One hour later we are back at Headcorn, mission completed and I help the cameraman disembark, taking the heavy Sony camera from him first. There are happy, goofy smiles all around and again, as one, they bow to me offering their thanks and I say my goodbyes. As I start my takeoff roll, I glance across and they are still standing in a line watching me as I leave and waving.

* * * *

There is an immediacy in open-cockpit flying that is lost in any other form of flying. Feeling the wind on your face, so cold sometimes your skin is numb, being able to smell the air, the cut grass, the bonfires a thousand feet below, the sulphurous industrial pollution, the cloud, the farm manure brings the whole experience of flying alive. You can feel the coldness of the air, not read it by a remote probe attached to the outside of the aircraft, hear the engine talk to you, and feel on your cheeks if the aircraft is in balance. I completely understand why Lindbergh, on his thirty-three-hour flight across the North Atlantic, chose not to fit the glass side windows but instead be open to the wind. Meticulous as he was about minimising every ounce of weight and every pound of drag above all else, he was prepared to accept the slight increase in drag caused by the air buffeting through the open windows in order to live the epic moment in full. You can directly see the tiny figures below, not through a window, you can shout to a friend. There is also a greater sense of achievement in a long flight in an open cockpit; the experience of mounting the aircraft on one grassy airfield and dismounting on a completely different but somehow similar stretch of grass is unique. Stepping onto the wing and throwing a leg into the cockpit to get in, is akin to mounting a horse. In fact, early Royal Flying Corps pilots were selected from the ranks of cavalry officers because it was recognised that the husbandry of aircraft was also similar to that required with horses (although it was wisely suggested that spurs were not taken into the aircraft). You don't switch off and go home after a flight in an old biplane, there are tasks to attend to. In the same way that a horse needs attention before the rider, so it is with the Tiger Moth. There is oil to be wiped from the engine bay and the underside of the fuselage; excess oil and wood and fabric do not mix well. The propeller needs to be wiped clean to remove the bugs, the oil level checked, the harnesses left tidy and the covers put on. Tiger Moth pilots need to be strong to move the aircraft. They are completely unmanoeuvrable in tight spaces so it's a question of lifting the tail onto your shoulders and wheeling her into the spot you want, either to the fuel pumps or into the hangar. However, whether by chance or design, once the tail is lifted to head height the weight of the engine exactly counter-balances the weight of the aircraft and it's easily possible to hold the tail up with one hand.

Old skills are re-learned in the Tiger - the art of 'dead-reckoning', for example. Dead-reckoning is the oldest navigational technique around. It's a corruption of 'deduced-reckoning' whereby you deduce your position based on your speed and heading with allowance for wind. Set a compass heading, start a clock and, if your wind estimate is correct after X amount of time you will be at your deduced, hopefully correct, position. The P2 compass that is fitted to the Tiger is very accurate and it is possible to fly to one degree of heading if you concentrate. I decide to put the art of dead-reckoning to a proper test one winter's day, when the conditions are ideal.

I am flying from Little Gransden airfield in Cambridgeshire to Langham on the North Norfolk coast for routine 50-hour maintenance with the legendary Henry Labouchere. The cloud is perfect for the experiment, overcast at 1,000ft along the route with cloud tops at 3,000ft. I get airborne and climb through the cloud, enjoying the wet smell of the mist around me. The grey blanket becomes lighter as I climb with the odd glimpse of blue and then I am in sunshine. You never get tired of the transition to blue skies no matter what aircraft you are flying in; it's magical. In a jet, the change is instant as you race skywards on pillars of thrust but in a Tiger Moth, it's very gradual with patches of blue teasing you over a period of minutes, coming and going before the cloud finally falls away.

Sitting in the bright sunshine, above a white duvet of cloud and with no ground references, I set a heading for Langham based on the forecast wind and settle down for the hour's flight. I know the cloud base at Langham is high enough to descend through the cloud and pop out safely well above the ground because I had called Henry before I set off. I work carefully to keep the compass heading exactly correct. Fifty-five minutes later I start the descent dropping down into the grey. The cloud envelopes me and I concentrate on my instrument flying using the very basic instruments the Tiger Moth provides. The temperature drops markedly in the cloud; I shiver and pull the sheepskin collar up around my neck. Four minutes later I am out of the cloud and looking at the dull Norfolk countryside with the coastline only a few miles away. I can see the sliver of grey on the horizon that is the sea. I get my bearings and look at the map - I am only a mile off my track; the dead reckoning had worked. I take time to marvel at Francis Chichester and his epic solo flight across the Tasman Sea in his Gipsy Moth in 1931. Flying from New Zealand to Australia, the first leg involved 450 miles of flying over a featureless ocean to find the tiny speck of Norfolk Island, barely four miles across. Hours and hours of accurate flying in an open cockpit while taking sun shots and keeping a navigational plot, it was an astonishing show of navigation. Keep the faith and hold the heading, as the saying goes.

G-AOZH at low level

Beneath the clouds the day is clear and the visibility is endless. As I approach the coast, I can see the huge expanse of sand at Holkham off to my left. Before landing at Henry's strip at Langham I swoop down and set myself up to run along the surf about fifteen feet above the water. The air, as always over the sea, is silky smooth and the smell of the sea is strong, salty and tangy. The water is a milky green-grey and I can see the seabed only a few feet beneath the translucent water. I am cruising at 75 kts, the Tiger's wheels only a few feet above the waves. In the distance are some grey seals resting on a sandbank that is just showing above the sea and I bank gently to take a closer look, being careful not to drop a wingtip into the sea and keeping my distance so as not to alarm them. As I circle the sandbank, some of them glance my way before slipping effortlessly into the water with barely a ripple. It is a completely magical experience, not a soul about apart from some distant walkers. Just me, the sea, some wheeling gulls and the grey seals.

* * * *

"I bet I could get there quicker in the TR."

Masey and I were having a beer in 'The Fox Revived' in June 1994. The 'Fox' became the oasis of choice after the crazy days of the Six Bells and was almost a second office for Interflight. I was recounting to him a recent trip I had made in G-ANDE with my girlfriend Bev to St. Omer in France.

"Really?" I countered, "I doubt it."

"Want to bet?" replied Masey, always the gambler. "Why don't we open a book on it and give the proceeds to charity?"

And so started the plans for a 'Wacky Races' style challenge between me in my Tiger Moth and Masey and Terry Rawlings in Masey's Triumph TR4. The only rules were these: we both had to start at the 'Fox' at 1030 sharp and the finish was to be at 'Le Bon Boeuf' restaurant in the town square in St. Omer. And I had to start the engine myself at Redhill Aerodrome – I couldn't arrange for it to be running already when I arrived at the aerodrome. Fair enough. Apart from that, we understood there would be no rules. The landlord John arranged for posters and sold a lot of tickets in the pub with people betting on who would win and by what margin. The proceeds would go to a local Hospice. My plan was for me and Bev to make our way to Redhill, fly to Calais, clear Customs and then fly on to St. Omer. There we would jump into a taxi and high-tail it into the town centre to the restaurant. Masey in his TR would have to drive like a madman up the M23, round the M25 and down to Ramsgate, board the hovercraft, get off in Ostend and belt down the motorway to St. Omer. I had the advantage of straight-line speed but had to get to Redhill in the first place and then clear Customs in Calais and get a taxi into town once in St. Omer. Masey had the advantage of not getting out of his car but had further to go and at a slower speed. And possibly have delays on the motorways. The planned 1030 start gave Masey and Terry a fighting chance of connecting with the drive-on/drive-off hovercraft in Ramsgate.

The day arrives, the weather is beautiful and set to be so all weekend. There is a big crowd in the Fox car park to watch the start of the race. Masey is revving his TR4 with Terry Rawlings in the passenger seat, eager to get going. I am waiting a few feet away with Bev and some friends and I can see Masey is looking puzzled, he is waiting for us to jump into a car when the whistle blows and is busy looking for it. Except that's not my plan. Unbeknown to him and in the dastardly spirit of the Wacky Races 'no rules', I have arranged for a helicopter, through Denis Kenyon at Redhill, to collect us from the field at the back of the Fox to whisk me directly to Redhill. Denis, being the legend and great guy that he was, agreed to do this for free in the spirit of the charity. Just then Masey hears the approaching helicopter.

"You bastard!" he shouts through the drumming of rotor blades and drops the clutch roaring off as the heli lands gently into the adjacent field right on cue.

"Well, we agreed the only rule is 'no rules'!" I shout back, but he is gone, tearing up the road towards the M25.

The race is on. We jump into the heli with some other guys and lift off for Redhill Aerodrome. Denis has provided no ordinary helicopter, this is a fast Twin Squirrel, with leather seats. I can see the Tiger as we approach Redhill, sitting outside the hangar on the grass ready to go and the heli alights close by just seven minutes after leaving the pub. I jump out and run to the Tiger. Bev hops in and sorts her straps out. I give the engine a quick prime and it starts first swing. I jump in and we taxi quickly to the active runway with me strapping myself in as I go. We're off.

The flight is smooth and uneventful and we even have a slight tailwind which is good as we will definitely not need to refuel in Calais. The sky is blue from hazy horizon to hazy horizon and the sun, gathering strength, hangs like a fuzzy orange to my right. It's a gorgeous summer's day and not for the first time I give thanks for the privilege of flying such an aircraft on such a day.

There is a mild chop from the rising air but as we coast out over the Channel the air loses its heat, as always and becomes cooler and smoother. I call Calais

ATC and am cleared straight in making a fast, curved approach to the grass runway landing fifty-five minutes after leaving Redhill. On finals, I can see the airport Customs driving out across the grass to meet us on the side of the runway in their little Citroen to clear us in. Thanks to an earlier phone call explaining to them, in my best French, the charity nature of the flight they have kindly agreed to do this which saves us a lot of time.

We're on the ground for only ten minutes while our passports and the aircraft documents are checked then it's time to chock the wheels, tie the stick back, set the throttle closed, select the magnetos on and swing the propeller. The engine is hot and starts instantly. I hop back in, buffeted by the warm slipstream, buckle up and taxi to the runway and then we are airborne again for the twenty-five minute flight to St. Omer. Again, I have called ahead before leaving England and I'm hoping they have a taxi waiting for us to take Bev and me into town as planned. Unfortunately, this hasn't worked but,

"No problem, Monsieur!" the airport manager beams, "My brozzer will drive you to le centre ville!"

He assures me he will take care of the Tiger until the next day and hangar it safely and I decide to trust him that he will do this safely. We pile into the old Renault and head off to the town square. Two hours after leaving the Fox Revived, we are sitting in the bar outside 'Le Bon Boeuf'. Not too shabby. Two beers and one hour and five minutes later we hear tyres squealing on the cobblestones and then spot Masey and Terry in the red TR tearing into the square looking for 'Le Bon Boeuf'. Naturally I adopt a bored, chilled pose, as though I have been waiting all day.

"You took your time!" I goad them.

"I've bust a wheel," Masey tells me, without preamble as usual, as I hand him and Terry a cold Kronenbourg each. "A couple of spokes pinged out on one of the roundabouts," he explained.

I look at the nearside rear wire wheel and can see the damage for myself. The TR looks like it's been driven hard, dirty and the windscreen is covered in bugs and Masey and Terry look wind burned and exhausted. Later in the afternoon the company King Air arrives at the airfield and disgorges more Interflight personnel and we all enjoy a good dinner at 'Le Bon Beoeuf'. Masey pays, another example of his 'work hard, play hard' ethos and the next morning, slightly hungover but with blue skies and warm weather still, we all make our way home by Tiger Moth, Triumph TR4 and King Air.

* * * *

Few things have given me as much pleasure, or required as much responsibility, as flying Henry and Eleanor in the Tiger Moth when they were little. There are times in life when you have to weigh up extra risk against gaining a life experience and strapping them into the front seat of the Tiger, sitting on a pile of cushions so they could see out, was one of these. Yes, there is an element of risk in putting those you love the most into a seventy-year-old vintage open-cockpit biplane but then how many kids get that experience and how many mothers would ever permit it? They both loved flying in the Tiger and came along at every opportunity. Henry went upside down before he was born as I used to do aerobatics with Amanda during her pregnancy with him. I was a little more cautious during her pregnancy with Els. Amanda never tried to dissuade me from flying with the children, keeping any disquiet to herself and as a result, their childhood was enriched without a doubt.

For years I flew my Tiger G-AOZH on so-called 'trial lesson' flights mostly from White Waltham and Redhill aerodromes. These flights are a legal way of getting around the requirement of having a full-blown Air Operators Certificate which would normally be required if taking passengers for so-called 'hire and reward' as mentioned before.

The CAA doesn't differentiate in this regard between British Airways flying passengers in a 747 or a sole trader taking a single passenger up in a Tiger Moth on a sunny afternoon – the all-powerful AOC and all the regulation and oversight that goes with it, is required for any aircraft if money changes hands. The AOC is expensive and onerous to obtain so the 'trial lesson' loophole was and still is, extensively used for pleasure flying. All that's required is that you are a current Flying Instructor and you fly an appropriately maintained aircraft and you fly from a licenced airfield. That's all. The fact that no one ever returned for a second lesson beyond the trial one is conveniently overlooked. The occasional accident throws the spotlight on these lessons and for a while the CAA get interested but they pick their battles carefully and happily this area of operations is a stone they leave undisturbed.

The trial lesson business was lucrative and, as well as paying the aircraft mortgage and maintenance, also enabled me to meet some lovely and very interesting people. Passengers were usually recipients of a birthday present or anniversary gift and often the whole family would come along to enjoy the experience. Frequently the passengers were old chaps who had learned to fly in Tiger Moths during the war and for them the experience of reliving a flight in the Tiger was memorable, as absolutely nothing has changed over the intervening seventy years or so. And some of them could still fly well - obviously some hard-nosed RAF flying instructors had banged the basics into them very well when they were young pilots.

I met some extraordinary men in the course of these flights, including Les Weaver who, incredibly, survived twenty missions during the war in the Lancaster bomber; a lovely man who was nearly 90 when he flew with me. In all the years that I did this I never had a bad experience with a passenger; every flight was a pleasure. That's not to say it was easy money as the days were long with sometimes between eight and ten flights to complete, each twenty-five minutes long. With positioning flights, breaks and refuelling that makes for a very long day and I had to be careful to keep well hydrated and take breaks – open cockpit flying all day is fatiguing and mistakes are all too easy to make, especially towards the end of the day.

A typical day for a summer day's flying at White Waltham would be this. I would wake Henry early in the morning, maybe 6 am and after a quick breakfast we would drive down to Lotmead Farm where I kept the Tiger Moth. Lotmead Farm was an organic dairy farm owned and run by Norman Parry, a very accomplished glider pilot and part-owner of another Tiger Moth that he also kept on the farm. Norman had flown his Tiger from England to Australia in the 1990s and then in 2016 flew it to Cape Town on the 'Crete to Cape' rally, thus ticking off the two classic pre-war Tiger Moth routes. The strip at the farm - organic grass, of course - was aligned NE/SW and was around 600m long, perfect for a Tiger although landing towards the NE required care as there were tall trees on the approach and a line of trees along the west side of the strip. These could cause turbulence on landing if the wind was westerly.

Henry and I would man-handle the Tiger out of the hangar - carefully manoeuvring around the farm machinery that littered the area - and wheel it the 100m or so down a slight gradient to the grass strip. A quick pre-flight inspection and I would chock the aircraft, tie the stick back and start the engine. Once running, I would get Henry settled in the front cockpit, pull on my sheepskin jacket, clamber into the rear cockpit and we'd be off. Thirty minutes later, say by 0830, we would be at White Waltham. A quick refuel to full tanks, five minutes to catch our breath and we would be ready to greet the first passenger by nine o'clock. It was a bit of a rush but manageable. We became well known as a father and son team and often Els and Amanda would come down to the airfield in the afternoon to help with the 'meeting and greeting'.

In the early days of pleasure flying, I used to throw in a 'loop-the-loop' as an optional extra for passengers just before landing but stopped this after a nasty experience when flying at Redhill. The passenger was a young lad who had been out celebrating his 21st birthday the night before. He was still topped up with beer when he showed up and was definitely up for a loop before returning to land. So, just before returning to the airfield, I found a quiet area away from habitation and started the manoeuvre. Down we went, accelerating to 95 -100 kts airspeed, pitched up firmly, added full power and a little bit of left rudder to keep straight on the way up and pulled firmly over the top. I released the back pressure going over the top to keep the loop circular and not egg-shaped and then flew down the other side and pulled firmly to flatten out the bottom of the circle. If you get it right you end up at the same altitude and airspeed you started at and you hit your slipstream, signified by a little bump as you pass through the disturbed air.

We had just done the loop when I began to suspect that all was not well in front of me. It's surprising how much you can tell about body language when sitting behind someone in a tandem aircraft. Happy campers are busy looking around and chatting. Those less than optimum don't move their heads, hunch their shoulders and stare straight ahead, fixated.

"You OK?" I shouted through the headset intercom. Silence. "Shall we return to the airfield?" I persisted.

A feeble nod and still silence. I knew this was bad and guessed what was coming. I turned immediately for the airfield watching him carefully. A couple of minutes later, his head went down, his shoulders heaved and he leant over the left side of the cockpit. I simultaneously ducked and applied full right rudder to skid the aircraft and attempt to deflect what I knew was coming my way but it was too late. In an open-cockpit aircraft, it's a bit like throwing a pint of water at a big fan and expecting to be able to control where it goes. What seemed like gallons of blackish liquid hit my windshield and the top of my head. Guinness and lots of it.

We flew back to the airfield in silence and landed. When we came to a stop outside the hangar, I switched the magnetos off to kill the engine and hopped out, leaving the lad in the aircraft trying to mop himself down. I knew where the hangar bucket and sponge were and filled the bucket with water.

"Here you go," I said, handing my hapless companion the bucket as he walked back to the hangar. "It's tradition. You throw up, you clean up."

* * * *

Flying old aircraft is a privilege enough but it is not often, in one day, to fly in three aircraft with a combined age of 173 years. Who says aircraft can't last forever? In spring 2008 I flew my Tiger Moth up to Langham on the North Norfolk coast to leave it in the tender hands of Henry Labouchere for its 50-hour check. Henry is a large character and an excellent engineer who understands vintage aircraft, especially all Moths, better than anyone. He could make them safe without trying to make them new – exactly what is required, after all, they are now decades old. There was no one else I would entrust my aircraft to and, although it was a trek to fly to North Norfolk each time for maintenance, the aircraft never let me down whilst in Henry's care. He is a very good pilot – in fact the only person I would trust my kids to go flying with apart from me. In his younger days he was a crop sprayer in Australia and as such is an excellent 'stick and rudder' man. While there bought his Tiger Moth which he owns to this day. It flies better than any other Tiger I have flown thanks to various tweaks over the years, and minor adjustments to the rigging that make all the difference. Henry's workshop occupied a corner of the old airfield, next to rows of huts housing thousands of turkeys that stank to high heaven in summer. During the war, RAF Langham had been home to Bristol Beaufighters on coastal defence and to this day the gunnery training dome for RAF pilots sits

Els and Henry in G-AOZH

G-AOZH in summer sunshine at Lotmead Farm

in a corner of the airfield, one of only six left in the country and now fully restored. Leaving the Tiger in Langham, Henry lent me an old VW Golf to drive back home in. A week later he called me and the Tiger was ready for collection.

"Drive the Golf to Lotmead, old boy, and I will come and collect you. The Fox Moth is in Rendcomb and we can fly up to Langham in that."

"What about the car?" I offered.

"Oh, don't worry, I'll collect it sometime."

Henry was always traversing the country in diverse aircraft and cars so that came as no surprise. He never drove if he could fly. On the day I was duly waiting on the strip at Lotmead when Henry arrived with his usual no-nonsense flourish in a Cessna 185 Skywagon. He landed with a perfect three-pointer in no distance and taxied back.

"Hop in Marcus," he shouted above the engine noise. For some reason, to Henry I was always Marcus never Mark. This Skywagon was built in 1975 but it had been equipped with some wing modifications so its takeoff and landing performance was greatly enhanced. I hopped in and we set off on the fifteen-minute flight to Rendcomb, duly ticking off the first thirty-three years of the 173-year total.

Rendcomb Aerodrome, is a Great War airfield in Gloucestershire dating from 1916. To this day, a sign outside the officers' hut reads 'MAKE SURE YOUR POCKETS ARE EMPTY BEFORE GOING ON PATROL'. Good advice indeed. Inside old graffiti covers the walls. There were no official runways on the field, only a windsock, and you just landed into wind as in the old days when crosswinds were to be avoided at all costs. Henry landed, taxied to the hangar, swung the Skywagon around and cut the engine. The de Havilland Fox Moth was waiting outside and we settled in. It's an immaculate aircraft that was built in 1933. There are the next seventy-five years of history.

The flight to Langham was uneventful. I sat in the forward cabin which seated four people in cramped and deafening conditions as it's directly behind the engine. At Langham, it was time for a quick lunch in a nearby pub before making myself comfortable for the flight back to Lotmead in G-AOZH. ZH was built in 1943 – and that contributed the final sixty-five years. At the time of writing, all these aircraft are still flying and the total airframe time would be an incredible 215 years if those three flights were performed today.

Henry was always generous with his aircraft - and sometimes with aircraft that weren't actually his. For example, I arrived at Langham once and saw a beautiful Bücker 'Jungmeister' parked on the grass just outside his workshop. I walked over to take a closer look. The Jungmeister is a diminutive German aerobatic biplane that first flew in 1935 and performed well at the 1936 Berlin Olympics. Powered by a lovely 160hp Siemens radial engine it is widely regarded as one of the best aerobatic aircraft ever built, the controls being light and responsive and the aircraft having almost neutral stability.

The first pilot to fly it in reported that it had "astonishing agility" which says it all. It is also very valuable, only a handful existing worldwide.

"Take it for a spin if you like", Henry said.

I looked at him blankly. "Are you serious? I've never flown one before!" "Well, you can fly a Tiger so you'll be OK. Just whatever you do, don't get below 80 on approach" were his parting words.

I climbed into the snug cockpit and set off, climbing to 3,000ft to get the

Bücker Bü 133 'Jungmeister'. Stock photo.

Henry Labouchere

feel of this lovely aircraft's handling. At first, I was hugely over-controlling. This was very much not a Tiger Moth, which required constant heaving of the controls, this was an aircraft that flew almost by thought. It was beautifully light and responsive because it had almost no stability – important in an aerobatic aeroplane so the pilot isn't constantly fighting the controls while manoeuvring.

I tried a roll and a loop and loved it; the aircraft was flattering even of my poor aerobatic skills. The landing, when it came to it, with Henry's warning ringing in my ears, turned out to be a non-event and I settled smoothly onto the grass. As I came to rest and the engine clattered to a halt I sat in the cockpit for a minute, taking it in, totally in love with this wonderful aeroplane. My Tiger would forever rest in its shadow.

* * * *

In October 2011 I got a call at home from the secretary of David Ross. He was one of the co-founders of the Carphone Warehouse Company, along with Charles Dunstone and Guy Johnson. My ears pricked up.

"Mr Ross would like to take his girlfriend Emma for a flight in a Tiger Moth on Saturday. Is this the sort of thing you do?" she asked.

"Yes, of course," I replied. "I fly from White Waltham and do twenty-five minute fights…." I continued on with the usual sales pitch.

The secretary listened politely and then said,

"Actually he wants to do the flight over the North Yorkshire Moors. Mr Ross is holding a shooting party and thought it would be fun for her to fly over."

Two things sprang to mind immediately. One is I am wary of shotguns near Tiger Moths having been shot at before when getting too close, low down, to a shooting party in Wiltshire and the second thing is that this was a hell of a long way to go for a flight.

"Sure, no problem," I said. "Let me look at the timings and I'll call you back with a price."

I grabbed a topo chart to work out a plan. Being October, the days were getting short so this would need looking at carefully to make it fit into the day but it would be a lot of money, so I wanted it to work. It would finish the season's flying off nicely. The nearest grass airfield near the Moors suitable for a Tiger Moth would be Bagby, a small aerodrome about three miles south of Thirsk, North Yorks. I figured out that if I took off at first light, I could stop at Leicester Aerodrome, fill up with fuel and continue northwards to Bagby. Allowing an hour and a half for meeting the passenger, doing the flight and saying goodbyes, I could head south again stopping at Netherthorpe, home of Sheffield Aero Club and just make it back to White Waltham before dusk. Tight in the shortening days of autumn and not march margin, but doable. It involved around seven hours of flying in total. The weather forecast looked fine for the flight, a little early morning mist but no more. I called the secretary back.

"I could be at Bagby Aerodrome by midday to do the flight. Would that work for Mr Ross?"

She agreed it would be fine. "Of course, this is a lot of flying so the price will be high, I'm sure you understand."

I gave her the price of £3500, then hesitated a little.

"I am afraid I will need payment in advance due to the cost involved."

After a little to-ing and fro-ing this was agreed although I could tell she was surprised that I had asked for the money upfront implying that Mr Ross was not an honourable man. I was sure he was but, in my experience, these agreements are generally dealt with by lesser minions and minor details like payments tend to get forgotten. I had been forced to chase money before (film companies are the worst) and there was too much money at stake here to risk a delay in getting paid. The flight details were agreed and the money was promised to be transferred into my account by Friday morning. This came and went. By Friday lunchtime, still nothing. I called the secretary to let her know and she assured me the payment was imminent. The afternoon went by, still no payment and then at the last moment at 5 pm the money was in my bank. The flight was on.

Saturday morning dawned misty as forecast. I woke earlier than I intended and as I left the house at 6 am it was still dark as I drove the four miles to White Waltham. The air at the airfield smelt rich with autumn scents as I removed the aircraft covers, which were stiff and soaked with dew. I completed the pre-flight by torchlight and then swung the engine. The sound of the engine shattered the early morning quiet and I felt very conspicuous. The exhaust stubs spat tiny blue flames in the dark.

The sky was starting to get the first tinge of lemon as I very carefully taxied across the wet grass to the nearest runway. It was 6.45. There wasn't a breath of wind so any runway would do for takeoff and I lined up to start my first and only night takeoff in a Tiger Moth. Lifting off into the dark was magical, feeling rather than seeing the airspeed on the ASI which was invisible in the dark.

Amanda and me with G-AOZH

The stick steady in my hands, the Tiger slipped easily through the silky air. I climbed to 1,000ft where it was a lot lighter and set heading for Leicester, looking down at the villages and the valleys filled with mist in the early purple light. Having made an earlier start than planned, I got to Leicester Aerodrome fifty minutes after setting off from White Waltham and too early for anyone to be about. However, just after 8.30 I eventually found an early riser to sell me some Avgas and offer me a cup of coffee and at 9.30 I set off for Bagby. The flight northbound was calm and uneventful and after dodging round East Midlands and Doncaster-Sheffield airports I arrived there at about 11 am.

Excellent, an hour in hand so I treated myself to a full English at the little airfield café. On the dot of midday, a Range Rover swept into the car park and out stepped Emma Pilkington, David Ross's tall, leggy girlfriend. She looked at the Tiger and turned to me.

"Are you the chap with the Tiger Moth?" she asked.

I looked around, no one else was in sight.

"I am. Ready when you are."

"Are you seriously taking me up in that?" She looked aghast.

"Absolutely," I assured her in my most enthusiastic way, "You'll love it when you're up, it's wonderful!"

I could see she wasn't convinced though and that she was more used to aeroplanes with jets, comfortable seats and full cabin service. And a roof.

The next challenge was to locate the shooting party, somewhere out on the Moors. That's a big area. I walked over to the driver, who was leaning against the Range Rover bonnet, smoking.

"Any idea where Mr Ross's party will be?" I asked.

He squinted at my map. "Around here, I think," pointing with a stubby finger, "I'm not entirely sure."

Great. Where he pointed to was close to the RAF Fylingdales, a highly sensitive defence early-warning radar station and not airspace to wander into. However, armed with this information we set off.

More by luck than anything else, after fifteen minutes flying towards and around Fylingdales, I located what I took to be the party, maybe a dozen men with shotguns and several 4x4 cars. Everyone seemed to be waving but I knew from experience that it's difficult to tell from the air whether people are waving at you or shaking their fists – as I found out when I was shot at that time in Wiltshire. On that occasion, I thought the people on the ground were waving at me until I saw someone turn towards me and the puff of a shotgun being aimed in my direction, so I stuck my head out and examined the party carefully. I was just outside the Fylingdales prohibited area so that was a relief. I did a few low-level passes and wingovers and flew back to Bagby, side slipping on approach to land with a soft and perfect 'three pointer'. To my amazement when Emma stepped out, she was grinning from ear to ear, so I considered my job done.

The flight back home was via Netherthorpe, as planned, the air smooth in the cool autumn air. I touched down at White Waltham around 4.30 absolutely deadbeat. Six hours airborne, in the open cockpit and always against the clock, with the limited daylight available in the early autumn, was exhausting. However, it had been a wonderful day and my Tiger had performed faultlessly, not missing a beat. I put my tired and oiled steed to bed for the night and listened to the engine ticking as it cooled down. There was a smell of warm metal and oil. I paused for a minute to reflect on the absolute privilege it was to own such an old and iconic aircraft even if only for a few years.

I knew that I must hand it on to another owner one day and that itself made each flight more precious. In the end, I owned G-AOZH for 17 years.

I set off stiffly for the bar and a well-earned pint, the roar of the engine still loud in my ears. The sun was sinking quickly into the autumn mist, pale and watery and it was becoming noticeably cooler. I shivered despite the layers beneath my sheepskin jacket; the cold was catching up with me. Sitting outside the clubhouse on the one of the wooden benches, as I used to do all those years before as a new instructor, I contemplated the day.

GLOSSARY AND SLANG

ABTA - Association of British Travel Agents
ACL - Air Contractors
ADF - Automatic Direction Finder
AFM - Airplane Flight Manual
Airspeed - speed through the air
AOC - Air Operators Certificate
AOG - Aircraft on Ground is a term used when the a/c is unserviceable. Also used to describe urgent spares
APC - Armoured Personnel Carrier (army vehicle)
APU - Auxiliary Power Unit
ASI – Airspeed Indicator
ATCC - Air Traffic Control Centre
ATZ - Aerodrome Traffic Zone
Avgas - Aviation Gasoline for piston aircraft
BA - British Airways
Base Check – a pilot proficiency check
Bob Hoover – the legendary American display pilot
CAA - Civil Aviation Authority
CAM - Client Aviation Manager (TAG lead captain)
CAS - Crew Alerting System
Chieftain - a twin-engined aircraft made by Piper Aircraft designated the PA31
CIS - Commonwealth of Independent States
Citation - A Cessna light jet
C of G - Centre of Gravity
Dash - slang for a bribe
Dead-reckoning - corruption of 'deduced reckoning', ie navigating by heading and time only
DFO - Director of Flight Operations
DME - Distance Measuring Equipment. Measures distance and groundspeed
Dry Lease – an aircraft lease without crew and support
F/A - Flight Attendant
FAA - Federal Aviation Administration
FBO - Fixed Based Operator, basically an airport handling agent
FCU - jet engine Fuel Control Unit
F/E - Flight Engineer

FIR - Flight Information Region (air traffic control regions)
FL - Flight Level (eg FL80 = 8,000ft)
FMC/FMS - Flight Management Computer/System
F/O - First Officer
GAT - General Aviation Terminal
Gen Dec - General Declaration form, listing crew and passengers
GLONASS - Russian 'Global Navigation Satellite System' (similar to GPS)
Gopher - a general dogsbody as in 'Go for this, go for that'
GPS - Global Positioning System
Ground Speed – speed over the ground
HF - High Frequency long-range radio
IAF - Israeli Air Force
ICAO – International Civil Aviation Organisation
IFR - Instrument Flight Rules
ILS - Instrument Landing System
IRE – Instrument Rating Examiner
Jeppesen – aeronautical charts used by most operators
Jet A1 - kerosene jet fuel
Kt/kts - knot/knots (nautical mile per hour)
Mach - a measure of the speed of sound, also written as M or m.
Medevac - Medical evacuation
Mhz - abbreviation for megahertz, radio frequency
MOR - Mandatory Occurrence Report
NAT - North Atlantic
Nightfighter - prostitute
Nm - nautical mile (15% longer than a statute mile)
NOTOC - Notice to Captain
NOTAM - Notice to Airman
Oleo - aircraft undercarriage shock absorber
Omega VLF - a Very Low Frequency global navigation system
Pax - Passengers
PF - Pilot Flying
Plog - Pilot's Log, abbreviation
PM - Pilot Monitoring
PPR - Prior Permission Required
Ramp check - A check by a national authority on the aircraft, crew and documents

SAAF - South African Air Force
SATCO - Senior Air Traffic Officer
TCAS - Traffic Collision Awareness System
Three-pointer – the landing technique on a tailwheel aircraft where the main wheels *and tail wheels touch simultaneously*
Titan - a twin-engined aircraft by Cessna, designated the C404
Topo chart - a topographical chart showing towns and terrain, for visual flying
TRE - Type Rating Examiner
TRI - Type Rating Instructor
ULD - Unified Loading Device (baggage or freight bins used on cargo aircraft)
USAF - US Air Force
VFR - Visual Flight Rules
VOR - a VHF Navigation aid
V1 - Decision speed on takeoff
V2 - airborne takeoff safety speed

APPENDIX 1 – COMPANIES IN DATE ORDER

1979 West London Aero Club - Instructor

1980-1982 Chess Wing - Line Pilot

1982-1984 Skyguard - Chief Pilot, TRE

1985 – 1986 South East Air - Chief Pilot, TRE

1986-1995 Interflight Air Charter - Chief Pilot, TRE

1996-2006 Hunting Cargo Airlines / Air Contractors - Line Pilot, TRE

2006-2008 BP - Line Pilot

2008 TAG Aviation - Chief Pilot, TRI

APPENDIX 2 – AIRCRAFT TYPES FLOWN

Piston:

Grumman AA-5A / AA-5B
PA23 'Apache' / 'Aztec'
PA28 'Cherokee' 140/180
PA31 'Navajo' and 'Navajo Chieftain'
PA32 / 32R 'Cherokee Six' / 'Lance'
Beech Baron 55 / 58 / 58P
Beech Duke
Tiger Moth
Stampe
Zlin
Bücker 'Jungmeister'
Cessna 150 / 152 / 172 / 182
Cessna 310
Cessna 404 / 414 / 421

Turboprop:

Beech King Air B200

Jet:

Airbus A300-B4
Boeing 727-200F
Challenger 605
Falcon 7X
Gulfstream GV/G550
Hawker-1B / -3B-Fan / -600 / -700
Learjet 35a
Lockheed JetStar 731

APPENDIX 3 – FOREIGN COUNTRIES AND AIRFIELDS VISITED

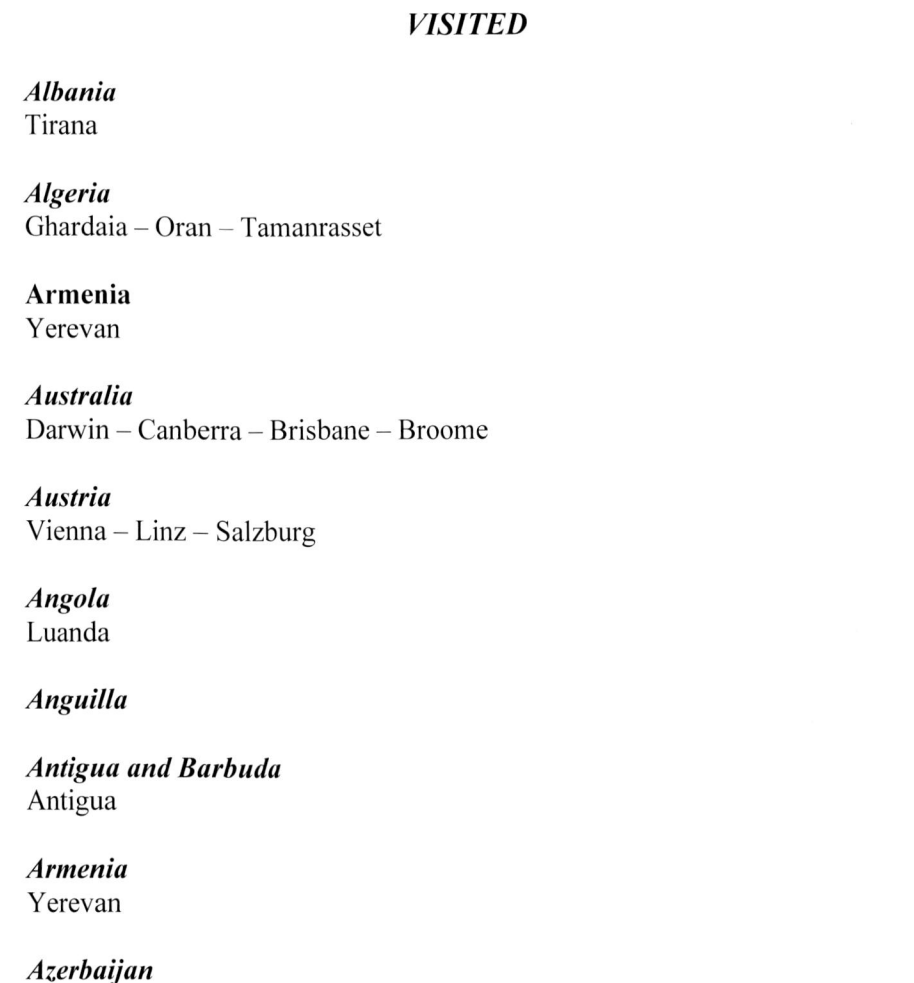

Albania
Tirana

Algeria
Ghardaia – Oran – Tamanrasset

Armenia
Yerevan

Australia
Darwin – Canberra – Brisbane – Broome

Austria
Vienna – Linz – Salzburg

Angola
Luanda

Anguilla

Antigua and Barbuda
Antigua

Armenia
Yerevan

Azerbaijan
Baku

Bahamas
Freeport

Bahrain
Manama

Barbados

Slovakia
Bratislava – Kosice

Slovenia
Maribor

South Africa
Johannesburg – Lanseria

South Korea
Busan – Seoul – Ulsan

Spain / Canary Islands / Balearics
Alicante – Almeira – Bilbao – Asturias – Barcelona – Fuerteventura – Gerona – Ibiza-Lanzarote - Las Palmas – Malaga - Madrid-Barajas - Madrid-Torrejon - Madrid-Getaffe – Mahon – Palma – Pamplona – Santiago – Seville – Tenerife-North - Tenerife-South – Vigo – Valencia – Vitoria – Valladolid – Zaragoza

Surinam
Paramaribo

Sweden
Borlange - Gothenburg-Save - Gothenburg-Landvetter – Halmstad - Lappeenranta   Orebro – Malmo – Stockholm-Arlanda – Stockholm-Bromma

Switzerland
Basle – Berne – Geneva – Samedan – Sion – Zurich

Syria
Damascus

Tanzania
Dar es Salaam – Zanzibar

Thailand
Bangkok

Trinidad and Tobago
Port of Spain

Tunisia
Jerba – Sfax – Tangiers – Tunis

Turkey
Antalya – Bursa – Dalaman – Istanbul – Izmir

UAE
Abu Dhabi – Dubai-International – Dubai Al Maktoum – Sharjah

Ukraine
Kyiv – Lviv – Odesa – Poti – Poltava – Simferopol

USA
Atlanta – Albany - Battle Creek – Burlington – Brunswick – Burbank - Broome County - Deer Valley - Duluth - Dallas-Love – Eagle – Falcon - Great Falls - Glen Falls - Houston-Hobby – Houston-Sugarland – Houma – Honolulu – Hartford – Lakeland - Los Angeles – Lexington - Las Vegas – Morristown – Minneapolis – Miami - Napa Valley - Niagara Falls – Oakland – Palm Beach – Portland - Palm Springs Poughkeepsie – Providence – Portsmouth – Rochester – Scottsdale – Sedona – Sugarbush – St. Louis-Lambert – St. Louis-Spirit – Sacramento – San Jose- Santa Barbara – San Diego – Smyrna – Tuscon – Teterboro – Whitefield – Westhampton – Washington DC- White Plains

Yemen
Hodeida - Saana

Zambia
Livingstone

INDEX

Adare Manor 10, 11
Air Transport Auxiliary (ATA) 5,9
Ajaccio 174-176, 178
Angel, Tony 36
Angola 95
Anyan, Rod 167, 168
Aswan 117-119
Bader, Douglas 2
Bagby Aerodrome 226-228
Balin, Pascal 187, 189, 190
Bampton, Al 163
Barnett, Al, 154
Barrow, Stuart 180
Barton, Louise 193
Bayley, Martyn 56-58, 76-78, 86, 87, 95, 104, 118, 119, 130, 132-140, 149
Berlin 102, 103, 223
Biak, Indonesia 180
Bonfield, Frank 89-91, 104
Borsberry, Ben 208
BP aircraft incident 182-183
Brough Aerodrome 18, 21, 22
Brown, Lord 179, 180
Bücker Jungmeister 223, 224
Bullard, Jimmy 140-142
Burton, Don 155, 158, 167, 172
Cairo 42, 116, 142
Chauffair 207, 208
Cobb, Roy 49, 50, 98, 99
Collins, Phil 59
COVID 223-225
D-Day 1984 commemorations 35
Daines, Don 37-39

Darrah, Colin 184, 185
Dead Reckoning 90, 144, 212, 213
Doc McDermott 80, 81, 96, 97
Eismark, John 140-142
Farthing, Dave 154
Geneva Airport 141, 142, 152, 153, 201, 202
Ghardaia 49, 118, 119
Gold flights 81, 82
Goose Bay 43, 144, 149
Gurney, Chris 204
Heath, Dave 173
Headcorn Aerodrome 209, 210
Hilton, John 8
Hodgson, Ron 154, 157
Hollands-Martell, Mark 187
Horse flights 159
Hotel Rossiya 100, 101
India 193-195
Inwood, Liz 3, 4
Jervis, Chris 154, 174, 178
Jersey European Airways, 38
Joyce, Alan 27, 34, 35
Labouchere, Henry 212, 220, 224
Lagos 78, 110-114
Las Vegas 196
Lear stall 132-133
Leavesden Aerodrome 18, 19, 22, 26, 28-31
Lindberg, Charles 204, 211
Lockerbie 104-106, 174
Lombardi, Frankie 191, 198-200
Looker, Maurice 1
Lotmead Farm 218, 222, 223
Maldives 196-198
Manning, Geoff 154
Marrakech 136, 137

Masey, Simon 40-45, 47, 49, 52-54, 57, 59, 65, 67, 70, 73, 75-80, 82, 88, 94-96, 102, 104, 107, 114, 117, 119-122, 126, 129, 135-137, 139-145, 149, 214-216
McEwan, Ian 46
McGowan, Pete 198, 200
Montenegro 107-110
Moore, Robert 148
Morgan, Pat 179, 180
Mr Myers 10-12, 14
Newcombe, Dave
Moore, Robert 134
Murphy, Con 175
Northrepps 204, 207
Odesa 99
Pacific flights 186
Paramaribo, Surinam 186-190
Parry, Norman 218
Pollard, Graeme 193
Probett, Nick 207-209
Rawlings, Terry 40, 214, 215
Redford, Robert 130
Redhill Aerodrome 207-209, 214-217, 219
Rendcomb Aerodrome 222, 223
Rijnmond Air Service 44
Rolls-Royce Viper 48-52, 60
Ross, Wally 157, 158
St. Lucia 198-200
St. Omer 214-216
Securicor 32, 33, 35
Simferopol 82, 88
Sokoto 78, 111, 115
South East Air 37, 39
Spencer, John 152
Star shells 90
Stanton, Paul 5, 16

Stokenchurch Mast 14, 15, 17
Sub-hunting 135
Tamanrasset 50, 52-54, 96
Tbilisi 82-88,
Tegucigalpa Airport 184, 185
The Vintage Aeroplane Company 208, 209
Thompson, Brian 96, 99, 107, 109, 112, 114-116, 123, 124, 128, 129, 137
Turbulence 47, 48
Uberlingen 169, 170
Veasey, Peter 25
Wacky Races 214-216
Wall, Nigel 180-182
Wass, Geoff 18
Weaver, Les 218
Wellcome Trust 34
Wennink, Mike 94, 117
Wham! 31
West London Aero Club/WLAC 1, 4, 5, 7
Werdenberg, Werner 154, 172, 175
Williams, Ceri 201, 202